Murder on the Reservation

A RAY AND PAT BROWNE BOOK

Series Editors
Ray B. Browne and Pat Browne

Murder on
the Reservation

American Indian Crime Fiction:
Aims and Achievements

Ray B. Browne

THE UNIVERSITY OF WISCONSIN PRESS / POPULAR PRESS

The University of Wisconsin Press
1930 Monroe Street
Madison, Wisconsin 53711

www.wisc.edu/wisconsinpress/

3 Henrietta Street
London WC2E 8LU, England

1   3   5   4   2

Printed in the United States of America

Library of Congress Cataloging-in-Publication Data
Browne, Ray Broadus.
Murder on the reservation: American Indian crime fiction / Ray B. Browne.
p.   cm.
"A Ray and Pat Browne book."
ISBN 0-299-19610-0 (cloth: alk. paper)
ISBN 0-299-19614-3 (pbk.: alk. paper)
1. Detective and mystery stories, American—History and criticism.
2. American fiction—Indian authors—History and criticism.
3. Indians in literature.   4. Crime in literature.   I. Title.
PS374.D4B765   2004
813'.087209897—dc22   2003020566

Contents

Acknowledgments

On this page of a book the author customarily expresses gratitude to all the people who assisted in its writing. First I would like to thank Peter Rollins for reminding me that the story of the man who wished he could engage in sexual activity as the squirrels he and the woman were watching appeared earlier in *The Grapes of Wrath*.

I want especially to thank the authors studied here for their willingness to strengthen the book by giving interviews, though by mail, to me and providing information not otherwise available but nevertheless vital. I sought no interview with Tony Hillerman because I felt there are enough conversations with him already available.

It is usual also to thank librarians for their assistance. I have been the recipient of such help for decades. Long long ago I worked for years in all sections of the Library of Congress, from the Special Collections to the Music Library, the Folklore Archives, and the general stacks. I discovered that after a reader became a familiar face and established his trustworthiness he could move around at will, taking books from one section to another, reading from the stacks in the very bowels of the great collection and thus discovering resources not hitherto suspected. I have always appreciated the opportunity granted under those circumstances. I am sure Thomas Jefferson, whose works originally served as the very beginning and core of the Library of Congress, and others have enjoyed even greater trust, being able, I am sure, to check books *out* of the Library of Congress and return them when they liked. That is the basis of trust and understanding.

Other special collections have provided me with great opportunities. I have also discovered that at times it is more satisfactory to possess one's own books. In the many novels needed for this study I have learned that sometimes it is preferable to spend the several hundred dollars required to get access to the needed books rather than to count on other sources. Sometimes, especially in the cases of the Jake Page and Robert Westbrook, clothbound copies of the works were not available. Therefore perforce the page numbers are to paperback editions.

Murder on the Reservation

Introduction

In the rapidly developing field of literature by and about Native Americans, ethnic crime fiction is a vigorous genre. In many ways this genre develops in the tradition of crime fiction in general, but it necessarily incorporates new materials and people in their own settings and cultures. Thus it is a new and different total environment for the age-old treatment of crime and punishment.

In literature, crime fiction—or detective fiction, as it used to be called—serves many purposes. Two major ones, seemingly contradictory, develop concurrently: One serves to maintain the status quo by picturing society in upheaval and the reestablishment of the status quo ante. The other, in opposition, points the way, as well as the danger, for altering society through violence and crime, because although law and order have been reimposed at the end of the story, society has clearly been affected and does not return precisely and wholly to the status it held before the disestablishment. Although each type of crime fiction in its artistic accomplishment provides a modicum of catharsis, both, especially the latter, provide stimulus to the imagination about the possibilities of leveling the cultural playing field through upheaval. In the presence of violence, especially along the horizontal gun barrel, all people are equal.

Crime fiction with its investigator who searches for the perpetrator is as old as Western time itself. In the Garden of Eden two instances of breaking the law were chronicled—Eve's eating of the Forbidden Fruit and Cain's murdering his brother Abel—and God was the first investigator, as well as judge and jury, ferreting out the guilty party and the reasons why Eve and Cain had broken His law. In later times, the biblical Book of Daniel gives perhaps the first recorded story of actual civil crime and investigator in the story of Susanna and the two elders who because she would not have sex with them accused her of infidelity and were in turn executed when proved guilty of false accusation. In classical times the historian Herodotus (490-425 B.C.) told a delightful story of how King Rhampsinitus (possibly Ramses III) was robbed blind by one of his trusted workers and how the mystery was solved through simple detective work.

In our own time, the oldest, classic Golden Age crime fiction, in the tradition of Edgar Allan Poe and his investigator M. Auguste Dupin, and Sir Arthur Conan Doyle's Sherlock Holmes, still examines a special segment of society that has been thrown into turmoil by murder or some other disuniting force. This is elite crime fiction, which is both intellectually and socially controlled. Elites, those in power, look at some of the diseased spots in culture—that of crime—and reexamine them cognitively, with the certainty that all will be put right again after the disruption has been discovered and isolated. In their world of fiction, at least, the status quo ante will be reestablished if the malefactors in society are brought to the bar of recognition if not justice. New threats are, of course, always sneaking into the world of Golden Age crime fiction, for example in the role of women in society and crime. They are included with an embarrassed concession that they should have been members of the club all along. Other challenges resulting from developments in culture, such as technology and the expanding roads to power and wealth, can be handled in Golden Age crime fiction in traditional ways with conventional conclusions about the natural return to order in society.

But challenges in cultural awareness and solutions demand direct confrontations. Life and literature have burst beyond the boundaries of their old dictates and speak in new voices. There are other threats to the status quo, and therefore another type of crime fiction dealing with everyday people and everyday crime and violence has been in large part returned to the people who commit and are affected by them. Raymond Chandler, our classic early exponent of "hard-boiled" crime fiction, more than half a century ago in "The Simple Art of Murder" argued that since the weight of crime ordinarily falls on the common man and woman they are the ones who should read and write crime fiction, and in their own language. Chandler was roundly Whitmanesque in his feeling for the universal power and understanding of the common man and woman. Chandler sums up his essay, in his frequently quoted passage, that person "talks as a man of his age talks, that is, with rude wit, a lively sense of the grotesque, a disgust for sham, and a contempt for pettiness. The story in his adventure is search of a hidden truth, and it would be no adventure if it did not happen to a man fit for adventure. He has a range of awareness that startles you, but if belongs to him by right, because it belongs to the world he lives in" (see Hoppenstand 508). Apt as these words are, for our purposes Chandler's most cogent observation in that essay comes in the paragraph following the one quoted above: "If there were enough like him, I think the world would be a very safe place to live in, and yet not too dull to be worth living in." Chandler's urge for crime literature to become more inclusive in subject and treatment was for both vertical and horizontal rearrangement. He wanted more democracy in literature and more democratic writing about it, more subjects and more angles of vision. The need was important then and in our world of growing ethnic assertiveness more insistent now. The drive is in fact irresistible.

Today there is a rapidly expanding growth in lateral inclusiveness in literature, especially in opening new fields of inquiry in ethnic crime fiction, which in general thrives on two driving forces: 1) All authors need to find and exploit new fields of human action and location in which to present material both different and exotic. In *The Ethnic Detective,* a collection of short stories by seventeen such authors, Bill Pronzini and Martin Greenberg call this a "handle." This handle for ethnic crime writers is useful since it provides an economical and comfortable form of geographical and cultural tourism, traveling to exotic societies and observing strange people and getting to know something about both the society and the people. It is an index, a short course in the education about a different people and society.

2) A second reason for the rapid growth of ethnic crime fiction is political-cultural and may be to a certain extent a matter of expediency in our time of growing awareness of the need for society to accommodate all cultural attitudes and persuasions. The reasoning here is that it is good politics as well as justice to give every minority group a fair hearing and equal opportunity in life. As democracy grows so does the feeling of self-conscious and guilt-ridden shame about America's treatment

of minorities, especially Native Americans, in the past, and authors of such fiction have begun writing about those actions in order to correct misconceptions or ignorance about people different from those the reader knows. This fiction is increasing rapidly throughout the world.

With the growth of many kinds of crime literature various new theories of creating the greatest effectiveness spring to mind. One of the more unusual ones is that of H. F. Keating, the distinguished British author of ethnic crime fiction, who thinks that the most effective examples in the genre build up from a sense of humor, through which can be developed the high seriousness of professional techniques. To a certain extent he is correct. Humor adds a helpful dynamic. It intensifies the reader's enjoyment and, since we all like to feel superior to someone else, it gives him or her a feeling of being in some way better than others, which allows a consequent condescension to all people in the story. Inside the story, as well, there are large expanses available for various kinds of humor, both ethnic and extra-ethnic.

Ethnic crime fiction differs stylistically from other types in the genre. It is much less contrived and self-consciously "literary" than so-called hard-boiled detective fiction and involves more frank and direct terminology but in a more realistic way. Sex, for example, is named and approached directly, not indirectly by metaphor and innuendo. It is physical, not poetic. Of all other kinds, ethnic crime fiction differs most dramatically from Golden Age or "cozy" detective fiction in being more straightforward. It has none of the hothouse atmosphere in which the older form develops in its several manifestations and tends instead to maintain a constant lifelike temperature.

Of the various kinds of crime literature ethnic crime fiction in several ways resembles that of feminist writers or that of any culturally disenfranchised segment of society fighting for its portion of the cultural pie. The consensus about feminist crime fiction seems to be captured in the criteria of Marty S. Knepper: such writing shows women "as a norm and not as freaks, women capable of intelligence, moral responsibility, competence, and independent action; . . . reveals the economic, social, political and psychological problems women face as part of a patriarchal society; . . . explores female consciousness and female perceptions of the world; . . . creates women who have psychological complexity and rejects sexist stereotypes" (Klein 201). Women are fighting, of course, for equal status in a normal society.

Ethnic crime fiction likewise talks about people seeking acceptance and normal treatment in society. Whereas feminist crime fiction centers on the demands of the female, ethnic crime fiction emphasizes the rights of the ethnic group, both male and female. Of the two groups fighting for their place in the sun perhaps the ethnic crime writers may have, to one degree or another, a slightly easier time achieving at least partial success attaining their goals, for a couple of reasons: 1) Because they represent a less immediate threat to the dominant society, ethnics can be granted at least some of their "natural rights," once those rights are established. 2) Females, on the other hand, represent challenges to the whole dominant society with much greater consequences, and therefore have a steeper hill to climb before reaching the level playing field.

In ethnic crime fiction a difference exists between male and female success as protagonists, with males more acceptable than females. But there seems to be a more level encounter where female protagonists can play the same kind of hardball at which their male counterparts succeed, and with the same degree of success. In fact, often it is comfortable for cultural conservatives to see females triumph in ethnic crime fiction because their field of accomplishment is somewhat detached and "other world," and therefore a less immediate threat.

At its best, ethnic crime fiction can provide great cultural or social satisfaction other than airing the just demands of people who have been culturally mistreated. It dramatizes the conflicts between cultures, reveals the rift of threat to the safety of the dominant society, provides humor, and, finally, covertly or overtly reestablishes the reader's feeling of safety from and superiority over other groups of people.

In his suggestive book, *Playing Indian,* Philip J. Deloria observes that Americans have for two hundred years been "playing Indian" and "There was, quite simply, no way to conceive an American identity" without Native Americans (37). Playing in all forms is an anthropological ritual that is part of the process of growing up. So as whites have played Indian they have also been growing up in regard to their feelings about the Indian. In this process of white maturation the Indians have perforce grown too, though to a much smaller degree, as they have been admitted to cultural maturity.

Playing Indian for adults is an exercise in keeping the real Indian at arm's length by the masquerade of reaching out halfway to the Native American in the form of playful reenactment and ritual but stopping short of embracing the cause and object of play. Ritual playing of all sorts lasts only for a designated period and is designed to allow a subjugated people or class to blow off a little steam but not to effect any lasting changes. In fact its purpose and function is formed by the release of the explosive power of resentment to prevent change. So playing Indian is a game in which the winner is always white.

Ethnic crime fiction about Native Americans is much more than playing Indian though. It envelops the Native Americans in the blanket of life through the genuineness of crime and punishment. That is ritual, but it is much more than play. In America the streets of life are the avenues of reality, and those streets are violent, crime-ridden, and mean — for Anglos, Native Americans, and all other ethnic groups. In crime fiction all groups search for cures for the common disease. This ritual of safety and purification is more than fun "play," no matter how important play can be in the development of human society. Crime fiction is serious play. No doubt then that the literature is one step away from playing Indian and one step closer to playing American culture, with all kinds of people in the game. If there are alpha individuals, they are chosen on merit from the whole pack, not from a select, historically "superior" part of that group.

Ethnic crime fiction has blossomed in the last decade because it concerns a generic quality common to us all. Such fiction, though generally thought to be a subgenre, is actually by one definition all-inclusive in subject matter and peoples. It has to do with differences in heritages, cultures, and behavior and therefore concerns all actions in the lives of everyone. To paraphrase Franklin Delano Roosevelt in his speech to the Daughters of the American Revolution on April 21, 1938, all of us, including Indians, are ethnics or descended from ethnics. So anyone writing about crime and punishment between one kind of people and another is an ethnic crime writer.

In addition to providing new fields and human actions in which to present life in different and exotic ways, crime fiction is an economical form of physical and cultural tourism, a trip to exotic societies and a meeting with strange people and ways of life, with exposure to but safety from danger. It is something like seeing the threats of the creatures in the movie *Jurassic Park* from a safe vantage spot or the thrill of experience in *The Godfather* without danger from the Mafia. It is, in other words, a parallel form providing us, who seem increasingly to demand them, with inexpensive and enjoyable thrills.

Ethnic crime fiction also benefits from the current American deep concern with political correctness. It is good politics as well as prescribed justice to give every minority group a fair hearing in society. So ethnic crime writing becomes a kind of affirmative fiction, beginning with remorse and showing atonement. It is usually called "paying back," by a great number of these Anglos for former commissions of injustice against the Indians. Although they represent only just a little above one percent of the American population and one among hundreds of ethnic groups Native Americans are being especially targeted because the need to "pay back" is a particularly open sore and the urgency to understand the pathology of the affliction urgently acute. To be sure, not all authors of Indian crime fiction are interested in paying back. Indian lands and cultures provide rich and complex backgrounds for authors who are interested merely in telling good stories and providing entertainment and have chosen this new field. Often authors, new authors especially, build on folktales and legends. In the novel *Shaman Pass,* Alaskan news reporter Stan Jones develops an Eskimo legend into a full-scale crime novel.

In this story, the Smithsonian Institution has returned to an Inupiat village the mummified head of Northwest Alaska's nineteenth-century prophet and social reformer Maniilaq (named in the novel Natchiq) who had wanted to take his message of preparation for coming times, especially for women, to Canada and set it in motion but was killed by whites instead. The mummified head has been placed in the local museum but one night is stolen by one of his followers to prevent its being exhibited and gawked at by white people. The robber is murdered and the mummy returned, but Jones, wanting to tell a good Eskimo story, nevertheless develops in his tale a sharp message about Eskimo-White relations.

As the desire to write historical crime fiction grows, some of the authors are more interested in writing authentic novels than in making any statement about present-day Anglo-Indian relations. As such they work Indians into the plots as needed to develop their stories. As they do, however, consciously or unconsciously they add to the public's general knowledge of and understanding of the Indian's place in American history and present-day society. Not all the stories are located on reservations. Some have the Indians representing their tribes in the neighboring white towns but most have touched on cities as points of travel or as places the Indian law officers have tried and abandoned.

For example, Stephen Lewis has published three crime novels that he calls mysteries of colonial times. Set in Massachusetts some fifty years after the arrival of the Puritans, these novels center on the injustices consciously done by whites to other whites and, almost as matter of course, to Indians. Sometimes they use conventional symbols. Lewis's novels, for example, reach back toward the concept of the Noble Savage and the ignoble renegade of James Fenimore Cooper.

In *The Sea Hath Spoken*, "A Mystery of Colonial Times," the action is set in Newbury, a pioneer seaside Puritan village. The obvious religious and political powers in the village are the minister and the governor. But the real power is a sixty-year-old widow, Mistress Catherine Williams, whose husband before death was the richest merchant in the village. Mistress Williams, as midwife, wise woman, and powerful personality, manipulates all the males in the village to her purposes. Her chief assistant, whose life she saved when the whites were killing off all his fellow chiefs, is Indian sachem Massaquoit, who acts as a reserved and dignified helpmate. They are opposed by the sly renegade Wequashcook, who has ingratiated himself to the whites and will work for anyone—white or red, honest or crooked—who will pay him for his services. In this novel, which historians term historically accurate, Lewis peoples the society with other Indians as needed for historical accuracy and in order to move his plot along.

Perhaps as the number of authors of ethnic crime fiction continues to increase, with their probing into human motivations and actions and the sameness of human beings of all races and cultures being revealed, the world, as Chandler tangentially suggested, might become a safer and pleasanter place to live, with greater justice to all. At least it will be a place where people have greater knowledge and understanding of one another.

One important result with as yet insufficiently understood consequences will be an outreach of democracy to more Americans and especially ethnic groups. People on whom light is cast through fiction become more aware of themselves and their accomplishments and potential. "I don't care what you say about me if you just spell my name right," is an outreach cliché applicable to ethnic groups as well as, apparently, to all individuals. We all want to be noticed. Indians want to be noticed with dignity. They do not mind being treated realistically and truthfully but they want a fair account. Louis Owens emphasizes that Indians are "a gallery of characters who can laugh at themselves and others, who are fully capable of cowardice as well as heroics, and whose lives can be every bit as tangled and messy as the worst scenario " imaginable (*Other Destinies* 29). Peter Bowen insists also that Indians have a "wonderfully pointed sense of humor," often centering on delicate females and approaching the pornographic, or realistic. Jean Hager, who writes about the Cherokee of Oklahoma, describes the need in his interview with the author: "You have to treat the culture of which you write with great respect even if there are negatives about that culture.

Your characters within the culture can make the comments to speak to the positives and negatives, but the author must treat the culture with great respect."

Bowen, in a letter to me, has the same slant though insisting that the term Native American is a non-Indian affectation that can be offensive to Indians.

> What any sentient human being wishes is to be treated like a human being and be judged on their merits, accomplishments, and character. Any race wants that from the dominant culture which, of course, prefers rather tribal exclusions. This applies in America to Blacks, Hispanics, Indians, poor whites, Samoans, and, lately, loggers and cattle ranchers. Other countries operate similarly with varying vilenesses. Indians have among them good folks, bad folks, murderers, saints, poets, people of courage and cowardice, child molesters, and, given the available pool of white guilt, numerous two-bit hustlers, literary and otherwise, since they possess not a few rank opportunists in their unrelegated unconformity.

Ralph Ellison, noted black author, wrote of the Black American male as the *Invisible Man* (1952), so unimportant he was not noticed. But groups other than blacks do not want to remain invisible either, in the shadow of dominant cultural awareness and opportunity. An invisible person is an ignored person. But a people increasingly the subject of literature becomes visible and strong. Critic Mikhail Bakhtin correctly feels that "novels level people on the plane of language, diffuse inequities of power, and give every citizen a chance to speak to other citizens about concerns such as the environment [and social and power inequities] and so offer opportunities for political [and cultural] change" (quoted in Teague, *The Southwest in American Literature and Art* 167).

Literature of all kinds is made stronger by being anchored deeply in the past and comparatively in the present. Historians have come increasingly to recognize that the power of their craft lies in storytelling. Indian scholar LeAnne Howe points out the breadth and depth of Indian history and stories:

> Native stories, no matter what form they take (novel, poem, drama, memoir, film, history), seem to pull all the elements together of the storyteller's tribe, meaning the people, the land, and multiple characters and all their manifestations and revelations, and connect these in past, present, and future milieus (present and future milieus mean non-Indians). (*The Story of America* 42)

Historian Sarah Maza lists substantially the same areas of human expression: "'Literary sources' in the widest possible sense of that expression, include oral narratives such as folk tales, both 'high' and 'popular' fictions, historical writing, stories for performance such as screen and stage drama, and certain forms of journalism." And she includes "narratives of sexual danger" (in other words, crime fiction), as well as "The judicial sources . . . that rely heavily on storytelling, such as witnesses' depositions, published arguments and pleas, lawyers' briefs, and accounts of trials in newspapers, pamphlets, and other media" (*Stories in History* 1494). Clearly, then, stories of crime and punishment, because they constitute such large segments in all societies, make up large and significant aspects of storytelling and story-writing.

Such empowering novels, as Bakhtin sees them, must exist in a polyglot world in which society is unified through language, especially conversational language, traditional storytelling, and tradition. Native American cultures are primarily oral communities, storytelling cultures for both conventional and crime fiction. Therefore novels about and by these Native Americans who stick close to their traditions are one step nearer to the power of the mainstream fiction.

Novels about Native Americans by both natives and non-natives often serve as Janus-faced observers and commentators, looking both backward and forward, into and out of Indian cultures. As such they are frequently what James Ruppert calls "mediational," that is, fronting one culture with another and explaining the two-way dynamics of a culture within a culture. He uses as his example the works of Leslie Marmon Silko, one of the most effective Native American novelists writing today. Ruppert refers to her novel *Ceremony:*

> Throughout Silko's goals are truly mediational as she seeks to translate the languages of the Other, but for both Native and non-Native fields of discourse, she must answer what has been asked before, acknowledge previous discourse, and advance cultural conversations. Yet she must also open up a field of access where Native implied readers can mediate their experiences just as the non-Native implied reader must. Ultimately, the text leads the reader to validate Native American epistemology—a central goal in the mediation of contemporary Native American literature—and to appreciate the new structures of meaning that mediation creates. (*Mediation* 75)

Native Americans and their past and present societies increasingly occupy a special place in our hearts and minds, not with soft-brained condescension but with the dignity that they and we deserve. This recognition has been a long time developing. Since Columbus's arrival on the shores of what to Europeans was a New World in 1492, Native Americans have suffered the fate of an outnumbered and outgunned society. The newcomers were fired by ambition to succeed in the new land of opportunity. For centuries they had been crowded in non-progressive societies without opportunity. Now, released, they looked on the New World as New Opportunity, and they were determined to exercise their newfound freedom and advance their own fortunes. This personal ambition was stimulated by religious zeal that drove the whites to force the natives to give up their misguided heathenish ways and convert to the gentle and proper ways of Christianity even if the cruelty and torture that often resulted in death were required to coax the conversion.

Columbus wrote to his queen that the natives of the New World were a kind and considerate people, who "love their neighbors as themselves, and their discourse is very sweet and gentle, and accompanied with a smile, yet they should be taught the Spaniard's ways of life and Spanish Catholicism." Along the Puritan frontier peopled by the English settlers, it was politically, culturally, and religiously proper to look upon Indians as devils in what the settlers called a howling wilderness. Both wilderness and devil had to be transformed to God's ways and purposes if the Almighty's purpose and potential were to be achieved. As is demonstrated in the folklore of the My Lai massacre in the war in South Vietnam (1969–73), for Americans with political and other drives sometimes a village, or a tribe or a people, had to be destroyed in order to be saved. As the Puritan frontier moved ever westward this mindset dictated that the best Indian was a converted Indian, or, in the view of Civil War general Philip Henry Sheridan, a dead Indian, often the latter being preferred—"The only good Indians I ever saw were dead," as he said, most often given in the vernacular as, "The only good Indian is a dead Indian."

Along with the notion of Indian as devil, the opposite romantic concept of Indian as Noble Savage developed. Since Plato, and probably a thousand years earlier, it had been believed, as it seems to be felt today, that natives in lands uncorrupted by the laws and restrictions of civilization were savage but noble. Nobility came with the territory. As seventeenth-century English poet and playwright John Dryden phrased it:

I am as free as Nature first made man,
Ere the base laws of servitude began
When wild in woods the noble savage ran.
(*Conquest of Granada* [1669-70] Part i, act i, scene i)

By the third decade of the nineteenth century James Fenimore
Cooper tested the concept of the Indian as Noble Savage in his popular
Leatherstocking tales. In these five novels Cooper reenacted life on the
frontier in the persons of regular citizens (usually members of the mili-
tary and females); of Leatherstocking, a guide and hunter who had been
raised among the Indians but did not want to be one of them; and two
kinds of Indians—the noble Chingachgook and his son Uncas and the
rascally reprobate Huron Magua. As the frontier moved farther and farther west and Native Americans were pushed and relocated toward the
setting sun, the concept of their being noble, though still a literary and
theoretical commonplace, was challenged more and more as whites increasingly coveted the space occupied by the red people, and in order to
justify in their own minds the takeover of this land demonized the Indians to whom they had only recently given it.

A dominant society always finds it difficult to accept a weaker minority group—especially one that is being persecuted and exploited—
on any terms other than rival and inferior opponent. So the Indians
were changed from noble—different—to opponent—wicked. Whites
recognized that there were at least three fields of association and conflict in White-Indian relations. Some Native Americans were friendly
to whites; some whites were friendly to some Indians; some whites were
unfriendly to all natives.

As the Indians became more and more second-class noncitizens because of the different paths they trod, they became at the same time
objects of scorn and of sympathy. Obviously mistreated like other minorities, the Indians consisted essentially of a nation apart, living *in*
America but not *of* America. More than black Americans who gradually
achieved some degree of importance and pseudo-equality because of
their increasing numbers and growing economic and political clout, the
Indians occupied a position as separate, lesser, and somewhat pitied
Americans, still native and outside the loop of civilization and culture.

In 1970, however, publication of Dee Brown's classic *Bury My Heart
at Wounded Knee: An Indian History of the American West* created a flood-
tide of remorse and desire for atonement. Brown's purpose in publishing the book was to "fashion a narrative of the conquest of the West as
the victims experienced it, using their own words wherever possible,"

and, he added, making his account of Western injustices a record of the whole continent. "Americans who have always looked westward when reading about this period should read this book facing eastward," he wrote (xvi). The book sold over four million copies and created a furor that in one way or another touched nearly every American and continues to resonate in a catalogue of horrors today. Jake Page, one of the authors studied in this book, in one of his novels fears that racial hatred may still exist in New Mexico, with a potential for more racial explosions as at Wounded Knee.

In the Preface to the 1990 reissue of *Wounded Knee* Brown commented that the occasion was the centennial year of the last battle of the Indian Wars, in which two hundred men, women, and children were slaughtered by the United States Army. "That ghost-haunted place itself, windswept and lonely," he wrote, "has become a modern symbol of unrequited wrongs." But he added that Native Americans who had been decimated at Wounded Knee and elsewhere have been pulling themselves up by their sandal straps through education and "use of the tools of law, economics and politics to benefit their people." Brown noted that the Indians "have created remarkable bodies of art and literature about themselves ranging through historical studies, polemical essays, current affairs, rich and powerful fiction, drama and poetry" (v). Brown was certainly correct in his observation and implied prediction. Increasingly courses in Indian literature and Indian culture are being taught in colleges and universities, and cloth and paperback books are standing out prominently on the bookshelves of college and commercial book stores.

John Cawelti suggests in *The Six Gun Mystique Sequel* that this new vitality in Native American literature "might be on the verge of a kind of literary and cultural awakening that occurred to another major American region, the South, in the 1920s and 1930s" (112). And for the same reasons, he writes, "In those years a new generation of Southern writers struggled to free themselves from the burden of Southern history and its dominant myths of white supremacy and the lost cause" (112).

Like the Southerners, the Indians still have several powerful oppositional forces to overcome.

One is the myth of the Southwest and its Indian inhabitants that has been long and powerful in white imagination. As Leah Dilworth points out:

> The American southwest is not simply a place. It is a region of the imagination, a "land"—of "poco tiempo," "journey's ending," and "enchantment"—on which Americans have long focused their fantasies

of renewal and authenticity. Characterized by its desert landscape and "tricultural" history, the Southwest—usually meaning Arizona and New Mexico—has been for the last one hundred years variously perceived as a kind of American Orient, a place conducive to utopian communality, and the source of a "lifestyle." (*Imagining* 2)

The people of such a district, many members of the dominant white society believe, she suggests, should recognize their Garden of Eden and act like its citizens—picturesque, docile, and indifferent to the hard and harsh world inhabited by those in control. They should be pleased that the whites in their paternal goodness will serve the inferior's needs and take care of them. But the natives are acting up and are developing a long list of literary spokespersons for themselves: Sherman Alexie, Vine Deloria, N. Scott Momaday, Louis Owens, Leslie Marmon Silko, James Welch, Louise Erdrich, Gerald Vizenor, and others. These authors of conventional literature are being joined by an ever-growing list of white, mixedblood, and fullblood Indian writers of crime fiction who are adding a new and powerful muscle to the literature of the Native Americans. These authors are trying to teach the world a new vision of Indian culture. "It is a holistic, ecological perspective, one that places essential value upon the totality of existence, making humanity equal to all elements but superior to none and giving humankind crucial responsibility for the care of the world we inhabit," says Owens in *Other Destinies* (29). Perhaps this is claiming too much virtue for the Indians and offering too much hope for societies at large under their guidance. But the joining of Indian cultures with others toward a nudging into greater responsibility can only benefit all.

Of all Native American crime fiction authors who are likely to lead that genre into a new literature, Owens is perhaps one of the more promising. He represents the goals and the possible restrictions that some powerful fullbloods and mixedbloods share. He feels the energy that is driving Indian authors, and what he calls marginal authors— "from westerners, from Native American Indians, from the children of Vietnamese 'Boat-People' and other Asian immigrants, from the growing richness of Chicano and *mestizaje* literature, from African Americans." He wants the literature of all these new and "different" authors to be read by everyone because it has truths that cannot otherwise be revealed. "To think that poems, novels, stories, or plays written and performed by Native people are not for all audiences is essentialist and absurd," he says (*Mixedblood* xv). Instead the fighting back against tradition and persisting culture breeds a new literature. As Owens believes,

"Out of this resistance, a new American literature is emerging, and American Indian writing—with all its anger, humor, bitterness, beauty, feuding, and deep sense of a real subject—is at the heart of this emergence" (xv). He also insists, following the hard pronouncements of critic Gerald Vizenor, that one does not have to be "Indian" to write about Indians. An author does have to be writing within his experience. In other words, he must know what he or she is talking about and write truthfully and realistically.

That observation is truistic. The authors of Indian crime fiction studied in this book all establish their bona fides in one way or another— being pure- or mixedblood, having lived among the Indians, or even to the point of visiting and having friends among the Indians. Without some knowledge one might write generally but not convincingly. But, despite the parallel argument being used among African Americans, one does not have to have Indian blood in his or her veins in order to write about them. In fact, one does not have to be "Indian" in order to write about "Indians," though it might ease the transition and add authenticity to the observations.

Owens seems to be joining forces with other fullblood, mixedblood, and nonblood intellectuals who write criticism and fiction insisting that the strength and potential development of great Indian literature lies in conventional approaches and types of art. "Today I think we are on the verge of a new wave of Native American Literature as poets, fiction writers, and playwrights are beginning to emerge in greater numbers from deep in the heart of 'Indian Country,'" he writes (23). And he appends a growing list of very accomplished Indian poets, novelists, and playwrights, and urges that increasingly young potential authors are coming along, writing and insisting that readers of all bloodlines must look into Indian literature for truth of Indian culture. Crime fiction is one of these important growing genres.

In his firm insistence on the development of Indian literature by and about Indians, however, Owens falls into the trap of seeming not to give full credit to much fullblood, mixedblood, and nonblood Indian literature, and Indian popular literature in general and crime fiction in particular. He is joined by other Indian literature specialists of the old school who want to establish and maintain some kind of canon, though at times it seems confusing what kind of canon they want. Apparently it is a canon of what they call "quality," which parallels that of the old school but extends outward to include all "serious" writers, never acknowledging that all authors are serious if they are published and successful. Robert Dale Parker *(The Invention of Native American Literature)* is one of the latest such authors who seem to be carrying water on both shoulders at the same time. As a working premise he reluctantly admits that Indian literature has "arrived" in the works of a few authors, who in their preeminence "take over the landscape of Indian writing and blot out the many other writers both past and present" worthy of study (vii). Parker's desire, as he says in his conclusion, is to bring in the unrepresented or underrepresented in Indian literature.

Other modern Indian scholars, often perhaps unconsciously advocating their narrow goals in their field, fail to see the full scope of such literature. Paula Gunn Allen, for example, a well-established and perceptive feminist Indian scholar, in *The Sacred Hoop: Recovering the Feminine in American Indian Traditions* insists that when scholars recognize the proper and historical role of Indian women in their culture new conclusions are inevitable:

> All the interpretations and conclusions scholars in the fields of folklore, ethnology, and contemporary literary studies will have to be altered, all the evidence reexamined, and all the materials chosen for exemplification of tribal life—which at present reveal more about academic male bias than about the traditions and peoples they purport to depict—will have to be redone. This is because the shift in focus from a male to a female axis recontextualizes the entire field. (266)

But Parker, Owens, and Allen look backward at the literature and canon of the past rather than the reality of the present. Notice that Allen, though she insists on a new interpretation of Indian literature and even of "contemporary works," which she calls "genre literature," is willing to recognize—or accept—only "classic categories" like westerns and folklore, when the new field of Indian crime fiction is doing far more to return power and dignity to Indian women than the western or folklore does.

This exclusion is especially interesting in view of the fact that although he is a perceptive critic Owens is also a powerful author of one of this rapidly growing types of popular literature, crime fiction. Another peculiarity about his authoring such literature is the fact that Owens had never read a detective story or crime fiction novel before he decided to write one. His admission does not say, however, that anybody can write an effective crime fiction work or that these works are not valuable literature. Perhaps almost anybody can write a detective story of some merit. But within the genre there are degrees of quality and achievement, just as in any other type. Owens writes crime fiction of exceptional merit. This accomplishment denotes the value of such fiction in art and cultural expressions.

The truth of the matter is that one writes, or should write, the type of literature that one writes best, no matter whether it is conventional or new, mainstream or marginal. Authors are always straining to write different kinds of literature within the conventional type—a new type of play, an experimental poem, canon-smashing conventional fiction, the "great Americana novel," as author Tom Wolfe does in his *A Man in Full* (1998). Wolfe's novel was criticized by some authors of conventional fiction but praised by such critics as George F. Will as "a high-octane moral judgment and exhortation" which "[rises] to literature" (*Newsweek*, 23 November 1998, 96), an evaluation testified to by the fact that the first press run was 1.4 million, with three subsequent printings. It would seem logical, therefore, to extend the margins of conventional literature and recognize that any quality expression of art or culture—especially done in a new and appealing form—can be very valuable. And certainly crime fiction is meritorious in at least two ways: it is an outward extending democratization of literature, and it is a rapidly growing expression attractive to the general public because of its intellectual appeal and because of its concern with one of the most basic drives in human existence, violence.

Owens expertly pictures both aspects of the Indian—that is human—experience. In two of his novels he has created a three-generational family soundly based in Indian tradition that moves freely from the Indian land of dreams and visions to the white's existence in so-called reality. Further, Owens seems one of a growing number of authors who write in their own form and language, expressing their own ideas regardless of how they are received, rather than modifying their ideas and language for commercial success. Owens, for example, claims that he would rather be published by a university press (University of Oklahoma Press, in his case) and have limited sales than be sold much more widely by a commercial press and be forced to write what he thinks is a prostitution of his principles. As he explains:

> I published *Nightland* with Dutton Signet, singularly the most unpleasant experience I have had as a writer; to those people Indians are defined by Hollywood westerns and romance novels, and Indians are either dead or in the process of making themselves vanish through alcohol and dysfunctional behavior. I had wanted to get away from the University of Oklahoma Press for one book. Now I'm going back to

OU Press with great pleasure. New York wants ridiculous, comically self-destructive Indians, mystical shaman-warriors, breathless and precious prose about imploding Indian communities and idiotic love affairs. (Correspondence with author)

Actually, New York publishers want fiction that will sell. Sometimes the editors and publishers have to be dragged screaming into accepting potential best-selling works, as witness the common occurrence of a dozen publishers turning down a manuscript which when eventually accepted and published will sell in the millions. We all remember the numerous examples of judges who stumbled badly in giving an opinion of a manuscript. Although situated at the bottleneck of control and advised by considerable experience, publishers quickly admit that they know very little about their trade. But they sometimes get it right and with their meddling improve the manuscript. Again, we all know the difficulty Maxwell Perkins had in whittling Thomas Wolfe's manuscripts down to a proper (long) length. Other authors trust the editors, or at least graciously give in to their suggestions or demands. Irving Wallace, for example, always wrote as freely and voluminously as he liked, knowing that his wife would take out objectionable words and phrases and the editor would remove at least one third of the manuscript as verbosity.

The world of publishing, especially fiction, is a high-stakes crap game, with the percentage of right combinations for success surprisingly low. But some authors learn to work within the self-imposed restrictions of the commercial houses, modify them as they can, and achieve remarkable successes both commercially and artistically. It is probably at considerable risk that authors learn to despise the desires of the reading public as understood and interpreted by the commercial houses who cater to their desires. Some do and succeed. Many others do and fail.

Authors of Native American crime fiction write about the Native Americans in three venues: almost exclusively on the reservation; the interaction between Indians and whites; and white-centered society in which Indians operate as Indians. Altogether, these authors, as Louis Owens points out, are fundamentally revising the view of Indian cultures and lives and are producing what Roy Harvey Pearce called for years ago: "a study of the Indian image of himself, a study of the idea of civilization as it at once has been interjected into the Indian psyche and helped to shape it" (*Savagism* 202).

Native American writers deeply and strongly share the general Indian animosity toward whites. With that feeling they still write novels that picture American cultures, warts and all, clashing in their ways to achieve a common goal. So these authors write fiction about what America has been, is, and hopes to be. Such fiction forms a powerful base for further development of the fiction itself and of Native American-White relations in general.

Usually this literature has worked in and carried on the long-used Indian oral tradition, in which lives the historical strength of Indian culture and ways of life. These authors' purposes are to speak in conventional literature in the traditional voice of the Indian in order to establish the Indianness of Native Americans in American culture, or perhaps more correctly the Native Americanness of Indians in American culture. In other words, to identify and reestablish Native Americans as a people with a past that needs to be reidentified to demonstrate the quality of the present-day people. That reidentification can be done through rediscovery and reuse of an oral tradition that was especially though not uniquely their own. As Paula Gunn Allen wrote, Indian authors "rely on native rather than non-Indian forms, themes, and symbols and so are not colonial or exploitative. Rather they carry on the oral tradition at many levels, furthering and nourishing it and being furthered and nourished by it" (*Sacred Hoop* 79).

Such an effort shows a determination to write a psychological geography of identity and importance, a literary declaration of rights that was largely destroyed by a more dominant culture that in its political construct largely wrote the Native American out of history. Gerald Vizenor calls this victimization: "The *absence* of the *indian* in the histories of this nation is an esthetic *victimry* (*Fugitive Poses* 12). Now the need is to cleanse that "victimry" by reinstatement of the Native American in his natural rights and accomplishments.

Another powerful movement in and about the Indians and their culture is speaking in Native American crime fiction. Instead of keeping the Native American on the cultural reservation in dignified and politically unequal tradition, crime writers of Native American fiction are endeavoring to identify and dignify their subjects' culture and join it to the larger Anglo society. Such writers would like to make the hyphenated Indian-American culture no more separated from general-American than that of other hyphenated cultures, say Italian-American or Polish-American, or, for that matter, English-American. In other words they want to Americanize their people.

Interestingly, in many ways the authors of Native American crime fiction are running counter to the general movement and in their own way achieving a different and significant status for Indians. These authors are trying to immerse the Indian in American life and in so doing reestablish his or her connection with the larger society. People who are not Indian or mixedblood may write this literature, and all these authors demonstrate that Indians are a part of American legal and political life and therefore deserve equal and included treatment. The literature suggests that if one has legal and political equality he or she ought to have cultural equality also. This literature, in other words, written by such people as Tony Hillerman and the other authors in this study, although keeping Indian culture visible and distinct before the reader, demonstrates that quite clearly all people are the same under the sky, that superficial differences are only color deep.

These crime fiction authors write with a sophistication, candor, and purpose that might not have been possible before *Wounded Knee* and the growth in understanding Native Americans that resulted from that book. The new attitude toward Indians is being spread through this literature to hundreds of thousands of everyday non-Indian citizens who might or might not have been aware of or interested in such affairs in the past, but having been made aware of Indian-White cultures they become more understanding. Popular literature, and especially ethnic crime fiction, is helping to level the cultural field and to meliorate or soften the antagonistic feeling toward Indians—and other minorities—held in the past and at the same time to bring identity and dignity to the subjects of such fiction by erasing the color and social lines and making them full-fledged Americans.

If to know is to understand and to understand is to be empathic, then ethnic crime fiction is doing Americans a good turn in helping to develop a society in which all members enjoy the rights and privileges promised by the Constitution. And it is accomplishing its goals to a degree other, more elite and therefore more limited, fiction cannot. Exposure to popular fiction may like the wheels of the gods grind slowly but it smoothes out inequities.

An excellent case in point is *The Man* (1964) by the popular novelist Irving Wallace. Always keen to write on subjects that would sell but also were of social importance, Wallace felt that a burning issue in American culture is society's reaction to the inevitable election of a black person as president of the United States. James Baldwin, before he died an active black elitist writer, protested to Wallace that a white man could not and should not write of a black person. Wallace insisted that the issue is of vital importance, that he reaches a hundred times as many readers as Baldwin does, and the more who know the issue the more widely the friction is reduced; therefore he should write about it. He was obviously practical and correct. If the powerful do not work for the weak, then who will, and who can do it more effectively? In a matter of as great concern as political and cultural rights, a group seeking those rights cannot afford to have only members of their group, no matter how effective, push for them. In changing the mores of a society, the more like-minded people working together, the faster the goal is achieved. In numbers there is strength.

Perhaps a more immediate example is found in the crime fiction of Father Andrew Greeley, who writes of a Chicago-based Catholic priest named John Blackmore "Blacky" Ryan. Numerous Catholics, from the Vatican out to the local level, have criticized Greeley for his rather steamy fiction, but he always defends and explains his position by asserting that through his fiction he is doing his and God's work of bringing wayward Catholics back to the Church and of converting people to the Church. And he has evidence in the form of numerous letters and other statements from people who say that through reading Greeley's fiction they were brought into or back to the Church. It is hard to argue with evidence of such solid success.

It may seem ironic that one way to lower the walls of antagonism between races is by linking the dominant White culture and the Indian culture through a threat common to us all—crime and violence. But it is historically valid. In his study of human nature, *Leviathan* (1651), Thomas Hobbes insisted that the unalterable nature of mankind is violence, a world of wolf versus wolf. But Hobbes was a social philosopher and not studying from historical evidence. Archaeologists today, however, are discovering that the history of all races of mankind includes warfare, and the conflict has been over dominance. The wolf versus wolf hostility has been for the food of survival. In a perceptive article in *Archaeology*, Steven A. LeBlanc observes that, "History shows that peoples with strong animosities stop fighting after adequate resources are established and the benefits of cooperation recognized" (25). In the book *Constant Battles: The Myth of the Peaceful, Noble Savage*, he expands his thesis that human beings have always competed with one another and fought over possessions. Throughout human history, "To the victor belongs the spoils," has always been obvious. But LeBlanc stops short of recognizing all the demands fought over today. The benefits increasingly demanded are the results of equality in all things. And equality in White-Indian cultures seems especially compelling.

In the remarkably viewpoint-reversing book, *Facing East from Indian Country*, Daniel Richter looks from west to east and sees the European settlers as invaders. Richter suggests that the Whites and Indians although they had only slightly veneered fear of and hostility to each other had to "*learn* to hate each other" (2), and the natives were consequently later written out of the Constitution and all other documents concerning the dominant Whites. What a culture has learned, hopefully, it can *unlearn*.

By implication LeBlanc and Richter say that apparently these goals of unlearning and changing can be achieved only through open and violent or subtle and continued conflict. But the results of conflict—slavery, cultural or financial dominance, tourism, familiarity with the customs of others, or continued peaceful or even hostile and other forms of intermingling—do wear down the walls of separateness and pull the teeth of the snarling wolves on the field between opposite cultures. It is obvious that after the initial shock of envy and hostility the more we know of the cultures of others the more we want to understand and be sympathetic to (and perhaps participate in) them.

Crime fiction gets to this main drive of human nature when treating the subject of conflict; it speeds up the process of smoothing discord and leveling society. Throughout time and at varying speeds, crime and punishment have demonstrated the development of democracy. All people must die, some in the grip of violence, some in the arms of justice, but at the point of death all people are equal. Crime fiction begins when society has been disrupted and hostility has been generated. Then by telescoping the process, the cause of disruption has been removed, hostility has been erased or minimized, and harmony restored. Crime fiction is therefore one of the outreaches of the artistic enactment of the great democratizer. Depiction of nature, and particularly political nature, in microcosm may have some beneficial effect on the millions of white readers who know little about the Native Americans as well as on the thousands of Indians who have left the reservations and moved to the city. Not in letting them see crime in the city, for most Native Americans crime fiction is not sited there, but in seeing crime fiction on the reservation. It is nostalgia. But other peoples—immigrants from India, South America, and other countries, for example—use entertainment from their homelands as ties to the cultures they left behind but do not want to forget. Perhaps if we can begin with that lowest common denominator, that is, crime, we can build up to a realization that we are after all more alike than different, that all share and must react to common occurrences in life, and when those occurrences threaten it is time to unite against them.

Then the remorse and atonement will have been at least partially successful, and we will have paid back some of the debt we inherited from our forebears and, far more important for our own activities, nurtured and promoted for the benefit of us all.

Indian crime fiction, like all crime fiction, is not only one of the many voices of popular culture but also a growing power both in subject matter and in the weight of importance it generates. Some advocates of Indian rights, like Fergus Bordewich in his book *Killing the White Man's Indian,* believe that popular culture has perpetuated what he calls "the fuzzy New Age myth of the Indian as the innocent child of nature" with its "shallow patina" (12) of misinformation and misconceptions. But such ideas are at best only partially perceptive and through the veil of this unrecognized elitist hauteur dismiss the strongest force in American correction of its prejudice against the Indian. Popular culture is the force that pulls prejudices and attitudes, though slowly, onto the level field of democracy. *Vox populi semper vincit,* the voice of the people ultimately prevails. Crime fiction is an ever-growing literary voice of that corrective movement. It should be recognized as such and encouraged in its effort. In a task of this magnitude there cannot be too many workers.

Tony Hillerman, perhaps the most respected author of Native American crime fiction working today, has been for decades the leading chronicler of our dominant society's injustices to the Native Americans and our debts to them. In his series of novels about the Navajo Indians and the crime fighters Joe Leaphorn and Jim Chee, and in his nonfiction, Hillerman has been a proponent for righting these wrongs. He feels, for example, that because the Indians are politically weak they have not been accorded all the freedoms guaranteed to other Americans, even small minorities who have come from Europe and Asia, by the First Amendment of the Constitution. This denial threatens the very soul of Native Americans: "While the United States recognizes religions imported from Europe and Asia, it has never given the same respect to the faiths of the people who were here when the Europeans arrived. In complicated ways, this double standard in our national attitude is destroying the cultures of Native American Tribes" (Greenberg 304). Hillerman is especially concerned with the freedom of religion that is necessary to the Indians because it forms the sinews and soul of their way of life. While the religious practices of other peoples have been respected, those of Native Americans have been scoffed into unimportance.

Hillerman points out that it is easy and proper to protect the holy places of recognized religions. We have strict laws against desecrating religious shrines and places of worship as well as worship itself. But Indian holy places are generally looked upon as physical natural wonders or geographical sites and therefore open for exploitation by those who do not consider them holy. As Hillerman comments: "Protection of tribal shrines presents a unique problem. Most are natural landmarks: mountains, lakes, springs, salt deposits, eagle nests high in mesa walls. They are never buildings. And the land where most of them are found is controlled by a dominant culture that hardly knows they exist" (306). The parallel with Ayers Rock in Australia as holy site is obvious. Whites look upon it as a fascinating tourist attraction and desecrate it in numerous careless ways, whereas to the Aborigines it is a sacred shrine.

Yet, as Hillerman says, "There are ways to grant full First Amendment rights of religious freedom to all Americans. We only lack the will" (Greenberg 307). And that will can grow only from pressure—political, financial, and moral—exerted on the dominant culture and its political representatives. Changes seldom occur, especially in the short run, merely because they are right. They have to be proved through pressure.

Increasingly, authors of ethnic crime fiction are trying to exert the power of moral suasion and hope for the resulting political action resulting from education. Experience has demonstrated that since frontier days, ignorance of Indian lifestyles has perpetuated the myths of savageness and strangeness and has helped keep them separate and strange and exotic and unequal. The American movie has been the most powerful force in casting this long shadow of ignorance to the American people. Wilcomb Washburn, in the Foreword to an informative group of essays in *Hollywood's Indian: The Portrayal of the Native American in Film,* stated the situation succinctly and comprehensively:

> The image of the American Indian, more than that of any other ethnic group, has been shaped by films. Why? Because the characteristics that define the American Indian are dramatically conveyed by this powerful twentieth-century medium. All American ethnic groups, of course, are defined—stereotyped, if you will—by Hollywood, but no other provides the opportunity to convey that image in a narrative form in terms of rapid physical movement, exotic appearance, violent confrontations, and a spirituality rooted in the natural environment.

Washburn goes on to emphasize that although the image of the American Indian has varied through history, "one is struck by the tone of admiration and frequent references to honor and nobility even in the context of cruelty and savagery" (ix).

The outlook of Americans now in our so-called Post-Boomer Gen X Age frequently shows a somewhat changed attitude, probably influenced or modified by movies, in fiction such as Max Brand's, Zane Grey's, and Louis L'Amour's. For example, prolific author J. F. Trainor insisted, in an interview, that as a child he, and apparently his playmates, never "thought of Indians as *the enemy*. If we were playing cowboy . . . I never had any objections to being the Indian chief. To me, they were fellow Americans of different customs and languages." Clearly older stereotypes and their resulting behavior are fading into the coolness of history.

This mixture of admiration for the Indian, in spite of or because of what some think is this reputed cruelty and savagery, has driven the myth of the Native American. Such feeling places the object on a pedestal yet in a position of inferiority, parallel to the attitude toward women that has persisted through the ages. But with an ever-increasing urgency we are recognizing that the more we understand the real, living Indian behind the myth and our ignorance, as with women and other "minority" groups, the faster our fears and antagonism to Indian cultures fade away. It is assumed that an educated public is a responsible public, and that when the dominant culture understands the lifestyle of an important minority culture—in this case Native Americans—and realizes the minimal threat it represents there will be more harmony between the cultures. Experience teaches that the more we understand different cultures, the weaker grow our fears of and antagonism to those cultures.

Ironically, one way to lower the walls of antagonism might be by linking the dominant White culture and the Indian cultures through a threat common to us all—crime and violence. Apparently the two great emotions people have are the Siamese twins love and hate, joined at the heart, the engine that propels all emotions, and driven by impulses that at times seem blind. Often love is achieved through violence or the threat of it. Feminist writers have discovered that the most effective way to elicit love is to demonstrate strength and, as an increasing body of female crime fiction authors have discovered, by making their protagonists equal to or superior to their male counterparts.

Often it is not easy to see beyond the power of violence, and various Indian authors discuss it with varying degrees of intensity. In an effective novel by Sherman Alexie, a Spokane/Coeur d'Alene Indian, America consists of two armed camps of cocked guns. *Indian Killer* is a novel of violence and murder, but not a detective mystery, where Alexie pictures the Indians and whites facing each other with genocide on the mind of the whites and murderous self-defense in the hands of the Indians. A murderer stalks the streets of Seattle, killing and scalping white men

with little identifiable pattern in choice of victim. Somewhat in retaliation and somewhat out of natural inclination, a small gang of white
toughs cruise Seattle streets searching for defenseless Indians to beat up
and kill. The city is thus split into the two camps: One—the white
toughs—operating in the security of societal dominance. The other
breathing the drugs of exclusion and insecurity; above all they want to
belong to their own Indian society and tribes.

Ironically named John Smith, an Indian was snatched from his Indian mother at birth and given to a white couple who were unable to
have their own child. In trying to determine who and what he is, Smith
gradually goes mad. He is, to paraphrase the despair of English Victorian poet Matthew Arnold in two of his most famous lines in *Stanzas
from the Grande Chartreuse* (1855), living in a world robbed of a future by
a people unable to conceive their own descendants. In similar situations
around Seattle, all Indians are alienated and hostile. One young female
in an Indian literature class taught by a white anthropologist at the University of Washington won't let him teach his class because although
he knows the literature and has lived on reservations for short periods
she thinks he knows nothing because he is not of Indian blood. As killings and beatings continue, the novel ends in mysticism and ambiguity.
Alexie does not clarify whether John Smith, the tribeless insane Indian,
is the killer, as he commits suicide in a way that melds him into tradition. But guilt of an individual is not important. The genocidal conflict
between Indians and whites has risen to mythological proportions. A
black man witnessing the conflict comforts himself by saying he is glad
he is black and thus free of the battle. But, Alexie intimates, the White-
Indian battle, now raised to the heroic level, will go on. It is not clear
whether the Indian killer is the pursued Indian who has been killing
whites or whites who have forced him into serial homicides. So the
novel is a mystery wrapped in uncertainty.

But the determination of the Indians to continue their fight is clear.
Alexie ends his novel in a paragraph of timeless determination on their
part. In what he calls "A Creation Story," Alexie places the killer after
death, wearing "a carved wooden mask, in an Indian cemetery where he
dances and sings on his determination, joined by other Indians who
learn the ritual and are joined by Indian animals and symbols. The
dance is five hundred years old and destined to last forever. The book
ends on a prophetic note: "The killer plans on dancing forever. The
killer never falls. The moon never falls. The tree grows heavy with owls."

With most Indian authors of crime fiction, however, the violence is less mythological and not so intense. It is more individualized and is person against system rather than race against race. As such personal remorse and atonement will have been at least partially successful. Sometimes the path of truth runs down the meanest streets to go through and reach various cultures. In the crime literature of Native Americans these mean streets frequently run through the swamps of four or five themes and motifs: 1) introduction of cocaine or other drugs into life on the reservation; 2) degradation of Indian land through drilling for oil or other minerals; 3) theft of Indian religious or other artifacts; 4) conflict between Indian desires to remain native or go out into white world; 5) imposition of some element of white culture on that of the Indians, especially the Romeo and Juliet convention that white women should not marry Indian men, an ever present subtheme in these works.

The writings of the thirteen authors in this study were chosen because of the quality of their novels and because of their backgrounds. Some are mixedbloods, some whites. Some carry in their hearts the leaden sins of their ancestors and are dedicated to trying to repay the Indians for the injustices they have suffered in the past. Others, because they know Indian cultures from having lived among them, write about them because they know Indian peoples and ways make good settings and characters. These authors have a primary purpose of writing to entertain and to sell. But regardless of leading purpose, all are doing all elements of American society a great service. Through the most elemental kind of fiction they center attention on one of the many cultures of our society. They realize that crime gives little distinction to social or cultural identity. It is more interested in vulnerability and accessibility. All people are vulnerable. All blood is red. In Indian crime fiction Indians are like all others and all others are like them. The authors try to picture the truth as they see it and through it to free us of prejudice and negative opinions. If they only partially succeed, their efforts have been helpful and, perhaps equally important, we have excellent crime fiction in the bargain. One could ask for little more.

My purpose in this study is to analyze and evaluate the individual works of the authors, and equally important, to point out how they comment, if they do, on the individual's reading of and attitude about the race relations between the several groups in the United States.

In investigating these elements we need to analyze the literature from four angles: 1) The Making of the Author; 2) Cultural Background and Development; 3) Protagonists, Associates, and Development; and 4) Literary Achievements.

CHAPTER ONE

The Making of the Author

In studying an author's development of an attitude and philosophy, it is imperative to see the writer's background and the shaping of his or her points of view. This is particularly significant in the analysis of authors of literature about Native Americans because of the power of the presence of Indians in American history and present-day culture. No person is without attitude and bias. In the case of white people's attitude toward Native Americans that bias exists close to the surface because of the importance of the frontier and the concept of the Noble Savage that has influenced our culture and because of our general sense of guilt and wrongdoing against the Natives who peopled the American Garden of Eden that the New World was thought to be.

The sense of wrongdoing against the natives of this Eden, which we were taught we had discovered, is a repudiation and a dirtying of the dream of Paradise and produces a sense of disappointment inside our psyches that is almost a religious disillusionment. If the natives in the Garden of Eden are not worthy of it, we think, then it must not be the ideal for which human nature has longed. This conclusion leaves us more desolate and hopeless. If civilization has also proved a profanation of Eden, then there is no hope in our continued search for other Gardens unless we are willing to reverse the irreversible flow of civilization and all go back to primitive cultures. That leaves us with nothing on earth that is better than mundane reality and smashes our hopes for all happiness except in the afterlife. The conclusions frame a dark picture.

In writing about Paradise destroyed, the injustices done to the American native, the hope for improvement in treatment, the author projects his or her own conscious or unconscious attitudes, the cognitive and physical environment in which he grew up and developed his dispositions both negative and positive. To a lesser degree these attitudes are influenced by the stereotypes and generalizations as part of the air around him. In the case of Native Americans, these stereotypes have been strong and graphic and difficult to negate because they present an inferior group that the self-styled superior people find comforting and reassuring to have in their view if not their midst.

But an author is what he or she writes and what she or he writes is what she is. Sometimes the author casts a short shadow, sometimes a long one. And the shadow, though at times crooked and tenuous, reveals the essence of the author, his spirit now and probably at least to a certain extent in the future.

James Fenimore Cooper, for example, could pen his Leatherstocking saga because his family had lived on the frontier and interacted with Indians. Herman Melville, one of the more contemplative authors of the nineteenth century, wrote his enigmatic "The Indian Hater" in an effort to convince his readers that American society's hatred of Indians, before and during his lifetime, was an attitude he found cancerous in the body culture. Mark Twain traveled throughout the world and lived in all sections of the United States; he visited the Mississippi of his youth, after moving away, only when he had to. But in effect he never left Hannibal. His wife, Livy, called Twain "Youth," but she might just as properly have named him "Memory" or "Nostalgia." He could not flush out the life-juices of his youth on the banks of America's mightiest river. He, for example, always used Tom Sawyer and Huckleberry Finn as investigators in his several crime stories. Helen Hunt Jackson wrote her idyllic novel *Ramona* (1884) because of what she had learned in her study of society's mistreatment of Indians and published as *A Century of Dishonor* (1881).

Authors sometimes write projections of problems or situations of which they are only distantly a part or are connected only through imagination. Such is the beauty and strength of creativity. Zane Grey and Max Brand, two of the three most popular authors of westerns of all time, had never traveled in the West when they wrote their stories. Irving Wallace wrote *The Man,* as we have seen, because he wanted to study the phenomenon of America with its first black president. Peter

Benchley wrote *Jaws* because of the vitality of the stereotype of the shark as "the perfect killing machine." Stephen King and Anne Rice feed richly today on America's fascination with horror.

The authors in this study, like others throughout our society, wrote their stories because they are who they are in the moment of history in which they live. They are mirrors reflecting and refracting that reality. All can look around themselves and some can look into the future. All to one degree or another want to leave notes of some life accomplishment on the bulletin board of history. They want at least a tick on history's roadway by which to be noted and remembered. All are propelled and guided by the generative force of their backgrounds.

Tony Hillerman

Native American crime fiction reaches its zenith, in the eyes of many critics, in the work of Anthony Grove Hillerman, acknowledged dean of ethnic crime fiction and CEO of American southwestern and Western literature in general. His works are the high water mark against which others are compared. Rightly or wrongly all writers of Native American crime fiction are weighed on Hillerman scales. His endorsement is sought by publishers on at least half a dozen manuscripts a month on all kinds of literature. He has turned to anthologizing various types of ethnic stories and Western fiction. He is the symbol of advocacy literature in crime fiction on native rights today.

Hillerman's background was propitious for the role he developed. He was raised in Oklahoma among Potawatomi and Seminole Indians and for eight years attended an Indian school for girls, where he acquired his compassion for the downtrodden and disenfranchised in general and Native Americans in particular. A veteran of World War II, he has been a reporter, news editor, city editor, political editor, bureau manager, executive editor, professor, and assistant to the president of the University of New Mexico. Currently, despite problematic health, he is active and frequently in the news.

To Hillerman ethnic crime novels seemed to be instruments for accomplishing two goals. They are "the ideal way to engage readers in a subject of life-long interest: . . . the religions, cultures, and value systems of Navajo and Pueblo Indians" (*Talking Mysteries* 27), and through that interest to sway public opinion toward a healthier attitude about Native Americans than that held historically.

To be most effective, a writer such as Hillerman, though not necessarily a blooded Indian, must be authentic and realistic. He or she must choose genuine settings and personalities. For his models in authors, Hillerman chose strong exemplars and developed his own stories vigorously. He began by deeply understanding the ethnic crime stories of the Australian author Arthur W. Upfield (1888–1964) and making them bone of his bone:

> I cannot honestly say that when I set about to write my own versions of the mystery novel, Arthur Upfield was consciously in my mind. Subconsciously, he certainly was. Upfield had shown me—and a great many other mystery writers—how both ethnography and geography can be used in a plot and how they can enrich an old, old literary form. When my own Jim Chee of the Navajo Tribal Police unravels a mystery because he understands the ways of his people, when he reads the signs left in the sandy bottom of a reservation arroyo, he is walking in the tracks Bony made 50 years ago. (*Talking Mysteries* 28)

Hillerman does it, of course, in a way different from Upfield's. The Australian writer wrote his mysteries as tell and show, Hillerman does his show and tell. Upfield gave the explanation and then the example. Hillerman gives the adventure then the explanation. Like Upfield's Bony with his marvelous natural tracking skill in his work, Hillerman has Jim Chee explain why Native Americans are excellent at this work, but there is a difference in Hillerman's attitude. Bony has a natural innate talent. Hillerman, wanting to place his Native Americans more in the mainstream of American society, insists that their tracking ability is cognitive and the result of training.

In *The Dark Wind,* for example, a white lawyer named Gaines, one of the associated villains in the work, says to Jim Chee, "I've always heard that Indians were good trackers." Chee responds, dignifying both the skill and the people who practice it, "Some Navajos are good at tracking. Some aren't. You learn it by studying it. Like law" (73). The details on learning the pages of the book on the art of tracking are explicit:

> You see a man walk by. You go look at the tracks. You see him walk by, carrying something heavy in one hand. You look at the tracks. You go again tomorrow to look at the tracks after a day. And after two days. You see a fat man and a thin man squatting in the shade, talking. When they leave, you go and look at the marks a fat man makes when he squats on his heels, and the marks a thin man makes. (73–74)

Undoubtedly, also, Hillerman felt the injustice voiced by Upfield done by the whites to the Australian Aborigines, since the cases with the original natives of Australia and America were parallel. Upfield voiced his indignation explicitly: "The first white man to set foot in Australia brought with him the Serpent from the Garden of Eden, when no longer was there in all the land law and laughter . . . only the slow progress of segregation into compounds and settlements of ever dwindling remnants of a race" (*Murder Must Wait* 125). Or Upfield's harsher criticism of the white man's abuse of the aborigines: "The bodies of Australian aborigines had rotted to dry dust in the hot sands of the deserts; had slowly perished in creeks and waterholes; had swelled with the effects of the white man's poison; and festered with the effects of the white man's bullets" (*Venom House* 69–70). Little wonder that Hillerman was inflamed by what he thought were parallel injustices to the Indians of America.

Not only a cultural commentator, however, Hillerman has been influenced by other masters in crime fiction who made the presentation of his thesis more effective, as he named them: Eric Ambler, "because he never wrote the same book twice"; Raymond Chandler, "a master of setting scenes which engage all the senses and linger in the mind"; Graham Greene; Ross Macdonald, who "taught every one of us that, given enough skill with metaphoric language, one plot is all you ever need for as many books as you care to write"; George V. Higgins; and Joan Didion, with her "superb journalism" (*Talking Mysteries* 27–28).

Hillerman learned his craft thoroughly and created his own territory for development different from others'. Whereas Upfield, for example, sometimes positions his characters, especially his protagonist Bony, in the epic tradition, Hillerman has made his protagonists grow against an authentic background with thorough cultural authenticity and analysis. As experienced journalist he has an eye for details, as avid amateur anthropologist he has searched for the essence of cultures, and as storyteller he has known how to weave in details for a captivating story. His reputation as chronicler of a minority culture is assured, quite different from that of Upfield, whose writings have been banned from the Australian Aboriginal canon because of a misreading of the texts and the author's purpose.

Hillerman is proud that both the Navajo and Zuni recognize their culture in his books and read them widely. "His novels are used in English classes in Reservation schools," writes Ernie Bulow, who knows both Hillerman and the Indians well, "and are immensely popular with the Navajo people, being passed from hand to hand until they literally fall apart with the reading" (*Talking Mysteries* 15). Hillerman himself, in his describing his pride in writing his stories authentically, quotes a Navajo librarian who says that when she and her customers read about Hillerman's Indians, they say, "Yes, this is us. But now we win. Like the stories our grandmother used to tell us, they make us feel good about being Navajos."

"As a fellow country boy, I am proud of that," Hillerman concludes (*Talking Mysteries* 43). Hillerman disclaims that his ethnological material is "intended to meet scholarly and scientific standards" but tries to make it realistic and authentic. As he admits in the Acknowledgment of *The Blessing Way*, "ethnological material as used in this book is not intended to meet scholarly and scientific standards," and he admits having taken his material from the publications of scholars, thus making it secondhand, as well as the advice and information provided by his own Navajo friends, thus making it subject to the interpretations of his informants. Because he is not a blooded Indian Hillerman is criticized by fullbloods and mixedbloods for writing about a subject for which he is not qualified, by blood, to be concerned with. But he cannot redo lineage and must work as best he can with what he has. To criticize him or anybody else for working on subjects that blood has not "qualified" them for seems not only shortsighted but also self-defeating. After all, Thomas Jefferson and George Washington and the thousands of other patriots who won the Revolutionary War were not qualified through blood for revolution. Quite the contrary. They were qualified by lineage to remain loyal to the throne. But they threw off the reins of heritage and lineage for new and higher goals.

Jean Hager

Authors of Indian crime fiction present their stories with varying degrees of Indian lore and culture. Some place their adventures in the white society so that they can have the Native Americans acting as a subculture in that more dominant society as well as the Indian society. Other authors, an increasing number, restrict their stories to the Indian community, reaching out to the surrounding white society only when logical reality demands the interaction. Both types, though striving to tell an engaging mystery story, in effect, willfully or inadvertently reveal the characteristics of Native American cultures, their differences from the dominant white culture, and the conflicts that result from their coexistence.

Jean Hager belongs to the type who writes of Native Americans as though they are essentially a semihomogeneous culture. She can do this because she is one-sixteenth Cherokee, and in the population of Oklahoma one of every seven people has Cherokee blood in his or her veins. Increasingly these people are conscious, even assertive, of their heritage. Their culture in America is dense enough to provide the setting for crime fiction. Although Hager feels she is an "outsider" from the Cherokee race, through learning and writing she tries more and more to become an insider, "one of them." Increasingly as she learns more about their culture, Hager can live in and write of it more convincingly and make it a self-contained community culture.

Her writing career has been long, but only recently has she turned to mysteries involving the Cherokee. She always wanted to write. She was encouraged by a librarian in elementary school and wrote short stories in those early years. At Oklahoma State University she took a course in creative writing and graduated with a degree, as most wannabe authors do, in English. While teaching school in Cleveland, Oklahoma, she nourished her desire to be a writer. She enrolled in a correspondence writing course and joined a writing group in Tulsa. After that, as we say, her history is one of writing.

She had read all the mystery books, like the Nancy Drews, as a child. In 1970 she wrote a children's mystery that sold locally to schools and libraries. Encouraged, she followed with a series of adult novels that did not sell. One was *Terror in the Sunlight*, written under the name of Amanda McAlester, which featured an English teacher as heroine. Perhaps its flesh was too close to the autobiographical bone. She wrote two other romantic suspense novels, *Evil Side of Eden* and *Shadow of the Tamarack*, under the pen name of Sara North. She found a literary agent through a conference for professional writers, which she attended at the University of Oklahoma, was encouraged to read romance novels like the Harlequin series, and turned out *Captured by Love*, whose heroine was a veterinarian.

Hager subsequently began writing for Harlequin but quickly "burned out" on these, as she says, and finally decided to write contemporary mysteries. She began the Irish House series about the closed environment of a bed-and-breakfast setting and the people who for one reason or another meet there. These "cozies," as Hager admits, are "total fantasy," and agrees with fellow Indian crime writer Jake Page that "the reader has to suspend reality to accept the whole premise." But Hager has "fun especially exploring the characters." Like all authors she claims she never knows the ending beforehand and is often "amazed at how the story happens and the end is often a surprise" (interview).

She continues to write these Golden Age mysteries while at the same time developing her two series on Cherokee culture. The first series involves Mitchell Bushyhead, mixedblood chief of police in the small town of Buckskin, Oklahoma, and his three fullblood deputies. A parallel series has developed involving Molly Bearpaw, an official with several Cherokee tribal associations, and her sometime love, D. J. Kennedy, a white police lieutenant. With already four novels about each of these protagonists, she plans two or three more. Unlike Tony Hillerman, who finally put his Jim Chee and Joe Leaphorn protagonists together in a series, Hager does not plan to have hers work in the same novel. So far she has written the impressive number of over fifty-five books on all kinds of subjects and is still going strong. Her most accomplished successes are easily the Bushyhead and Bearpaw series.

Jake Page

One of a half-dozen most powerful authors of Native American crime fiction is Jake Page, who has published five such novels so far. His tribe of choice is the Hopi of New Mexico and northeastern Arizona. He centers on their life and activities around Santa Fe, New Mexico, a city for which he has a love-hate relationship—love of its beauty and tradition, contempt for its commercialization of its facade and its pretentiousness. Santa Fe, Page has his leading character say, has "various social tribes that effectively define the city," and those tribes "have two overriding convictions. . . . One is that Santa Fe is as close to the original Eden as mankind has come since Adam and Eve were banished" (*Gods* 13).

The second is that Santa Fe is a small city, with all the advantages generally associated with a town of that size. Page thinks both personal convictions about a geographical site may be pushed too far. His evaluation comes from a cool dispassionate analysis that reveals all kinds of serpents in the Garden, such as pride, greed, blatant ambition, desire to shine in the public eye, and self-nurtured ignorance. In other words, Santa Fe is or is coming to be like Albuquerque, which Page hates, and other American cities.

Page, who has no Indian blood, writes of the Hopi Indians because he has lived and worked among them with his photographer wife, Susanne Anderson, since the early 1980s and knows them well, not, he says in the "sappy way a lot of people are who meet Indians and want to wear feathers or whatever" (this and following quotes are from personal interview), but in a much profounder and more respectful way. Knowledge breeds respect. He respects the Hopi and they know they can count on him for friendly assistance whenever he can help, as he has on several occasions.

A Hopi tribal chieftain once asked Page if he would publish magazine articles about the theft of four Indian gods, a matter of profound importance to the Hopi. Page wrote such an article for the *Smithsonian* magazine, which turned it down because, Page feels, it "implicated a sister museum" in the trading of Indian religious artifacts," a crime against the federal government because the tribes fall under the jurisdiction of the Bureau of Indian Affairs and therefore are policed by the FBI. Page subsequently wrote another article, for *Connoisseur Magazine*, which also turned it down because, Page felt, it "would be offensive to galleries" (interview). Having been forced to drink the gall of the injustice of the art world's treatment of less powerful cultures, Page decided to write a novel on the subject, the kachinas, the religious artifacts that he considers splendid and deserving of the praise voiced by one art historian as "the most profound works of art in North America."

In his first novel, *The Stolen Gods*, Page shakes a large fist of accusation at art collectors and dealers who by hook or crook get control of and sell Hopi art to outside collectors who cannot understand and are indifferent to its religious significance. Callously and greedily they deprive the Indians of the soul of their existence, fattening on the commercial exploitation of religious artifacts. Page scornfully labels such practice *simony* in the biblical sense of the word.

Page does understand the significance of the kachinas, their use in religious practices, and other manifestations of spirituality in the lifestyle of the Hopi. He wants to pay back the Indians for the sins of his fellow Americans and freely and fully offers his personal, family, and racial remorse and atonement for the misbehavior of fellow whites: "Over the years," he says in the Author's Note to his first book, "many Hopi people have enriched my life and my family's lives in ways that one does not count. This tale is offered, in one sense, in the spirit of reciprocity to those people and will, I trust, be taken as such. They call it *paying back*" (*Gods* 2). Page feels that he and his family are not alone in their need to pay back. It is a national, cultural debt, not in money but in recognition and respect.

Sometimes Page pays back in heroic proportions. For example, in *The Deadly Canyon* he supplies a Coda in which he has Mo, the sculptor-investigator hero in all his books, unveil a sculpture, about which he has been talking, at the Desert Research Center in the high Chiricahua Mountains. It is "an Apache woman warrior. Indian women, they're strong of heart and will. Always were. And I thought you folks might like a reminder about those people who used to live around here," Mo says in a short and pithy dedicatory speech (*Canyon* 237). Such tributes to the Indians could hardly be more straightforward or go unappreciated.

Like fellow Southwest author of Native American crime fiction Tony Hillerman, Page personifies the remorse and debt owed to Indians and makes every effort to atone for mistreatment of them in general and the Hopi in particular. Throughout his novels, however, like Louis Owens, he carefully avoids what he calls the "sappy" sentimentality of people who see only the surface of Hopi life, the feathers and dances, and feel remorse for abuse of the superficial offenses.

Page treats the Hopi with profound respect. Sometimes his villains are Hopi Indians, sometimes they are naive and gullible. Generally, however, Hopi society is in one way or another victimized. And Page's atonement is for the American nation in general. He universalizes his atonement by developing a hero who grows through the generality of folklore into mythology and thus to Everyman or at least Every Ethnic Crime Fighter.

Aimée and David Thurlo

Aimée and David Thurlo, a husband and wife team also living in New Mexico, have written some thirty novels under their own names and pseudonyms, as well as various other kinds of materials in such publications as *Grit, Popular Mechanics,* and *National Enquirer.* Their novels, including such titles as *Timewalker, Black Mesa, Spirit Warrior,* and *Strangers Who Linger,* have appeared in more than twenty countries. Their latest series, involving Ella Clah, Rose, Clifford, and Wilson Joe, promises to be even more widespread. Individually and collectively the two work well together because their interests dovetail and are very compatible.

Aimée, after coming to the United States from Havana, Cuba, when she was seven years old, went to Catholic boarding schools, then Louisiana State University in New Orleans. She moved to Albuquerque and settled next door to David, who had been born there and raised on a Navajo reservation. He went to college at the University of New Mexico, Albuquerque, and while a student met and married Aimée, then continued on to graduate studies. He taught science in Albuquerque for twenty-five years and has just retired.

Aimée began her first novel around 1979, and David helped as he could, by editing and, as he says, playing "devil's advocate." The manuscript was placed with a publisher after about six months. From that first endeavor the two learned how to work together as collaborators on the same work of fiction. David tells of their collaborative technique:

> We soon learned that my strength was plotting, action and detail work, and Aimée was best at dialogue and characterization. Nowadays, I write the basic story outline, Aimée does the first draft, then we take turns with drafts, both adding whatever we think is needed, and editing extensively. Working together, we go through 4 to 5 drafts before a novel is finished. (This and following quotes are from personal interview)

Apparently they are perfectly in sync novelistically. "Though our work is very demanding," he says, "we always manage to decide on what's best for the manuscript. . . . We've developed ways of solving our writing problems by talking things over. I think one of our advantages is that our strengths are in different areas, and we trust each other."

Like most effective storytellers they want to be primarily novelists and not propagandists or do-gooders. Both have a "deep respect and admiration for the Navajo culture and people," about whom they write, instilled in David "at an early age." Like all of the effective authors of Native American crime fiction, they "try to write respectfully and honestly" about the Navajos and their culture, "hoping that the readers will appreciate and respect the Navajos as a unique culture." In that unique culture there are good guys and bad guys, good Indians and bad Indians, but the Thurlos try to "represent the majority as the decent, honest, patriotic citizens that we've seen them to be."

The Thurlos are not interested in having white society "pay back" the Navajo for the sins of their forefathers. "The tragedy with most 'payback,' in my opinion," David says, "is that it usually benefits those who weren't maligned by hurting those who weren't responsible for the original suffering. We're not here to teach any lessons or function as advocates or spokespersons."

Instead of any anachronistic, postdate payoff or compensation, the Thurlos want instead a level playing field with equal dignity and respect for all participants. "The dignity we give our characters, and to the Dineh (the Navajos) in general, is something every culture is entitled to receive, and we don't need a soapbox to justify that to the reading public."

Remorse and atonement are not a conscious part of their purpose. "We're trying to entertain the reader, and if they are enlightened a little at the same time, that's good too." But because they are successful authors writing on a subject pregnant with offspring that move in the positive cultural directions, in presenting the Navajo realistically they edge over toward correction of inaccurate attitudes.

Successful novelists—especially popular culture novelists—seek entertainment as their primary goal. Not to be entertaining is to be not read and therefore not further published. But entertainment wears at least two faces. A writer can entertain negatively, presenting characters and actions as undesirable: stereotypically evil, sly, malicious, murderous, destructive in every way. Or a writer can entertainingly present their people and culture as decent, honest, law-abiding, and desirable in most if not all ways, in other words, realistically.

Each presentation influences readers or watchers, or at least we think it does. Most of us are convinced that the positive presentation of violence—for instance—on TV and in movies influences behavior negatively. Copycat violence seems to be the latest manifestation. All of us know that advertising—which to be most effective must be entertaining—influences, commodifies, and directs attitudes that drive behavior. Some entertainers have done more harm than they admit to or intended, while others certainly have accomplished more good then they might have hoped. Apparently the Thurlos may be in the second category and their fiction may be positive in ways not foreseen but certainly desirable. They authenticate their works but at the same time at least hint at a second, a "higher," purpose. With other authors that "higher" purpose always looks out in different ways. It is from behind stage in the works of Dana Stabenow.

Dana Stabenow

Ethnic crime fiction is fast catching on and developing in Alaska. That growth should be expected. Alaska, our forty-ninth state, is a strange and fascinating country, where existence is challenging, and the people who survive in the outback must be hard and assertive, and are likely at times to be stirred to violence. Some authors of crime fiction in this venue use the setting as background for conventional works, where the emphasis is on the crime and its solution, as in the works of John Straley, a Sitka private investigator, and Sue Henry.

Of a different nature, using the uniqueness of Alaska for an entirely different achievement is the effective writer Dana Stabenow, who uses characters as well as the magnificent and challenging natural world to develop Aleut culture, people, and crimes.

Stabenow was raised in a half-Aleut half-Filipino family in Seldovia, Alaska. Wanting to write from childhood on, she has experimented with numerous kinds of literature. She began her career with a science fiction novel, *Second Star* (1990), and has recently turned to crime novels. With the success of seven books featuring Kate Shugak, Stabenow has signed with Dutton to "write a new series featuring an Alaska state trooper and his significant other, a bush pilot, which will be set in Bristol Bay, Alaska, the salmon-fishing capitol of the world," she wrote to me.

The new Liam Campbell series will have to be exemplary to outshine the seven so far produced in the series featuring Kate Shugak, her main character, her significant other Jack Morgan, and the really splendid creation, Kate's grandmother, Emaa. In fact the first Liam Campbell, *Fire and Ice,* departs from the Alaskan natives personnel and merely uses Alaska as setting for a fascinating action story of murder through use of an airplane propeller. It is a fine story but not to our point.

Stabenow writes of the Aleut, not Alaskan natives in general. In clarifying the several kinds of peoples in Alaska, Stabenow is explicit: "Aleuts are not Native Americans, they are Alaska Natives. Same with Inupiat, Yupik, Athabascans, Tlingits, Haida and Tsimshian. . . . Inupiat and Yup'ik do not take kindly to being called Indians, and Athabascans are averse to being called Eskimo." In other words, the Alaskan "melting pot" does not generate enough heat in this climate to blend cultures that naturally through frigid centrifugal cultural forces continue to be thrown into their many constituent parts. Stabebow's works are included in this study because they are about one of the minorities in the larger American dominant culture.

In this land of conflicting constituent cultures Stabenow is strong on adventure in her fiction. Her novels carry the sharp imprint of life among the Aleut. She has two kinds of novels—those which are strongly action oriented and the others which are more character development. Those of action—*Dead in the Water* and *A Cold-Blooded Business*—are so tense with activity that it tends to overwhelm the main characters. The action drives the plot and forces the characters into the background. Stabenow's other novels have less physical action and allow the personalities and the crime fiction aspects to be the major points of interest. Sometimes the novels are pastoral, if indeed Alaskan landscape can be termed pastoral. They open on a setting to allow crime to intrude and break up an otherwise quiet and peaceful world. These books define a different kind and pace of character development, in which the conventional modes of sleuthing are more apparent.

Stabenow differs from such authors as Jake Page, Jean Hager, and Tony Hillerman in purpose or in degree of purpose concerning the people about whom she writes. But in the end she joins them in not being averse to trying to "pay back" prediscovery Americans for the wrongs that have been inflicted on them through the centuries. Her declared purpose is "to entertain. I'm not a teacher, or a sociologist, or an anthropologist, or a booster. I'm a writer. I write popular fiction. You could even call me a performer. I want to make 'em laugh, make 'em cry, make 'em shiver. If I make 'em think, too, that's just the icing on the cake," she wrote to me.

But that's her strength. She has plenty of icing. We all know that presenting a way of life of people in a different society compels readers to think. No one, for example, could have walked away from Leonard Bernstein's *West Side Story* without having been touched to one degree or another with the humanity of the members of the Cuban-American street gangs presented so effectively in that musical. No reader of *Gone with the Wind* laid down the book without some kind of reaction to the Civil War and the terrible aftermath. No one read Dee Brown's *Bury My Heart at Wounded Knee* without experiencing a strong reaction. No one, likewise, reads of the Native Aleut in Alaska in Stabenow's works without being better informed and without having developed some degree of empathy for them.

Stabenow knows this. She also knows that she cannot write about them and be merely an entertainer. She is their back door advocate. Her feelings run deep.

> The people indigenous to this area had been, by the time I was born into it, so assimilated into the predominant Western-White culture that their own culture had almost ceased to exist.
>
> Almost. They're recovering it now, slowly, due in large part to the lands and money they acquired through ANCSA. Land and money means power, a commodity in which they were largely lacking until 1973. In the past twenty-four years they've made a good start at running the BIA out of business, taking over the administration of NA education, health care and housing programs.
>
> I remember when I was growing up in Seldovia. People would try to hide their Native heritage. Now it is a matter of pride and spiritual sustenance. It is a wonderful thing to see.

In the final paragraph of this section of her letter Stabenow makes clear one of her purposes in writing the books: "It's a wonderful thing to write about, even if only in fiction."

Many issues of importance boil to the surface in Kate Shugak's world. Among them are Native sovereignty and fishing rights. And in future works Kate "will definitely be concerned with both," Stabenow promises. In one of her latest Shugak books, in fact, Kate goes far beyond such issues, important as they are, and reaches out to hover over one of the basic issues of society, women's rights. In *Hunter's Moon* Stabenow and Kate are concerned almost exclusively with women's rights. Kate is the universal feminist. But Stabenow is essentially the universal author, and she will choose and develop any topic that comes to hand or mind.

Louis Owens

It may not be necessary to have Indian blood in your veins to write crime fiction about the Native Americans and the injustices they have suffered at the hands of whites, but it can add a natural vitriol that fuels caustic comments. Add to that vitriol a lot of academic detailed knowledge and friendship with other mixedblood academics, like Gerald Vizenor, perhaps the outstanding scholar of Native American literature, and we have the author Louis Owens, a mixedblood of Choctaw-Cherokee-Irish extraction. His Indian blood drives him to present his characters in a manner unlike other authors of Native American crime fiction. Owens is a mystic, like James Doss, and much more. He lives naturally in the Indian world of mystery and the white existence of reality.

His books are filled with this characteristic of Indian culture. Owens says that he has always believed in perceptions that are not intellectual or rational and "in communications that might be termed extra-rational, in spirit, in dreams, etc" (This and the following quotes are from personal interview). Such experiences came with his mother's milk and food, and he has had "direct contact with what people might term 'ghosts' and so on. That's simply a part of a larger reality that figures in my fiction. Either a reader crosses that threshold or he doesn't, but if he doesn't then the fiction probably does not work." In continuing amplification and explication on the roots of his fiction Owens says:

> In addition to writing about reality as I have always perceived it, including dream reality, I also want to extend my readers' consciousness and challenge them by urging them to see beyond ordinary limitations. I cross boundaries as much as possible, with characters who are of more

than one culture and ethnic heritage and with characters who inhabit more than one kind of reality. I think you will find a lot of . . . mysticism in writing by and about Native Americans in large part because Indian people tend to see the world in this way, tend to believe in realities beyond "perceptual or intellectual apprehension but central to being." I don't personally know any Indian people, for example, who do not take dreams very, very seriously. And I have immediate, personal evidence that Indian people share experiences and communicate through dreams.

Owens is professor of English and author of five thrillers, *Wolfsong, The Sharpest Sight, Bone Game, Nightland,* and *Dark River.* His protagonist in two of his novels, Cole McCurtain, in the second book teaches Indian Studies at the University of California, Santa Cruz. Owens, being Choctaw-Cherokee-Irish, creates a protagonist with yet another strain in his blood—Cajun—the net result for both author and character makes for complicated reactions to culture and to white intrusions into it.

Peter Bowen

This same, though even more complicated mixture of bloods, animates Peter Bowen. His varied background includes stints as a carpenter, a barkeep, cowboy, folksinger, and fishing-and-hunting guide; he currently writes an outdoor column for *Forbes FYI* under the name Coyote Jack. He is author of five crime novels featuring Gabriel Du Pré, a Métis, that is, a combination of French-Crow-Choctaw and other Indian bloods, people who were chased out of Canada by the British and went to Montana or, in the case of the Cajuns, to Louisiana, where they regrouped as mixedbloods and continued to hate the English with undying passion.

Crime fiction writers try to create mystery solvers who are distinguished not only by their mental acumen but also their physical appearance. In pulp fiction in the 1920s these physical attributes ranged through all conceivable abnormalities making people deformed or in some striking way different from normal. In Native American crime fiction the most striking is, perhaps, Jake Page's Mo Bowdre, who stands six-feet-two-inches tall with a full white beard and a black Stetson to match the dark glasses over his blind eyes. Bowen's Gabriel Du Pré, though not so noticeably large, is the likes of which you don't see except perhaps among the hippies of the 1960s or their present-day throwbacks. He lets his hair grow long, is always drinking, and is indifferent to appearance. His companion, a Métis lady named Madelaine, is very careful about her appearance because she is vain and always trying to arouse and respond to Du Pré's sexual drive. Together, and with several other strong characters who resemble them in many ways, these two form the nucleus of a society not seen outside Faulkner's Yoknapatawpha County or the worlds of Snuffy Smith or Dogpatch, speaking in a language that Du Pré insists is Montanan and which at times needs some translation.

Margaret Coel

The Arapaho Indians live on the Wind River Reservation in Northern Arizona. They supplement their income by leasing land for oil and gas development and with income from casino activities. They are the subject of six novels by Margaret Coel, called "a master" by no less an authority than Tony Hillerman. Her novels analyze the Native's evil and the impact the dominant white society has on it and the resulting conflict between the two.

Before turning to the Arapho for subject matter, Coel wrote numerous articles on the American West that appeared in the *New York Times*, *Christian Science Monitor*, *Denver Post* and *American Heritage of Invention and Technology*. She is the author of four nonfiction books. For *Chief Left Hand: Southern Arapaho* (1981), Coel initiated the research needed to tell the story of an Arapaho chief in the mid-1800s. This research stimulated her interest in and concern for Arapaho culture and led to her fiction works about them.

During her research into the Chief's life, Coel met many Arapaho people, made steadfast friends, and felt a deep kinship to the Indian culture. "I like the culture very much," she says in our interview correspondence. "There are many things about it that appeal to me and, over the years, have changed my attitudes. For example, the Arapahos believe human beings should strive to live in harmony and balance with one another and with all of creation—the earth, the four leggeds, the wingeds—that every creature has value. I like that. They believe old people are wise and sacred, and it is wonderful to see the respect with which they treat their elders. When the Arapahos lived on the plains in the Old Time, they were well known for their hospitality. They are still hospitable and generous. No matter how little they may have, they will share it."

Her first Arapaho novel was *The Eagle Catcher,* and it vindicated their trust in her. The Indians were so appreciative that they held a celebration on the reservation for the author, with a feast, music, dancers, and a master of ceremonies. Coel felt it was "great."

Coel's fondness and respect for the Arapaho sparkle through her novels. Her plots, she says, originate with newspaper accounts of real issues affecting the Indian tribes. She knows the intensity of these issues because she visits the Wind River Reservation every year and talks to her friends there. They were not, however, always friends and hospitable. The Arapaho, Coel feels, are a private people with what they consider reason to distrust outsiders. It took Coel some time to prove herself amenable and reliable before they placed their trust in her. She has not let them down in her writings.

She begins her first novel "dedicated with respect to the Arapahos, people of the plains and of the blue sky," and in an "Author's Note," among other things asserts that, "for more than a century, European-Americans have continued to devise a host of ingenious methods to defraud American Indian tribes across the West." Also, despite the fact that some of the Arapaho characters in her books are drunks and violent individuals, she often has her characters talk about the injustices of whites and how the Indians hate their oppressors.

In her second novel, *The Ghost Walker,* Coel points out further the feeling of trust that the natives have for one another. On the reservation, for example, Indians don't lock their cars. "If someone came to take your material possessions, well that person must be in great need. That was the Arapaho way" (interview), but in the corrupt white world you lock or lose. Most Indians are likely to be corrupted when they go off the reservation into the white world. And whites invade the reservation for their own nefarious and dangerous reasons. Coel's sensitive observations catalogue the many nuances of Arapaho life.

The Dream Stalker, her third novel, involves a standoff between Indians and whites who want to lease a portion of the Wind River Reservation for a nuclear waste storage site. Vicky Holden, Coel's protagonist, seeing death and tribal disaster in the future, will not bear the thought of such misuse of reservation land. Because of her opposition, she becomes the object of would-be murderers.

Coel's fourth novel, *The Story Teller,* takes up a subject common in Indian mysteries, the theft of Native American artifacts and their sale or display in museums. The Native American Graves Protection and

Repatriation Act (NAGPRA) authorizes Indian tribes to recover such artifacts. But when such items have been returned to the Arapaho, certain items, notably a rare and beautiful ledger book, worth millions, is missing, and the museum says it never had such an artifact. Vicky and Father John, priest of a failing parish, must begin a search for the missing book and for the murderer of an Arapaho student who died mysteriously while working in the ledger.

Her fifth novel, *The Lost Bird,* is a study in nostalgia, the years of the past when the Arapaho Nation was more of a community before whites began exploiting the People's most prized possessions, their babies, and the whole nation's future. Greedy whites take advantage of the reality of polluted water in a housing development and circulate the "medical opinion" that most Arapaho babies die at birth from this pollution. Actually the babies are being shipped out to be sold to whites for large fees. Vicky Holden and Father John must suffer threats and difficulties to uncover the truth in this situation.

James D. Doss

Artifacts, through their fascinating and informative languages, lure many authors into writing about Indians. These artifacts come from various sources. Throughout the western United States, and especially the Southwest, they are sold and exhibited in roadside stands and museums as contemporary arts and crafts with rich intrinsic merits. They come also from legal and illegal digs that provide us with materials of the cultures of the past. Illegal obtaining and theft of Indian artifacts provides the backbone of many of the plots of books by authors in this study.

Arrowheads are the Indian artifacts that have impacted the American people most. Almost from the day little boys step out of their rompers they begin to search for arrowheads. Having found one, the child puts it into his pocket and constantly touches and rubs it as a talisman that will bring good fortune. Or he hides it in his most sacred treasure trove as a prize. Wherever it is treasured, the arrowhead provides a link to a culture, a people, and a way of life that fueled by dreams of the Edenic paradise of the past sprouts wings on which one soars into dreamland. It is the simplest but one of the most effective cultural stimulants.

This dreamland is one of the great myths of human existence, and especially of America, where the Frontier, the West, the Great Beyond the Hills has always fueled the American wanderlust and dream. It was at first nurtured in the concept of the Noble Savage and his assumed bucolic way of life. Interestingly, this way of life of the Noble Savage, strengthened constantly by movies, TV, and popular literature, is now being brought full circle and is increasingly appreciated by environmentalists and others who see much inherent value and beauty, as Louis Owens says, in the Indian way of life. These people are now trying to recapture some aspects of the Old Time, and in so doing are directly or indirectly paying back some of the debt we feel we owe because of injustices of the past to Indians.

James D. Doss was one of those kids who early on succumbed to the lure of the arrowhead. "I grew up in the midwest, mostly in western Kentucky," he wrote in interview correspondence with me. "One of my greatest pleasures as a youth was to find flint arrow-points in plowed fields." From that early stimulation he began to get more professionally involved. "When I was about 12, I joined archeological societies in Illinois, Indiana, and Ohio so I could have a subscription to their journals." His interest in Indians has been lifelong and grows more intense every day.

Doss writes about the Utes in Wyoming, Utah, and Colorado. Despite his long-lasting interest in Indians, when he started to write novels he did not intend to write about the Utes. That interest began to intrude because his novel (which was going to be about college professors who steal from their graduate students) needed some local color in the person of an Indian. That Native American became Clara, dispatcher in the Granite Creek police station. Doss's interest in Native American culture was rekindled and the characters grew in number. As he tells the development:

> With even a single minor Ute character, it was necessary to learn something about this group of tribes who once controlled much of the central Rockies. Little has been published, but I found a rather academic report (*Ethnology of the Northern Utes*, by Anne Smith) in our local library. It was here that I discovered *pitukupf*. Once I had learned about this remarkable "Ute Leprechaun," there was no turning back. I visited the reservation and found a fellow who was willing to tell me about the dwarf. The shaman, Daisy Perika (Clara's aunt) was a necessity because someone had to show up at the end of the tale and reassure Scott Parris. I liked Charlie so much that he became a major character in the second novel *(The Shaman Laughs)*, the third *(The Shaman's Bones)* and will continue to work for the author. (Interview correspondence)

Doss is a weekend author. He works full-time as an electrical engineer at the Los Alamos National Laboratory. On Friday nights he hurries away to his mountain cabin in the Sangre de Cristo Mountains of New Mexico and works feverishly until time to return to Los Alamos. As he writes, his interest in and knowledge of the Ute life continues to grow. A meticulous worker, he researches the sites of his novels, the Southern Ute reservation, the Ute Mountain reservation at Towaoc in Southwest Colorado, the Uintah (Ute) reservation in central Wyoming, the home of the Arapaho Indians about whom Doss's friend Margaret Coel writes. He also frequently visits the library at Fort Lewis College, Durango, Colorado, which has a splendid Ute collection, and whatever other sources that become available. His achievements so far are valuable.

Like Louis Owens, Doss is a mystic. He and his characters move from daily reality into spiritual existence with an ease and abruptness that is sometimes difficult for the non-Indian to follow. But the two worlds are necessary and must meld into one and the same if the total reality of Indian life is to be realized. On this aspect of Indian life, Doss and Owens write with the same pen.

Mardi Oakley Medawar

One of the more effective authors is Mardi Oakley Medawar, an Eastern Band Cherokee who lives in North Carolina. Her main character, named Tay-bodal, is a nondescript Kiowa medicine man who is not only one of the most important persons among the Kiowa but is also the stumbling investigator who through various nonapproaches to the problem of finding the murderer always finds his man.

Tay-bodal, whose name means something like "meat-carrier" or "rear end of a cow," depending on the translation Medawar gives it, is the Rodney Dangerfield of Native American crime fiction. He is of the lower order of tribesmen, though he is married to one of the upper class, and can do nothing to climb into the higher social bracket, though he associates with them because of his skill in medicine. He gets no respect from anybody, the upper class or his own lower class. He is married to a hellcat wife who berates him, her fellow tribespeople, and all others, including the enemy whites.

Medawar is the most humorous of the writers studied in this book. She has a relaxed, honeylike style that allows her to bring in a great deal of Indian lore but also at the same time to develop humorous episodes and attitudes, especially toward her fellow Indians. She spares no one and no gender; she is just as humorous-minded toward women as men.

She is delightful reading for those persons who like to spend a long cup of coffee with an author who is delightful in character development.

J. F. Trainor

The larger than life character of the Anishinabe princess Angela Biwaban (pronounced *bih-wah-ban*), created by and for the author J. F. Trainor, proves to be a remarkable achievement in Native American crime fiction. As is often the case in the dream and real world in which heroes and heroines are conceived and names created, Angela's birth was the result of unexpected fortunate coincidences.

Trainor writes in his interview correspondence with me that growing up in the 1950s and ever wanting to write, he was always addicted to the West. When he visited it for the first time in the 1980s, he found his favorite part of the National Addiction was the North Shore of Lake Superior in Minnesota. Trainor had already decided to write about a female detective comfortable on both sides of the law who would be a female equivalent of the Lone Ranger in the tradition of Cervantes's Don Quixote, so that he could have some fun with the gripping myth of the West. Trainor believes that he has succeeded with his Angela, who "is the Lone Ranger, although in *modus operandi* she's probably a lot closer to the Scarlet Pimpernel." Whatever literary allies she resembles, Angela is a commendable creation.

Trainor describes her comprehensively:

> Instead of being a strong, resolute, strapping six-foot-four Western Marlboro Man, she's a petite five-foot-four heroine. Instead of being a straight shooter, she's devious and manipulative. Like Scheherezade, the archetypal Moorish Princess, Angie uses words as her weapons. She is defending truth, justice and the American way with an endless series of lies. She wants to love and be loved, yet she rejects the traditional female role her family, most notably Aunt Della, has set out for her—husband, children, a family and home of her own. The basic immaturity of her lifestyle is self-evident. Angie is still playing the Black Canary, just as she did when she was seven years old. (This and following quotes are from interview correspondence)

How did Trainor find a name sufficiently strong and descriptive for such a character? Perhaps the tale can best be told in the words of the creator. At first planning to name her Brunilda Barros, perhaps a kiss of death, he allowed coincidence to lead down a more magic avenue to inspiration:

I happened to be browsing in a large gift store on Firehold Avenue in West Yellowstone, Montana, and I saw for the first time a large poster based on the oil painting *The Great Man's Daughter* by the Western artist Bill Hampton. I saw that painting and I was stunned. *There she is,* I thought, *there's my heroine,* And the name literally popped into my mind—ANGELA.

But in American society, which is some steps away from the mythological, heroines need second, family names. Working out the family name required some effort on Trainor's part:

Angela what? I racked my brains for a surname. At this time I was planning on making Angie a Lakota. But then I realized that I didn't know enough about Lakota culture to make the character real. But, having been to the Northland and the reservations at Fond du Lac near Cloquet, Minnesota, Lac Courte Oreilles near Hayward, Wisconsin, and L'Anse, Michigan, in the United States. I knew quite a bit more about, and felt far more comfortable with, Anishinabe culture. So I hunted for an appropriate surname for Angie. I came across *bidaban,* the Anishinabe word for dawn or sunrise, in Father Baraga's dictionary. It sounded just a little too harsh for English-speaking ears. I remembered then that one of the Iron Range towns near Virginia, Minn. is named Biwabik. So I made the name Biwaban, a blend of the two words. To me, it is perfectly pronounceable and euphonious—*bih-wah-ban,* But you'd be surprised at how many editors have stumbled over it. (Interview)

Trainor has novelized the amazing adventures of a profeminist woman who spoofs the tradition of the old West, sometimes being the Good Woman and sometimes the Bad Gal, always walking precariously on the razor edge of law prepared to leap either way in order to achieve her purpose, but making one of the more appealing fictional characters for all readers of Western crime fiction, both male and female. And that's no spoof.

Thomas Perry

In Native American crime fiction quite often an Indian plays the role of detective and investigator, yet another strong storyline is that in which a Native American occupies a position that is less directly investigatory. This individual for one reason or another acts as Indian contact between Native Americans and whites. These types of novels serve a slightly different purpose, since the leading character is not a crime investigator.

Instead that character's role can be that of interpreter, speaker, revealer, government official, or other. These characters serve as guides in national parks, as federal agents of some kind, or some other role outside mainstream detection. In all, however, they use Native American culture and lore to speak of and for the Indians, and in most cases they use that lore and culture to reveal how the Indians have been mistreated by the whites, and how their cultures—which are generally revealed in considerable detail—work, how they are committed against white incursions, and how the Indians still cling to the cultures that distinguish them from the whites. Although perhaps intended for a slightly different readership, these novels serve very well in our survey of paying back by remorse and atonement since all in one way or another turn on the breaking of the law and criminality.

Thomas Perry is one of the stronger authors in this category. Perry was born in Tonawanda, New York, in 1947. Like so many successful authors who have taken up the subject of Indians in fiction, Perry has a varied background. With a B.A. from Cornell in 1969, he went on to earn a Ph.D. in English literature from the University of Rochester (1974). Since then he has been a laborer, maintenance man, commercial fisherman, weapons mechanic, university administrator and teacher, as well as television writer and producer. His earlier works include *The Butcher's Boy* (1982), *Metzger's Dog* (1983), *Big Fish* (1985), and *Sleeping Dogs* (1992).

Perry's protagonist is Jane Whitefield, a five-foot-ten-inch brunette who is in the "research and consulting" business, in which she aids people who want to disappear from their present surroundings and take up new identities. It is a hazardous occupation.

In the midst of telling Whitefield's story, Perry writes also of intense traveling and gives much Seneca and Iroquois lore, including the many reasons the Indians hate the whites. He recounts, for example, that since 1779 the Seneca have always called every U.S. president "Destroyer of Villages" for the early depredations ordered by George Washington. On one occasion in *Vanishing Act*, when Whitefield is being pursued through the forests and her only recourse is killing, she thinks of the old time Seneca who, even under torture by whites would say, "I am brave and intrepid. I do not fear death or any kind of torture. Those who fear them are cowards. They are less than woman"(304). Torture was a white man's trick.

In *Shadow Woman*, his second novel in this series, Perry continues reiterating the reasons the Seneca hate whites. At great length he describes how the French king Louis XIV had ordered annihilation of the five Iroquois Nations because they were disrupting the fur trade. The French burned and killed villages and villagers, and the Iroquois in retaliation "made New France from Mackinac to Quebec a very dangerous place for a couple of years. They attacked Frontenac and Montreal, killing hundreds and carrying off hundreds more" (24). Americans were no better than the French, for they were dedicated to "scheduled extermination" of the Iroquois. Jane Whitefield is one-half Seneca and can exterminate virtually anyone who opposes her or her Seneca relatives.

She demonstrates her physical prowess in *Dance for the Dead*, Perry's third novel about Whitefield's marvelous adventures. This time she changes from her usual subjects to take care of a poor little rich boy who has millions of dollars and dozens of enemies. In combating the evil of whites, Jane will take on any cause and any adversary.

In his 1998 book *The Face-Changers*, Perry backs off a little from intensely featuring Jane Whitefield; he returns to the development of her character in ways similar to the straightforward adventures of his characters in action books written before the Whitefield series. Working in Jane's name, the "face-changers" are doing evil rather than good. In the development of this story, Jane's new husband, Carey McKinnon, instigates her participation and is therefore more directly involved in the story than in any other preceding novel.

Robert Westbrook

Robert Westbrook is a new kind of star rising in the sky of authors of Indian crime fiction. He has a different attitude. He is less reverential of Indian customs, of white's feelings of remorse and atonement over former mistreatment of Native Americans, and writes with an unconventional leaning toward traditional attitudes about sex and the use of it in his fiction. He is, in fact, a well-armed, hard-boiled author of Indian crime fiction. He flavors his crusty writing with an outstanding sense of humor, not deliberate and slapstick but subtle, offhand, and quick-witted. He seems to be satisfied if he can chuckle at his own humor, whether the reader gets it or not. He works as a jazz pianist and perhaps brings some of the improvisation associated with the magic of the keyboard to his verbal skill. Withal though he may not revere Indian customs and rituals—and life—he knows how to use them to advantage and creates informative and interesting fiction.

He is first and foremost a writer who wants to craft an effective novel. Humanistically he is a cynic who sees the human race as a species of grudgers determined to take advantage of other people before they take advantage of them. Not all whites, in Westbrook's view, are necessarily prejudiced against Indians except where the prejudice benefits them. Indians, likewise, are not necessarily prejudiced against whites except where they gain from it. Whites generally agree that Indians are the victims of discrimination.

Westbrook uses people with somewhat different backgrounds and foregrounds as his main characters and gives different slants on their development and behavior. The two main characters are Jack Wilder and Howard Moon Deer, who run the Wilder & Associates Detective Agency in the small town of San Geronimo, New Mexico, close to Four Corners in the northwest portion of the state. The town is more white than Indian though there seems to be no animosity between the races. There even seems to be little hard feeling between the rich and the poor, though the former are very wealthy and the latter dirt poor.

The owner of the agency is Jack Wilder, one of a growing number of blind detectives, three of them in Indian crime fiction. Like Jake Page's star Mo Bowdre, Wilder lost his sight fighting crime. He is an ex-captain of the San Francisco police force who was blinded on a raid on a dope gang. Constantly reminded that he is blind, he accepts the situation philosophically, at times even using the unsightliness of his blind eye sockets to advance his causes. As a result of his blindness Jack has developed his other senses to a keen degree. People constantly talk in his presence about being blind, speaking blindly, etc., and apologize to Jack for their thoughtlessness. But he reassures them that he is not offended. Like the usual blind detective in crime fiction, Jack is aided by a woman, this time by Anna his wife, and his seeing eye dog. At times both seem to be more insightful or luckier than Jack.

Wilder's action is provided by Howard Moon Deer, called "Howie," a Sioux Indian who grew up on the reservation and freely admits that he took advantage of every opportunity whites offered him. Two of his white teachers on the reservation cradled him under their wing and got him into Dartmouth College because the college was established to educate Indians. From there, after a period sowing his wild oats in Paris, he went on to Princeton and has finished all the work for a Ph.D. except his dissertation. Wilder and Westbrook call him an "overeducated Indian," but there is no criticism in the description. Howie knows that the only thing "Indian" about him is his DNA. He once claims that he doesn't hang his coat on deer antlers. Otherwise he enjoys in a heroic way the joys of being a superior human being. His dissertation subject is something of a joke. He tells Wilder that he is interested in "culinary psychology." That is he is trying to show "how the cultural divide in America between the Left and the Right is connected to how people eat" (*Ghost* 49). Although Howie is still interested in the subject he is more concerned with how people behave in general. He tells his partner that he knows nothing about crime and certainly nothing about detective work, but he is a quick learner. Howie moves freely in and out of white society, and especially in and out of women's beds, and learns human nature at every move. The Agency, led by Howie, sees everything in life as the conflict between good and evil—dark and celestial—and Westbrook's most effective novels begin high with supernatural conflicts between man's nobler and baser conflicts. They are literally "out of this world."

The superiority of the two is enhanced beyond Jack's blindness and extrasensory perceptiveness. Their association began in a "supernatural" manner. Howie one day is feeling frisky and out riding his bicycle when a rainstorm overtakes him. Rain showers down and "lightning crackled" but Howie is indifferent to and superior to the weather. He pedals out of the high-rent part of San Geronimo into the mixed section of both poverty and newfound financial security. Lightning strikes in front of him when, "Through a break in the clouds, San Geronimo Peak in the distance was bathed in single swath of sunlight, fantastical." In the windstorm Howie sees a gray-haired man outside an old adobe house trying to tie down a tarp to protect his food. Howie stops to see the conflict of man against nature and reads it as man wrestling with god: "The tarp was flapping wildly in the wind, as though he were wrestling with an angel. The scene was almost biblical." It looked like the wind, obviously a demonic force, was going to carry Jack "into the black heavens" (47).

Of the two, Jack—the head of the agency and supposedly the brain force—is really the superior, with his extrasensory perception. He is more inclined to sit at home, like Nero Wolfe, think through the crime and solutions, and have Howie investigate and prove his theories right or wrong. Howie is the everyday helper. Given to indulgence in sex, common sense and action, Howie represents not so much the Indian as the ambitious American (human being) filled with empathy and willingness to enjoy self- and human fulfillment.

Westbrook shades his fiction off the beaten path of Indian crime fiction, tincturing it with a new strain of vinegar that might change the chemical balance altogether, driving it more toward typical old-fashioned unsentimental fiction in a Western context.

He also delves more deeply into the ever-increasing salaciousness of pornography or pseudo-pornography. Jake Page uses good old-fashioned sex to develop his stories. Westbrook at times uses it for its own ends.

An unusual theme in the crime fiction of both Jake Page and Robert Westbrook is development through music. Page restricts himself to some form of popular or folk music, while Westbrook branches out into jazz or classical music. An accomplished jazz pianist, he knows the literature of both and uses it to enrich the atmosphere of his stories.

In *Warrior Circle*, for example, Howie and Aria Waldman have sex and she immediately jumps out of bed and says she has to leave. She departs to the notes of Puccini's *Turandot* on the car radio, and a little later Howie is awakened by the strains of Luciano Pavarotti singing "Nesum Dorma" from the same opera and suspects that evil has befallen her. Later, with another woman, Claire Knightsbridge, Howie recognizes her sight unseen by the fact that he hears her playing Bach's Suite No. 1 for Unaccompanied Cello. Later, Howie's and Claire's fortunes seem to be thrust upward on the strains of Schubert's string quartet *Death and the Maiden*. He uses music conventionally elsewhere, but one of the more unusual statements is when Claire undresses before they go to bed for sex and starts to play the cello, in which she is musically adept, and Howie finds a naked woman playing a cello "almost unbearably erotic."

Westbrook's Indian world is more integrated with that of the white's than the other authors of Indian-White crime fiction.

Laura Baker

Other authors of Native American crime fiction and other heroes and heroines in their actions and statements demonstrate the need for "paying back" what many writers and readers feel is a long-overdue debt. One of these authors is Laura Baker. She owns two Native American art galleries in Albuquerque and to date has published three novels on Navajo culture. The first, *Stargazer*, an out-and-out romance, is hot in both Indian legend and romance. Its stretch of the imagination sees a handsome fullblood Navajo do a little time warp travel and come to present-day society from the days of the Indians' friend, Kit Carson, who died 130 years ago. Lonewolf, the traveler, is a stargazer and singer who when he is working with the magic pouch from Navajo tradition sees the Seven Sisters in the sky in alignment and feels the throb of the stars vibrating in him. With the help of the stars he is able to cure a sick boy of a malady the regular M.D.s could not touch.

Baker is not content with that bit of Navajo shamanism. Her interest lies in recapturing and saving the Navajo past and their artifacts. She has Navajos robbing burial sites to seize artifacts to protect them for the Indians. Then there is conflict between Indian factions about those artifacts and their proper disposition. Further, the novel is steamy with throbbing bodies and sex, as a halfblood female agent of the tribal police is torn between the reality of her profession and the love of the handsome shaman.

In *Legend*, Baker's second published novel, FBI agent Jackson Walker's psychic abilities have made him successful in past investigations, but now he is faced with five savage murders in his native Navajo land. His prime suspect is a beautiful shaman's daughter named Ainii Henio, who tends sheep and weaves rugs.

The outsider invasion of a bucolic setting is the natural venue for the development of legend. And that is what grows here. The story reads like a legend brought into an everyday vernacular setting. It is romantic; it maintains the Indian past to authenticate the development. As legend it leaves some parts unexplained—as, for example, how a human being dressed up as a wolf can run seventy-five miles per hour. That's stuff of legend. But in general the translation of legend into reality is made understandable.

In telling the story, Baker echoes the writing of novelist Henry James in worrying that individuals—here both Jackson and Ainii— must face the beast within, weakness and indecision, and free themselves from its grasp. As it was with James, to Baker, "Writing is a way for me to explore the human heart in conflict with itself: What makes the person who he or she is" (interview correspondence).

In effect the individual human heart in conflict with itself is also a tribal weakness. The larger moral is that the Indians must come out of their legendary existence and face themselves and current reality.

In developing her novels, Baker is stylistically direct and clear. She clothes her people and events in powerful figures of speech. Walker, the FBI man, for example, is "a primal force." Ainii is a "perfect conduit," a "lightning rod" for bringing the primal force into reality. Baker knows, describes, and uses Navajo tribal lore and culture. In telling the story Baker sometimes speaks through a biblical megaphone, as she makes acceptable the murderer's philosophy that some wicked people deserve to be murdered—or at least to die. Her books are Navajo primers.

They are also human primers, for Baker, as she outlines in a letter to me, is interested in Navajos as human beings. "What gets me jazzed," she writes,

> is writing about two protagonists of equal intelligence with sympathetic goals and very deep convictions—it's these deep convictions within the protagonists which I want to rock to the core and crack and make them reconsider by the end of the book. And the convictions must be about how they see *themselves* in the world, not how they see their gender, or their race, or their culture. Writing is a way for me to explore the human heart in conflict with itself: What makes the person who he or she is.

Like many novelists Baker is primarily interested in telling a good story, not in having whites "pay back" Indians for former mistreatment. But she knows of potential side effects of her works:

> Certainly my relationship with Navajo artists and friends was a "spring board" for my interest in their culture. But as I researched more, it was their core of beliefs which really drew me in and left me powerless to go in any other direction. Their belief in duality and search for balance spoke to something inside me. Indeed, I think the search for balance is a universal quest. You see, when I write about the Navajo, yes I am trying my best to be true to their culture and beliefs, but I am also depicting human beings, just like the rest of us, with hopes, dreams and fears. The journey to find our place in balance with the world is not exclusively Navajo: The conflicts I describe are within all peoples.

Baker, like most authors who write about and is read by Native Americans finds them enthusiastic readers of her works. In her correspondence with me she recounts two interesting anecdotes:

> Yes, I do have many Navajo friends and they seem to admire my work. I have two stories in that vein. When I was writing *Stargazer*, I approached one of our silversmiths for an opinion of the plot. Besides being a well-known silversmith, he is also a medicine man and, at the time, was on the staff of the Navajo President. I outlined the story, from the time-travel of my hero, to his ultimate goal of saving the life of the next Starway Shaman. My friend sat there very quietly, even after I finished. Then, without the slightest change of expression, said, "Reminds me of the story my grandfather would tell us." To this day, I don't know what part of the story he meant, or whether he was pulling my leg. He still comes to the store to sell us jewelry and always asks how my books are doing. Another artist, also an older man, picked up *Stargazer* at the gallery and took it with him. About a week later, I was

standing outside my gallery when a silversmith approached. Instead of going to my husband, who does all the buying for the gallery, the Navajo walked straight to me. For the first time in the 11 years I have known him, he gave me a hug. He stepped back and said, "I have been reading *Stargazer*. Now my wife has it and my kids want it, so I don't know when I will get it back to finish the book. Can I have another one?"

As such, though unrealistically romantic, these books spread the word about Native Americans and thus to one degree or another modestly further the notion that Indian society is worthy of receiving recompense for past injustices visited upon it. If Baker begins to emphasize the crime element in these stories over the romantic, they will have to be included more thoroughly in future studies of Native American crime fiction.

These are the main authors in that category, and looking at the works in greater detail reveals how deep and varied the debt is and how its repayment is being approached.

CHAPTER TWO

Cultural Background and Development

Authors of Native American crime fiction agree that in order to authenticate their material their stories must grow in and from genuine Indian culture, which includes not only present and past earthbound beliefs and practices but also a great deal of mysticism that is difficult for non-Indians to find credible. For example, we can easily understand the Navajo belief that everything should be kept in balance; that is reasonably close to Socrates' teaching that all things should be taken in moderation and even similar to eighteenth-century English philosophers who suggested that all things should be balanced out. But some Indian practices of the past and present—being able to get lost in the spirit world, even through the use of drug-induced trances—is too close to present-day drug use for the general public to put much positive spin on the practice among the Navajo. What was an outreach into the spirit world for the Indians has become for us a mind-warping into irresponsible and dangerous self-indulgence from which might easily spring of all sorts of evil. The difference lies in the purpose for which the drugs are put: positive religious experience or free libertine personal indulgence. Although there are many aspects of Native American cultures that are similar to our own, there are differences even from one Indian tribe to another that each author must catalogue and develop.

Jean Hager

In order to present their stories in an authentic setting, authors utilize their backgrounds in ways best suited to their purposes. Some have to do considerable research to resurrect their materials. Jean Hager, for example, despite being one-sixteenth Cherokee, feels she needs a lot of relearning if she wants to steep her stories in credible Cherokee lore, and that is necessary because most of her part-Cherokee fellow citizens are no longer conversant with the culture of their ancestors. She must in fact teach the general public. Hager had done her previous writing in conventional subject matter and traditional detective stories until she turned to Cherokee culture for her materials and her two protagonists, Bushyhead and Bearpaw, and stories associating them with that culture. To make the switch she did considerable research, and she learned thoroughly. Because she is in effect working from the outside in, from library knowledge rather than participatory understanding, she often has to wrap her stories in Cherokee legends, bringing them in and reshaping them for her purposes rather than letting them grow from inside out in a natural development.

Although not a lone worker in Cherokee crime fiction, as other authors studied in this book demonstrate, Hager claims to be the first and is certainly one of the more important writing today. Her works are sincere since she wants to record the old ways of the Cherokee, because, she laments, "so much has been lost." "I am trying to record the heritage of the people from whom I came," she asserts in correspondence with me. She is also, of course, spreading knowledge of that heritage among all Americans. In so doing she strives to be as precise and detailed as possible.

Wherever and whenever she can she maintains the Cherokee persona. "My characters speak English although occasionally I use a Cherokee phrase for both the effect and because it sounds right in its original voice." Sometimes the Cherokee words best give the needed atmosphere and feeling, as in this naming of the Cherokee evil witch:

> When Crying Wolf had returned to his cabin yesterday, the power of the talisman had been broken by *ul(i)sdu:dwanv:hi*, a Door Closer, because he had been in the vicinity of a corpse. Now he must cleanse the root so that its power would return. (*Medicine* 58)

Sometimes Hager uses Cherokee words to best express the Indian feeling about the surrounding society:

> Zeb stared back at him with his black-marble eyes. "You talk like a *hi-yo'ne'ga* (white person). Telling me things for my own good." He was now speaking English, for Conrad's benefit. "That's what they always say. We must speak the white man's words for our own good." His voice gained volume as he warmed to his subject. "And give up our land and take up the white man's religion and stop making medicine." He peered darkly at Conrad. "Look it up in your white man's books, Nephew, and you'll see I'm right." (*Stones* 11)

For authenticity of other kinds in her books, Hager relies on primary sources. From an old Aunt who was in a nursing home she gleaned background information for her novels. Hager visited the aunt and listened to her memories of Indian folklore, thus gaining a realistic vividness not otherwise available, and, of course, carrying on a Native Indian tradition of having the elderly tell their stories to the younger members of society.

Further, Hager continues to do research and to enrich her books with Cherokee culture. She takes her research seriously. "It is no different than the history of England or Colonial America," she insists. Her "best source" is the three books on Cherokee folklore by Jack Frederick and Anna G. Kilpatrick: *Walk in Your Soul: Love Incantations of the Oklahoma Cherokees, Run toward the Nightland: Magic of the Oklahoma Cherokees,* and *Friends of Thunder: Folktales of the Oklahoma Cherokees.* All are readily available in the library at Northeastern State University at Tahlequah, Oklahoma, which she visits often. The printed word is her major source of information. She does not get particularly inspired by non-print or non-oral sources, for instance Indian paintings, as do other observers of Indian life. In order to discuss Hager's books comparatively both with one another and with those of other ethnic crime writers we need to see the plots and developments of each.

The Grandfather Medicine: An Oklahoma Mystery is a village procedural, or perhaps more accurately a small-town sheriff procedural. Police procedurals are by definition novels that to one degree or another use in their investigations the procedures followed by police in everyday work. To quote George Dove, one of the authorities on that type of crime story:

> The term "procedural" refers to the methods of detection employed, the procedures followed by policemen in real life. Where the classic detective solves mysteries through the use of observation and logical analysis, and the private investigator through his energy and tough tenacity,

the detective in the procedural story does these things ordinarily expected of policemen, like using informants, tailing suspects, and availing himself of the resources of the police laboratory. This qualification almost automatically suggests another one: the policemen in the procedurals almost always work in teams, sharing the responsibilities and the dangers, also the credit, of the investigation, with the result that the resolution of the mystery is usually the product of the work of a number of people instead of the achievement of a single protagonist. . . . The conventions of popular fiction demand that there be a main-character detective in the procedural, but he or she does not solve the crime without the collaborative efforts of other police. (*Procedural* 2)

In *Medicine* Chief Bushyhead, a mixedblood, and his three assistants, Virgil Rabbit, Charles "Roo" Stephens, and Harold "Duck" Duckworth, all fullblood Cherokee, have to investigate why Joe Pigeon, local Indian artist married to a white woman, has been killed. Bushyhead has had hard feelings with the town Council members, who immediately begin pressuring him to get the murder solved. Bushyhead is friends with George Turnbull, president of the local bank and head of the Council, who begins to play an ambiguous role. Bushyhead believes a local lawyer named Derring, who always successfully defends, at great personal gain, the Indians that Bushyhead accuses of guilt, committed the murder. Derring is going to marry Valerie, Turnbull's wayward and promiscuous daughter. Led by promising evidence, Bushyhead follows a lead that takes him to a cave in the forest that he discovers is the storehouse for large quantities of marijuana. Turnbull catches Bushyhead in the cave and is going to kill him because the Chief has found the cache that the president of the bank, in conjunction with some Las Vegas mobsters with whom he has come to do business to try to repay a $40,000 gambling debt, is importing. As Turnbull is about to shoot Bushyhead, Valerie, his daughter, rages onto the scene with shotgun in hand and blasts away at her father because it was he who murdered Joe Pigeon, with whom Valerie was in love and by whom she is pregnant. She respects Cherokees, whereas Turnbull, though he is their successful banker, does not.

Bushyhead, narrowly escaped from Turnbull, is in need of relaxation and recreation. So at 10 P.M. he calls Lisa Macpherson, the schoolteacher friend of his daughter Elly, and asks if he can come over. Knowing his intentions, Lisa asks Mitch if he is now free of the ghost of his dead wife, who died of cancer a year earlier. When Mitch says he has exorcised that ghost, Lisa tells him to come on over. They can enjoy a companionship free of ghosts and demons.

The novel is rich in Indian lore and customs. Tony Hillerman was right when he said in a quote on the book jacket that the work is "not just an intriguing mystery but a clear-eyed evocation of the Cherokee culture." One example will illustrate. Hager's story begins deep in Cherokee magic. Crying Wolf, an aged shaman, has been asked to use his magic and incantations to break up an adulterous sexual liaison. To do so he uses the strongest kind of tobacco magic. Tobacco is the Cherokee's chief vehicle for use in working magic. It has no inherent magical power, so the magic is worked in through saying or singing a magic text over it.

Tobacco is usually "remade" at dawn and preferably alongside a stream, which intensifies the power. While "remaking" the tobacco the shaman usually faces east. Sometimes the "remade" tobacco is held up to the rays of the sun for curative purposes, but this is never done if the tobacco is to be used for sinister purposes. Most texts read over the tobacco are repeated four times, occasionally seven. Sometimes one recitation causes the magic to work, sometimes they must be repeated four days, sometimes seven, running. Expectorating and blowing into the tobacco, if the shaman is in perfect health, strengthens the power. If tobacco is "remade" at sunrise, it is held in the left hand and kneaded with a counterclockwise rolling motion of the four fingers of the right hand while an *i'gawe':sdi* is said over it. If the remaking occurs at sundown or midnight the rolling is sometimes clockwise. Obviously this is a practice that requires much memory and practice.

According to the Kilpatricks:

> "Remade" tobacco is customarily used in one of four ways: it is smoked in such proximity to the individual who is its target that the smoke actually touches that person; its smoke, sometimes on a set schedule, is merely projected toward the victim, or the direction in which he is likely to be; it is smoked in such a fashion that its fumes pervade a general area; it is not smoked, but instead placed where the person for whom it is intended comes into contact with it. (*Nightland* 11–12)

If the "remade" tobacco is to be used to separate two lovers, the names of both are first stated, and the separating chant is this:

> You Two Little Great Wizards, You fail in nothing
> Very quickly I have just come to tell you two the word.
> Very quickly I have just come to cut you upon your right side
>   with the Red Knife!
> Very quickly I have just come to cut you upon your left side
>   with the Red Knife!

The chant can be altered to fit individual circumstances or shortened as needs dictate (*Nightland* 65–66).

Another example in the same book testifies to the richness of the lore. Crying Wolf, the leading shaman in all of Hager's Indian stories, is telling Mitch Bushyhead about a dream he had. Recognizing that Mitch has Cherokee blood but was raised white, Wolf says that he will tell the story in English because Mitch will not understand "his father's language." Here is his story:

> The *Uk'ten'* was a monster, like a very big snake. He had spots on his body and horns and claws and his breath was poisonous. When the *Uk'ten'* lived on earth long ago, a man could even be killed by walking in the *Uk'ten's* path. At that time men had to live in caves, they say, to be hidden from the *Uk'ten'* because the *Uk'ten'* roamed about looking for people to kill and eat. (*Medicine* 178)

In telling the story, Crying Wolf's chanting voice was deep, like that of a folk story teller. He continued:

> A brave man who lived in that long ago decided that the *Uk'ten'* had to be killed or men would always live in caves like animals and fear to walk on the earth. This man—I do not know his name—was told by the old men of his clan that he would have to hit the *Uk'ten'* on his seventh spot to kill him. The first time he drew his bow, he missed. The second and third time the arrow went under the *Uk'ten'*. The fourth time he drew his bow, the arrow hit right upon the seventh spot. (179)

Mitch is captivated by the richness of the story and its revelation about his ancestors. Crying Wolf finished the myth:

> Then, the *Uk'ten'* fell over and floundered about and thunder came, louder than any we hear in these days, and lightning flashed all around, they say. Thunder and the *Uk'ten'* had a fight to decide which one would live among people. The *Uk'ten'* caused it to rain hot fire, and the fire rained until he was completely dead. The people came from their hiding places after that. (179)

Mesmerized more completely, Mitch comprehends Cherokee culture, and we the readers understand more fully the appeal of the Hager novel.

According to the Kilpatricks the *Uk'ten'* are monsters similar to European dragons, gigantic reptiles with a deadly breath. They live in marshy or rocky places, are horned and have claws to tear human flesh. To the Cherokee the *Uk'ten'* symbolize satanic evil, but the scales of a defeated *Uk'ten'* provide protection and healing. So evil can be turned to beneficent purposes by overcoming it.

Like the mythical cultural monsters, the *Uk'ten'* has a vulnerable spot. In her recounting of this battle, which resembles the Old English story of Beowulf's battle with Grendel, Hager varies the details very little. In *Friends of Thunder* the Kilpatricks describe the business this way:

> He [the one who killed the *Uk'ten'*] was told to hit him upon the seventh spot. The first time he drew his bow, he missed; the second time he drew his bow, it [the arrow] went under him [the *Uk'ten'*]; on the fourth time that he drew his bow the arrow hit right upon the seventh spot. Then he [the *Uk'ten'*] fell over and floundered about and tremendous thunder and lightning appeared all about, they say. It continued to thunder and flash lightning.
>
> The *Uk'ten'* and Thunder were having a fight at that time. That was when Thunder was given help. They [human beings] loved Thunder very much.
>
> The *Uk'ten'* was very poisonous. One could be killed by walking in his path. These two were fighting to decide which one would live among people. They used bows and arrows to hit him under the seventh spot. After he fell and floundered about, he caused it to rain hot fire. The fire rained until he was completely dead. The people came from their hiding places after than. They say that's what happened long ago.
>
> This *Uk'ten'* who lived long ago could have devoured all the people. But that's the way God willed it: that people should live, multiply, and love each other. The reason that we are here is that God is powerful. No man on earth has made things the way they are. It is God, who is so powerful, that has made everything the way it is. (*Thunder* 44)

In rewriting and redesigning the Kilpatrick folktale, Hager made it more artistic and pointed. She has, in *The Grandfather Medicine* and the books that follow, indulged in a new transitional subgenre to ethnic crime romance, at least in the ending.

Her second novel in this series, *Night Walker*, demonstrates that Hager had better control of her Indian folklore and medium. The beginning four chapters constitute a tightly controlled dramatic situation in which it is clear that the clash between Indian sexual customs and modern liberalized sexual behavior will end in disaster.

Graham Thornton, owner of a lodge built on an Indian burial ground, is obnoxious and hated by everyone. He coerces his women employees into sex, fires his employees arbitrarily, and mistreats all Indians. His latest sexual victim is Joy Yeaky, a young woman who submits to his sexual mistreatment because she needs her job and knows that Thornton will fire her summarily if she refuses. She fears that her young impetuous husband will become violent if he learns of the liaison. Thornton is grotesquely murdered and placed in the open cab of Joy's pick-up on a cold Oklahoma evening during a snowstorm. His several past mistresses, all the women he has fired in the past and all Indian employees, are suspected of being the murderesses. Suspicion swings to Thornton's sister, who hates him, and to others, even his mother, who it turns out had been regularly beaten by Graham's father as well as by their son and was actually the murderess.

The murder story is enriched by the splendid recountings of Indian lore and ceremony. Early on, Hager creates the atmosphere of impending doom in the legend of the Night Walker:

> Children were warned not to go out alone at night, lest they meet an evil night walker. In all likelihood, if that should happen, they would not recognize the witch until it was too late, for witches often assumed the form of an animal or a bird. A screech owl was a favorite disguise. If one heard a screech owl three nights in succession, it was almost certainly a night walker seeking to further his evil designs.

Hager's novel is lightened somewhat by a parallel story of the teenage rebellion of Mitch's daughter, Emily, who in her self-assertion performs a foolish and irresponsible act but which, in fact, leads to the solution of the murder. Thankfully, Mitch's new girlfriend, Emily's schoolteacher, has gone to California and therefore does not bring romance artificially into the story. But sex is present. The novel fairly oozes it as the motivation for the action and the plot.

In *The Fire Carrier* Henderson Sixkiller has escaped from prison because he could not bear being shut up. Now he is going back to the town where his beloved sister, Jessie, is being abused by her husband, white Tyler Hatch, who is director of the Job Corps Center. Because of his position Hatch is able to coerce women into having sex with him. Sixkiller has only one thin blanket to shelter him from the cold and is forced to hole up in a cabin without heat.

In the woods he sees a witch, a fire carrier, moving around generally with two lights instead of the usual one. Hatch has beaten his wife again and she has been moved to the house of Rhea Vann, the local medical doctor, as protection against his sure return to beat her more. He does come to Vann's place, threatens her, and she hits him twice on the shoulder with a table leg. When Hatch is later found murdered, he has been hit four times with some kind of club, and Vann is questioned as to whether she is sure she hit him only twice. Meanwhile it turns out that somebody has been robbing the horsy set of farmers of both their prize livestock and their valuable trophies. Two young locals have been renting or stealing moving vans over the weekend, and it turns out that these activities furnished the fire carrier lights seen in the forest. The plot takes an unexpected turn and throws Hatch's murder back upon itself as justifiable homicide.

The Fire Carrier, the third work in the Bushyhead series, demonstrates Hager's growing mastery in the use of Cherokee folklore. It shows also how close that folklore is to that of other cultures.

Other societies have much lore about mysterious lights floating around in the dark. Alabama folklore, for example, has dozens. The mysterious bright yellow lights can stand still or move rapidly around. Sometimes the light rolls rapidly across the path of people on foot, horseback, or in automobiles. Superstitious people usually think it is a supernatural manifestation of some evil force, though a more rational explanation ties the lights to vapor that rises from swamp gas or other elements of decaying material or, occasionally, ball lightning, which of course lasts only a split second.

For comparison with Hager's account consider this Civil War story about the injustices of executions of soldiers during the war:

> At Appomattox some deserters were shot. They was lined up and made to stand in their coffins, then they was shot. Well, later some other soldiers returned to this particular part of the old battlefield one night, and as they stood there, they looked off to the place where those deserters had been shot and they saw a ball of fire playing over the very same place. Just floating back and forth over the place where them soldiers had been shot. (Browne, *Night* 149)

While writing the Mitchell Bushyhead series, Hager has also been developing Mitch's counterpart in a female operator named Molly Bearpaw, whom she writes about in a different series. Like Mitch, Molly is half-Cherokee.

Ravenmocker begins the series and establishes Bearpaw's credentials as a qualified spokeswoman for the Cherokee and their able assistant in fighting crime and injustice. Molly, like all heroes and heroines, comes from a star-crossed background. She loved her white father but he abandoned her Indian mother when Molly was a child. Her mother had been an alcoholic who committed suicide. So Molly was reared by her maternal grandmother, who is still alive and a source of counsel and comfort. Molly lives alone, in a garage apartment owned by a retired college professor named Conrad Swope, who comforts Molly in times of stress and offers an occasional frugal meal. She also lives with a dog named Homer, who causes her many moments of relief and pleasure. Molly is investigator of the Native American Advocacy League, "a national organization charged with upholding the civil rights of Native Americans" and is always around to be called upon when any Cherokee are threatened or find themselves in trouble.

The Ravenmocker, also known as Apportioner, Thunder, Slanting Eyes, the Red Man, accord to the Kilpatricks, is "the witch or wizard who changes into a raven for the purpose of gaining access to the bedside of someone ill and stealing that person's life-force. . . . Among the tribal conservatives elaborate precautions are still taken to protect the ailing from a visit by *kolun'ayelisgi* (raven-imitator)" (*Friends* 147).

Thunder is the universal friend and benefactors of the Cherokee. There are numerous tales to illustrate this relationship. The Kilpatricks, under their category "The Friends of Thunder," write a lyrically descriptive paragraph:

> The noblest, most moving myth that we have heard . . . was the beautiful relic of that last cosmology that deals with the eternal question of the choice between good and evil. . . . The hero symbol is not that of a man, but that of a child. The choice was made in the innocence of youth, not through knowledge but through pity; and the reward was not power but love. (*Friends* 50)

They then follow with several folktales; some are long and poignant and conclusively demonstrate the tradition Hager had in which to create the pathos of the plight of the Cherokee elders in the novel.

Hager's story begins in a nursing home where eighty-four-year-old Abner Mouse is dying. It is hot enough outside to "cook fry bread," and Thunder is mad at the Cherokee for abandoning the old ways. Most Cherokee "don't even know what clan [they] belong to nowadays,'" says the shaman in disgust. Abner's son Woodrow gets Vann Walkingstick, a medicine man, to use Cherokee magic to try to save his father's life because the nursing home doctors say there is nothing they can do. Abner dies, and so does another person in the nursing home. It soon becomes apparent that the deaths were not natural but had been delivered by the introduction of carbon tetrachloride into the drinking water of the nursing home. The motivation for the murder was, as usual, greed.

This novel differs rather sharply from the successful Mitch Bushy-head series. It is more domestic, more "cozy" or Golden Age. Hager had a special problem with this move from Mitch Bushyhead; he is an "outsider" from the Cherokee community, and so is Hager, and there-fore she could handle him with greater confidence and expertise. With Molly Bearpaw, the heroine of this new series, Hager wants to become a cultural "insider," as Molly is, and it is not easy for one who is not thoroughly a member of the Cherokee community to move in and feel comfortable. Hager will agree with the careful reader by admitting she was not entirely successful in the move and this novel. Becoming Cher-okee insider requires more than a nodding acquaintance. It is more a matter of blood than brains, experience rather than knowledge.

In order to move toward if not into the Cherokee community, Hager roots this novel deeply in Cherokee legend as a kind of living shell with feeder cords running to the story. In it she produces a satisfactory village procedural novel, which spins around a combination of Cherokee lores. At the beginning the old Cherokees are afraid that Ravenmocker, the Apportioner, has got mad at the Indians, as Hager recounts it:

> It was the Apportioner who, in the dim long-ago, had brought death to the people. Walkingstick wondered if Mercer was right about the an-cient Cherokee gods being mad at them. Maybe the Apportioner was thinking up more ways to punish them, even now. He squinted up at the blank blue sky, forgetting for an instant that the Apportioner be-came very angry when a man didn't look straight at her but screwed up his face. That was why she had brought death to the people in the first place.

To appease the Apportioner one must repeat an incantation four times:

> Listen!
> Red Man, quickly we two have prepared your arrows for
>   the soul of the imprecator.
> He has them lying along the path
> Quickly we two will take his soul as we go along
> Listen! O Blue Man, in the Frigid Land above your repose.
> He has them lying along the path.
> Quickly we two will cut his soul in two. (6)

The folkloristic atmospheric beginning, which sets the stage for the drama, is neatly wrapped up in the conclusion. Mercer Vaughan, who has been Abner Mouse's roommate in the nursing home for two years, takes his walking stick and goes out into the night to a cave where he sees the Little People, who look exactly like the Cherokee except they are smaller and more harmless and fun-loving. They cure him of his personal pains and reassure him about the safety of the whole Cherokee Nation. Thunder is no longer mad at the Cherokee. And the reader is pleased with the novel.

The Little People, who bring reassurance and peace to the Cherokee, are key characters in Hager's novel and Cherokee culture at large. According to the Kilpatricks, Cherokees "subsume several classes of Little People, each of which possesses distinctive attributes." They footnote that "A certain race of Little People, according to Cherokee belief, dwell in cliffs and rocky sites. The Eastern Cherokees have a term for this specific class of spirits" (*Friends* 80).

The Redbird's Cry, the second Molly Bearpaw novel, is more tightly drawn than its predecessor. The action derives from a conflict between a group of radical Cherokees calling themselves the True Echota Band, thus representing the true sentiments of the Echota Cherokee who led their people along the Trail of Tears, and the more conservative Cherokee Nation at large. The title comes from Cherokee legends about the Redbird, one of the Cherokee's key animal icons. In some recountings Redbird has taken on characteristics of Trickster, Coyote, or Brer Rabbit, one of the Cherokee's favorite wise animals. The Kilpatricks state that "the Redbird *(totsuhwa)* and the Yellow Mockingbird *(huhu)* are assigned roles in several of the most beautiful of the myths of the Eastern Cherokee. They are starred together in this fragile and evanescent mythic idyll of the Western Cherokee:

THE YELLOW MOCKINGBIRD DESIRES TO SEE ICE

The Redbird and the Yellow Mockingbird:
The Yellow Mockingbird had never seen ice. The Redbird said to him, "I'll save you some, and when you return, you must examine it."

"All right," said he [the Yellow Mockingbird], and went south.

When winter came, ice was saved for the Yellow Mockingbird. When the Yellow Mockingbird returned in the spring, he said, "Where is the ice?"

"Well, just two days ago it melted," he was told—Tsisqua *told the Redbird.*

That's all. (*Friends* 9-10)

Hager's story begins with an idyllic setting—the beauty and peace of Oklahoma in the autumn. But suffusing this bucolic picture is the poignant fear of impending winter and associated doom. Again we are given the Cherokee myth of death. Tom Battle, a lawyer who had opposed the True Echota Band (TEB), while reciting a myth of Cherokee lore, is shot by an arrow from a blowgun at the museum during an Indian ceremony and drops dead instantly. Two young radicals are suspected of the murder because when Battle was killed they were playing with two blowguns and one even shot an arrow that hit Battle. The arrow is found but the point is missing and therefore is assumed to have been covered with poison.

Molly Bearpaw, is called in to look around, and she does so with her reasonably intimate legal assistant, D. K. Kennedy, a lieutenant in the local police force. The arrow point is found and has no poison on it, so new methods and new motives for the murder must be discovered. Two tribal wampums are stolen from the museum, introducing a new motive into the murder. The plot and development are complicated enough to keep most readers away from the solution until it is revealed. The motif begins and is tied to Grandmother's premonition dream in which Molly is running away from danger in a red sea. It blends with a scene in a chapel in which Molly is about to be killed on a red shag rug by the real murderer. But as with the biblical red sea the red shag rug opens sufficiently for Molly to be saved. The mystery is, of course, solved.

Seven Black Stones, Hager's next Bearpaw novel, is a success, though not as tightly woven as the story immediately preceding it.

Zebediah Smoke, an old "crazy" Cherokee, lives next to the site of a proposed bingo hall to be built by the Indians but which he opposes. Bearpaw spends a lot of time with her grandmother, Eva Adar, who raised her when her drunken mother separated from her father and committed suicide. Dot Whitekiller's husband Ed is shiftless and can't hold a job but does keep his daughter's though not his wife's respect. Dot is jealous of this affection. Ed is sleeping around, currently with Susan Butler. Ed and Susan spend Sunday afternoon in a Stillwater motel. George, Susan's husband, comes home early, discovers Susan's affair and suspects her paramour. Ed is in his garage when someone comes in, knocks him out, places him on the back seat of his pickup truck, turns on the motor, and murders him with carbon monoxide, then places seven black stones, the curse of the East Cherokee before their removal to Oklahoma, in the back seat of the pickup truck. Dot insists her husband committed suicide but daughter Maggie refuses to accept that verdict. She makes Molly and the sheriff investigate.

One of the two workers on the bingo building had noticed that the concrete building blocks they were using regularly got shifted around. Suspicion is that Zeb killed Ed because of the seven black stones that had been left in the back seat of the pickup which are a Cherokee symbol. Then the man who had noticed the shifting in the cement blocks is found murdered. And Zeb's house is set on fire and he is almost burned to death. The fraud comes to light. The contractor building the bingo house, named Moss Greenleigh, was buying superior cement blocks, having them inspected, then changing them for inferior ones, selling the superior ones and pocketing the difference. Ed Whitekiller learned of the switching and tried to blackmail Moss. The man who had worked on the building was going to report Moss, and Zeb had observed the switching. That is the end of the main plot but there is a second one.

Molly's friend Moira is a bimbo who should have long since been married but has resisted. Now she is ready to get married and does. But instead of marrying the man she has been dating and was scheduled to wed, she marries his new office mate she has just met because he's "cute." The book ends with Moira reporting her switch marriage to Molly and D.J., who have decided to spend the night together. Such an ending ties together all the loose ends but it is artificial. It concludes the story but not the theme of the book.

Masked Dancers, Hager's latest Native American novel, is about a trying experience in the legal career of Mitchell Bushyhead and his assistants. But it is more than that. The novel further develops Hager's concern with the tension and conflict between individual Cherokees and the Cherokee community with the white dominant society. But she is even more concerned with developing the idea of family and extended community within the white society and the whole society around it. In other words, this book, more than Hager's earlier ones, examines the dynamics of community development and stability.

Hager usually builds her episodes around an integral part of Cherokee lore. This time the episode is more closely developed in and from an important aspect of Cherokee culture, the burlesque fun dance immediately preceding the Eagle Feather Dance and then the dance itself.

A game warden is found murdered close to the body of an illegally killed eagle. Inquiries implicate the high school principal who, although a respected member of society and his profession, is known to supply Cherokees with illegal eagle feathers, which they use in their religious rites, especially their eagle dance. There is a radical hate group around Buckskin who fight the government and the Indians. The son of the leader of this group is the assistant vice principal of the school. He masquerades as another persona who has dedicated himself publicly to opposing the politics of his father.

Family connections drive the novel. Vian Brasfield, the principal, has a checkered past that includes one murder. His wife is bisexual but terrified of having to live without the protective shield of her husband. The leader of the hate group, Dane Kennedy, intemperate in behavior and language, frightened off his wife, the mother of his son and daughter, because he discovered that she was having an affair with the principal's wife. Vian killed her after he discovered that in addition to having an affair with him she was doubling with an affair with his wife. Three murders result from this skein of twisted sexual and personal drives.

Two forces characteristic of Hager's series propel this book. One is Hager's concern with the value of family as community. Here as always Mitch is concerned with the safety and future of his thirteen-year-old daughter, Emily. She is young and very vulnerable. But already she is growing up and has an almost matronly concern for her father's safety and welfare.

Emily has also developed an extended family of two girlfriends whose activities impinge on hers and Mitch's. In the past Emily's school companions led her into serious and hazardous scrapes, once almost getting her killed. In this novel the girls behave like normal school girls but to the extreme that they break the bonds of security and help solve the mystery. One is taking photographs of the eagle dance for an article she is writing for the school paper. In so doing she pushes into adult behavior by providing an important clue that breaks the murder case.

Mitch too brings society and community into the story. He has been a widower now for two years. In earlier books we saw him struggling with present sexual needs in conflict with memories of his wife. He has lived a widower's life but aches for sexual and domestic satisfaction. Here he gets involved with a lady lawyer and for the moment achieves the closure needed, but of course he cannot seal that closure because he must remain the widower searching for happiness for forthcoming books. But for the moment the open wound of unfulfilled community close and personal needs are stanched.

The novel builds around and develops on the core of two Cherokee ritual dances. The first is the so-called booger dance, in which seven masked figures dance around in all kinds of comical poses and gestures, having fun and making light of the onlookers. Its purpose, like that of the Mardi Gras and other festivals, is to allow the underprivileged to blow off steam. The actors are masked in order to prevent detection and to achieve supernatural powers through their playful ladder to heaven.

This mocking dance is followed by the more serious Eagle Feather

Dance, which is an effort to communicate with the gods through ritual. But Hager spends more time with the mocking dance because it is the exercise that is more disruptive of society and as such contributes more to the disintegration of society through murder. Hager uses this disuniting dance as the commentary on the disruptive power of murder but she also uses it as a means to solve the murder. In other words, she is demonstrating that the Cherokee Nation dissolves its splitting forces through ritual while whites resolve theirs in actual murder. As such, it opens the gates for the construction of the development of community.

Hager points out how Kennedy's murders disrupted the community. "You made him pay, all right," Mitch said. "But the fallout is doing major damage to four families, including your sister's and your own. Was it worth it?" Mitch agrees to plea bargain for Hunter Kennedy, the murderer, because that way Kennedy's wife and kids and the other families "could get on with putting their lives back together again" (28).

Hager is a major author of Native American crime fiction for several reasons. She is an accomplished writer who fills her prose with splendid and graphic allusions and figures of speech, many strongly sexual, which shows that her fictional world consists of real-life people. In addition she is effective in accomplishing her goal vis-à-vis the Cherokee about whom she writes. She develops her novels closely on legends and mythology of the Cherokee, always improving the traditional materials she uses as references or guides to her novels. She is a powerful addition to the small army of mixedblood Americans who are trying to bring equality and justice to not only the Native Americans who suffer injustices but also to those who impose them.

Tony Hillerman

Tony Hillerman is proud of the authenticity with which he records stories about the Navajo, happy that the Navajo and Zuni "have recognized themselves and their society" in his books, which have been "heavily used in schools and on reservations and . . . throughout the Indian world by other tribes" as authentic chronicles of their cultures. Hillerman disclaims that his ethnological materials are "intended to meet scholarly and scientific standards" since he always has been essentially a reporter turned novelist. He keeps his eyes on facts but tries to make his writings realistic and authentic so that they will be credible and effective. As he states in the Acknowledgments of *The Blessing Way,* "ethnological material as used in this book is not intended to meet scholarly and scientific standards" and admits having taken his material from publications as well as "the advice and information provided by his own friends among the Navajo people." Hillerman's strength is the Midas touch with which he turns the everyday ores into gold.

In developing the Indian and sometimes Indian-vs.-white cultures, Hillerman blends Native American and white ways of life, showing that they are more closely related than the citizens know or want to admit. It is the sameness instead of the differences that Hillerman emphasizes. Sometimes he pushes this with a gentle suasion even though the events surrounding the lesson in anthropological morality are fierce and deadly. Generally there is a lot of talk in Hillerman's development, describing rather than engaging in deadly activity.

Knowledgeable Native American experts generally agree that Hillerman is sometimes incorrect in his details, though he continues to learn and is more nearly correct in later books than in the initial productions. Ernie Bulow, an authority formerly with the Bureau of Indian Affairs, says that when he first heard Hillerman reading from *The Dark Wind* he realized that the author knew nothing about how to pronounce Navajo words, did not realize that there are not and probably never will be Navajo policemen like Leaphorn and Chee, and that Hillerman frequently got details wrong, as in *The Ghostway* when he has Chee take a sweat bath by pouring water over hot rocks when he should have known that Navajos take their sweat baths dry (*Talking Mysteries 17*).

But such quibbling is irrelevant and threatens to dry up poetic and novelistic license, which all authors must have. And Bulow agrees with most readers that details aside and relatively unimportant, Hillerman is unexcelled as storyteller and depicter of Native American life. He has exerted tremendous influence on such other writers of Indian crime fiction as Jake Page, Jean Hager, Peter Bowen, and Aimée and David Thurlo, whose torches of exposé of injustice burn more fiercely than Hillerman's. In the works of these writers, Hillerman's books alone of all authors of Indian crime fiction are frequently found lying around in bookstores and in homes. He is their point of reference and guide, and their aid.

Hillerman depicts the intricacies, subtleties, and differences of various Native American cultures—Navajo, Hopi, Zuni, and others—as well as Spanish and Southwest Anglo, against the harsh dry and yellow landscape of the Southwest. He concentrates on the Navajo.

In picturing the ancient home place of these Americans, Hillerman graphically details the age of the land on which they live and mankind's pitiable newness and weakness when pitted against it. People of different cultures adjust to nature in various psychological, physical, emotional, and religious ways. Although Hillerman's characters are caught in the web of old fashioned ways warring against new ways of dealing with life, Hillerman is particularly concerned with the reasons whites sometimes do not respect Native American cultures, attitudes, and customs. He is particularly chagrined that white cultures do not grant Indians the same religious freedom other minorities are given. Other cultures are guaranteed their religious icons and rituals, so Hillerman calls for ending "the harassment of the Pueblo people and others who make ritual use of eagle feathers (and eagles) in some religious rites" (Greenberg 305). The impact on the environment would be inconsequential, yet the effect on Indian religion would be monumental, Hillerman believes.

Hillerman's fiction moves with the rhythm of Indian attitudes and life. The sun rises and crosses the heavens at its own pace. The Indians have adjusted by developing their own Indian time. Even in a life-threatening emergency Jim Chee and Joe Leaphorn, Hillerman's policemen who have every right to be impatient and hurried, question a Navajo patiently while the native in turn answers indirectly. That is the Indian way, which Chee and Leaphorn understand and respect.

Writing of the soul of the Indians' civilization and culture, Hillerman concerns himself with the spirit of his characters and not their physical appearance. Their physical descriptions grow incrementally, one part here, another there. By the end of half a dozen books, the reader knows what the two look like, whereas we have long since understood them psychologically.

Hillerman downplays dramatic prose. Instead he is a steady and clear stylist who lets life develop at its own pace and on its own terms. Frequently the reader must accept some things on trust. Eventually the ends will come together despite the fact that those ends sometimes are moved by people who seem not to have sufficient motivation for their actions.

Leaphorn and Chee, sometimes together and sometimes working individually, police the twenty-five thousand square miles of the Navajo Reservation in Arizona and New Mexico, in tune with the pace and customs of the natives, their fellow Navajos.

Leaphorn was the first to be introduced, in *The Blessing Way*. Although the main character in this first book was an academic named Bergen McKee, Hillerman placed the setting on the Navajo reservation because he felt that their lifestyle and homeland "would make a captivating setting for a mystery novel, which otherwise might not be very good, because I didn't know if I was going to be a good mystery writer"

(Greenberg 53). In revising the story for publication, Hillerman realized that Leaphorn carried the potential for a strong and new protagonist and a vehicle for picturing his desire to demonstrate the conflicts between Indian and white cultures and the means for their potential harmonious reconciliation. His role and function were therefore enlarged.

Leaphorn plays that role very effectively, though with some characteristics that keep him and the white McKee at arms length. Leaphorn has been married to Emma, a woman of the Bitter Water family, for some thirty years. She dies of cancer in *A Thief of Time* because of clumsy medical treatment. Through the years in subsequent works Leaphorn gets noticeably older, puts on weight, grays a little, grows stiff in the back, and generally earns the reputation of being hard to get along with. In *Talking God* the character Janet Pete calls him "grouchy Joe." He suspects the motives of nearly everyone who is not Navajo, and even some of those.

In this early, and slightly stumbling, novel, Hillerman gets his point across about how to bridge the gap and to meliorate the hostility that separates Indian and white cultures. McKee, a knowledgeable and understanding archaeologist, has little sympathy for the Indian belief in witches who shower destruction on the people. Leaphorn, being one of the Indians, shares their beliefs, though just barely. There is friction between the two. But Hillerman brings the conflicting viewpoints together here as he will throughout the series in a more modified way, through the most ancient of primitive customs. He has McKee's hostile "white" blood replaced with Indian blood. Wounded and unconscious for two days, McKee has to have a massive transfusion, about ten gallons, and then suggests that McKee has more Navajo blood in him than Leaphorn blood. With this new blood McKee has moved closer to the Indian point of view, and Hillerman has used an extreme method of joining the conflicting races that he will not employ again.

The book smelled of the library. Most readers agree with Ernie Bulow that many details were askew. Bulow recognized that "the ethnography of the book was shaky," and that Hillerman "had never slept in a hogan with fifteen other people or stood still in the cold until dawn three nights running to follow an Enemy Way, smelling piñon smoke and feeling the throb of the drum." Even Hillerman, in later years, agrees that the book has its shortcomings (*Talking Mysteries* 13–14). Hillerman has always had some difficulty in leaving the campus of the University of New Mexico, with which he has been associated for many years. He frequently writes of professors and other campus folk, and they generally are not his strongest, not his most commendable characters. He says he admires academics but they often fall short of more "natural people."

They do fall short in Hillerman's second novel, *Dance Hall of the Dead,* the follow-up in the Leaphorn series. Hillerman is unusually passionate here in his study of Navajo lore. He still sees the world through university glasses. An anthropologist whose reputation as the world's authority on the disappearance of an Indian tribe is being threatened by later research, which will disprove his theory. With his disciple and fellow worker he is out in the field searching for proof to substantiate his theory. Since he cannot find evidence he begins salting the dig. Some Navajo and Zuni kids find evidence of the deception and the anthropologist kills them to protect his secret. But detection of the homicides does not convict the man in the eyes of Leaphorn. The Indian policeman destroys the evidence, asking the anthropologist, "Who would believe a Navajo cop?" "I'm trying to learn more about white men," he says a moment later in a kind of self-justification for his act (166). The surprising thing is that Hillerman, weighing cause and effect, feels no bitterness over the outcome of the episode.

Listening Woman, Hillerman's next novel, strictly speaking a police procedural, is considered by some to be his most effective work featuring Leaphorn as a solo sleuth. The plot turns on conflicts between two cultures. It opens with Margaret Cigaret, blind medicine woman, visiting Hosteen Tso in his hogan to cure her of an illness. She believes that a witch has "messed-up" some religious paintings and thus imposed the illness, by violating Navajo religion. Tso tells Cigaret that he must talk to his grandson, "who went on the Jesus Road," (329) before he himself dies. He and Cigaret's niece Anna Atcitty are murdered. The outside world is introduced when a doctor in the Public Health Service thinks his disappeared daughter has been murdered and brings pressure on the FBI to coerce the Tribal Police to find her. The daughter turns up alive but the death of the two Navajos allows Hillerman the opportunity to comment on different attitudes toward death held by the whites and the Navajo.

Indian trader John McGinnis tells Leaphorn that though Navajos might kill in a drunken brawl or in a fit of anger, they are not deliberate and pre-planning murderers. "Any killings you have, there's either getting drunk and doing it, or getting mad and fighting. You don't have this planning in advance and going out to kill somebody like white folks. Right?" To the Navajo, McGinnis continues, "Even the death of an enemy in battle was something the warrior cleansed himself of with an Enemy Way ritual. Unless, of course, a Navajo Wolf was involved. Witchcraft was a reversal of the Navajo way" (363). This different attitude toward death, even the Navajo's difference from that of other Indians', clearly distinguishes the ferocity of whites from that of the gentler Navajo. Here Hillerman is not trying to bring the two cultures into closer proximity. Clearly, with Navajo culture superior, he would like to keep them separated because though superior, Navajo culture is still more vulnerable.

Having written three books on Leaphorn, Hillerman wanted to do three on a younger man with a different experience and outlook. Jimmy (Jim) Chee, this new creation, appears first in *People of Darkness*. A young tribal policeman, Chee is offered a job by a rich lady to find a stolen box of "keepsakes" which belong to her husband but have been stolen. The local Navajos think that the husband, a hunter named Benjamin J. Vines, is a witch and therefore will not work for his wife. Chee, however, though somewhat chary, agrees to think about taking the job. He is confused when told by Vines that the box said by his wife to be stolen is not missing. The whole episode is tied in with a killer named Colton Wolf who is trying to find his long-lost brother and mother. Wolf is demented and remorseless, willing to kill anyone and everyone casually or causally. For example, Chee is temporarily a patient in a hospital when Wolf enters his room to kill him. To escape, Chee climbs through a hole in the ceiling and hangs on until Wolf has left the room. But before he goes, Wolf, out of annoyance and pique, kills the patient who was Chee's roommate.

Jim Chee, it is generally agreed, is superior to Leaphorn in character and in Hillerman's works. In introducing the new man, Hillerman wanted a more naive tribal policeman who was at the same time more attracted to white culture. He is stretched on the rack of attraction to both cultures. Chee, looking toward the white world, has taken the exams and been admitted as a student at the FBI Academy in Virginia, to which he is supposed to report in a month. If he attends he might return to the Reservation and work among the Dinee (the term used by the Navajo to mean themselves, the People) but he will be pulled away from the customs and religion of the tribe. Trained from an early age in the tribe's religious practices, he had desired to become a "singer," that is, someone who performs oral chants and participates in the rituals that sustain the Navajo theology.

Chee is tempted to go white but has several reasons for staying Navajo. He realizes that the world off the reservation is complex and dangerous. A young white lady friend on the reservation named Mary is also a part of his dilemma. She recognizes Chee's problem and tries to help him in his decision. She is not Navajo (Dinee) and is also living in two worlds. The trouble is that Chee wants Mary to become Navajo so they can get married, but Mary recognizes that she probably can no more become truly Navajo than Chee can become lastingly white. Nevertheless, they decide to risk the marriage and plans are made, though arrangements will take weeks—picking the site, spreading the word, getting the proper singer, arranging for the food. When the marriage is over both supposedly will go again "with beauty all around" them (282), blended into one attitude and race.

But the two do not succeed. Before the ceremony, Mary realizes that Chee can never become white and she can never become Navajo, so the two are bound to be irreconcilable. She disappears from his life. She returns to Wisconsin, thinking of their reconciliation and possible life together. She invites him to come to see her and although she writes him a time or two and he thinks of her occasionally, she decides that she will not become a Navajo and he can't adjust outside the Dinee culture. Chee later will find an alternate romantic interest in Janet Page, a half-Navajo working for the Navajo tribal council.

This is a compelling novel, realistic and cuttingly painful, especially graphic in its character Colton Wolf. There are pathological killers like Wolf in society, as the estimated two hundred serial killers loose in the world today attest, and often they are easily successful in getting access to victims. The story is rich in Navajo lore, in the growing debate over the role of Navajo society today, and for the purposes of Chee and his future. We see the formation of a major figure in Native American crime fiction as he works through his personal agenda and remains trying to walk in beauty.

The novel becomes one of Hillerman's strongest. Colton Wolf might well be the author's most vivid creation in villainy. Abandoned by his mother and searching for his brother, Wolf has spent twenty-seven years as a loner, building up hatred for all people, since all have mistreated him and deprived him of normal happiness. In fact the theme of conflicting hatred and love keeps the tension at a near breaking point. The arrogant Vines and his wife Rosemary have their reasons for hating everybody. Wolf is indeed a beast. Chee and Mary are on a different mission of trying to walk in beauty. The two threads keep the novel at a feverish pitch. John L. Breen calls this Hillerman's "best novel to date" (Greenberg 23).

It becomes increasingly apparent in this work how much Hillerman admires the Navajo culture and what he is doing to influence respect for it from others. Despite the fact that Hillerman recognizes that he is writing entertainment and needs to keep the novel form in mind because "readers are buying my mystery, not a tome of anthropology" (Winks, *Colloquium* 142), he is in fact writing a mystery of human compassion and culture. John Reilly glances at this higher purpose in pointing out that Hillerman's attitude toward the Navajo's culture "is respectful," (Reilly 7) and that Hillerman also seeks to create sympathy and respect for Chee's Navajo culture.

Indeed he does, but his purpose goes much further than a modest effort. Hillerman is pointing out the differences between the two cultures, the parallel development of those cultures under the rubric of humanity and charting the directions they should take as they bend ever slightly toward each other. The goal does not require a conscious, deliberate intent, only a profound recognition of the underlying and spiritual makeup of the materials themselves and an honest and fully dignified effort to allow the cultures to speak for themselves.

The Dark Wind, Hillerman's next Chee book, is a man's story, a triangle of interests and conflicting forces. Chee represents the Navajo, and is aided more than usual by his superior, Captain Largo. A second force is the customs of the Hopi, with a different lifestyle and needs. This nation is represented by officer Cowboy Dashee, a Hopi policeman whose behavior won him the name "Cowboy." Both, sometimes with common interests, sometimes with slightly varying goals, are against the Anglo element in the novel, this time represented by two suitcases of high-class cocaine and an FBI agent. Both the FBI and Washington are hated because they stand for outside forces trying to disrupt Indian culture. In this novel, Chee and Dashee work with the FBI agent in trying to locate the suitcases of cocaine, which have mysteriously disappeared. The agent, however, is a mole who wants the cocaine not for turning over to the law but for his own purposes. So he is again the enemy. He is destroyed in a neat turn that puts Hillerman at the top in matters of tricky plotting.

As in his other books, implicitly or explicitly Hillerman emphasizes that Native American cultures must be respected. "My uncle taught me," Chee says, "He said we must always respect the old ways. That we must stay with them" (87).

After three books each on Leaphorn and Chee, Hillerman felt the urge to try having them work as protagonists in the same book.

Skinwalkers brings them together in this experiment. Although the joining allows Hillerman the opportunity to experiment and develop in different ways, there is some question whether the fiction benefits from the jointure. Both Leaphorn and Chee develop characteristics that have been only hinted at or underdeveloped in previous stories. Chee is getting more doubtful that anything will ever come of his relationship with Mary Landon, and he has now met Janet Pete, a lawyer for the Navajo Nation's Legal Aid Society. Leaphorn is becoming more human and agreeable. But the tension between the two, hinted at or stated explicitly in earlier novels, now comes to a head. The older officer thinks Chee naive, excitable, and unobservant. Leaphorn doubts the direction of Chee's investigation into Navajo religion, but Chee won't stop unless and until ordered to by his superior, that is, Leaphorn. Further, Chee feels intimidated by an irascible Leaphorn and does not respect him as he should. By the end of *Skinwalkers,* Chee and Leaphorn have, however, harmonized their differences and seem set for peace and cooperation.

But the next work starring both begins with the harmony forgotten and the former animosities restored. Of course, this is one of Hillerman's techniques for developing the novels and keeping a tension there that could not exist if the personalities did not conflict. But rekindling old fires in each book only to have to let them die out at the end prevents a kind of development that might otherwise benefit the fiction as a whole, and Hillerman's cultural message.

A Thief of Time, Hillerman's next and personal favorite and one that appeals to most readers, is more complicated than usual. It begins with the quietude of Southwest nature, broken by the invasion of human beings, and ends with that invasion corrected, in a paean of harmony of two individuals perfectly at peace with themselves and the world. The introductory paragraph is especially peaceful:

> The moon has risen just above the cliff behind her. Out on the packed sand of the wash bottom the shadow of the walker made a strange elongated shape. Sometimes it suggested a heron, sometimes one of those stick-figure forks of an Anasazi pictograph. An animated pictograph, its arms moving rhythmically as the moon shadow drifted across the sand. Sometimes, when the goat trail bent and put the walker's profile against the moon, the shadow became Kokopelli himself. The backpack formed the spirit's grotesque hump, the walking stick Kokopelli's crooked flute. Seen from above, the shadow would have made a Navajo believe that the great *yei* northern clans called Watersprinkler had taken visible form. If an Anasazi had risen from his thousand-year grave in the trash heap under the cliff ruins here, he

would have seen the Humpbacked Flute Player, the rowdy god of fertility of his lost people. (1–2)

The full novel plays on the idea of two people searching for Anasazi pots in a cliff dwelling, one legitimately though illegally, the other illegally and illegitimately. Eleanor Friedman-Bernal, a Jewish anthropologist, discovers that the dig she wants to explore has been despoiled by someone else, obviously recovering the priceless treasures to convert them into cash. Out at the dig in the middle of the night a "humped shape that was coming out of the moonlight into this pool of darkness" (10) approaches her. Ellie, though armed with a 25-caliber pistol, is terrified, as she has a right to be. As a result of this encounter, Ellie disappears and has been missing for two weeks before Leaphorn and Chee are asked to investigate. Indians report that she has been destroyed by the devil.

Leaphorn and Chee are called in from separate points. Leaphorn, is out of pocket because he is set to retire from the Police Force because Emma has died needlessly, during an operation for a brain tumor that should have been 90 percent safe, but from a blood clot she had developed.

Chee meanwhile is off larking with lawyer Janet Pete, who is interested in buying a used Buick. Out testing it for Janet after a mechanic friend has told him it is a lemon, Chee meets a wanted suspect on the highway, makes a U-turn to chase him but winds up in the sagebrush in a Buick considerably damaged. Pete then claims that car dealers always mislead women about automobiles.

Leaphorn and Chee get together at a revival meeting of the Navajo evangelist Slick Nakai, a known dealer in illegal Anasazi pots. Chee abandons his research in used cars and helps Leaphorn investigate the disappearance of the anthropologist. Perhaps because Leaphorn is on terminal leave and will abandon the Force in ten days, Chee does not have to defer to the older man's authority, and they work well together, without the suspicions and tensions ordinarily growing from their association. After Friedman-Bernal has been found and rescued, the novel ends on an upward note. Leaphorn decides not to leave the Police Force and has developed a new attitude toward his junior police officer. The book concludes in a beautiful closure of their association, professionally and spiritually:

Jim Chee notices Leaphorn was watching him.
"You all right?" he asked.
"I've felt better," Leaphorn said. And then he had another thought.

He considered it. Why not? "I hear you're a medicine man. I heard you
are a singer of the Blessing Way. Is that right?"
Chee looked slightly stubborn.
"Yes sir," he said.
"I would like to ask you to sing for me," Leaphorn said. (209)

The singing and the song bring temporary amity. For the moment,
at least, two Navajos, though separated by age and experience and thus
some philosophy, are drawn together because of their blood ties. Individually and together they work effectively to control the crime within
the tribe and to oppose invasions from the outside society. They are
clearly working for the advancement of the Navajo Nation, at least as
they see it.

As we turn next to Louis Owens, a mixedblood with strong feelings
about the ability of non-Indians to write on Indian cultures, it behooves
us to pause a moment and recapitulate on Hillerman's accomplishments.
With a varied background in journalism and many nonliterary activities,
Hillerman was not sure that he could become a novelist. His attitude toward white mistreatment of Indians had been formed and developed
since his days in a Native American girls school. So only his medium of
expression had to change. In *The Blessing Way* he learned that with practice he could succeed as a novelist and he has demonstrated this success in subsequent works. These works have been appreciated by non-
Indians, who might easily be mislead by the charm of art, and by real-life
Indians, who live too close to reality to be seduced by pretty words and
stories. They know what Indian life is, and Hillerman's occasional lack of
real knowledge can be easily forgiven in light of his greater truths. Perhaps Indian and non-Indian authors of literature about Native Americans need to keep in mind that although the lifeblood of literature may
start out with varying amounts of oxygen in it, all indeed runs blue until
depleted and forced to come back to the origin of life to get new strength.

In the matter of an author of one culture being able to write on that
of another, particularly Indian, Owens says in *Wolfsong,* "You don't have
to be an Indian. It just matters how you feel, what you think. Your
dreams" (104).

Louis Owens

Louis Owens writes a somewhat more intellectualized and angry series
in which the Native Americans live uncomfortably in and at least rhetorically antagonistic to a dominant white society. So far he has four

novels to his credit, two about Cole McCurtain, a mixedblood, and one, the latest, the strongest of the quartet, involving two poverty-ridden half-Cherokee farmers in Oklahoma.

The first of his novels, *The Sharpest Sight,* volume one in the University of Oklahoma Press's American Indian Literature and Critical Studies series, is a story of maturation, of growing up, of discovering who one is. It develops in conflict between the white and the Indian cultures. Attis McCurtain, a Vietnam veteran, is hospitalized for mental disorder. He is lured out of the prison by someone who cuts a hole in the fence surrounding the compound and then murders Attis alongside a raging river and lets him fall back into the water and be swept away. The river symbolizes the passions of humanity. For most of the year — during most everyday human life — it, the largest stream in the United States and perhaps the world, is dry, the water running underground. But in the heavy California rains of winter — in other words, in the outbreak of hatred and passion — it swells into a wide rushing stream, carrying everything before it.

Mundo Morales, Attis's friend and deputy sheriff, as he drives over the river sees Attis's dead face in the water and starts a search for the body despite the fact that everybody says the sight was only one of Morales's fantasies.

To escape the Army draft, Cole McCurtain, Attis's brother, flees to his Uncle Luther in Mississippi but returns to California and because of a bad heart escapes the draft. While in Mississippi, Cole is taught by Uncle Luther the old ways of the Choctaw. In Oklahoma, Cole's father, Hoey, becomes obsessed with the determination to revenge Attis's murder. But he has an overriding kind heart. He suspects a man named Dan Nemi of the murder and stalks him to assassinate him. While observing Nemi's house, Hoey sees Nemi's daughter, Diana, a lusty and promiscuous eighteen year old, return to the house in distress. She has been raped by Jessard Deal, a giant who runs the town saloon. Deal is a cynic who lives by the despair in the works of the American minister Jonathan Edwards and his defense of original sin. Deal says he is savage because he wants somebody to kill him but nobody will do him that favor.

The whole society is filled with illusions, smoke, and mirrors, where apparent reality is no more tangible than in the land of Oz. After the rape of his daughter, Nemi enters the saloon to kill Deal, sees him and fires. But he has shattered Deal's image in a looking glass, and standing behind Nemi, Deal taunts him for killing illusions and then cuts his throat. Hoey, in to avenge Deal's rape of Diana, sees the real person by standing behind him and kills him. Because he is Indian, Hoey can distinguish between reality and mirror illusions, as whites cannot. Living in the mystical world of Indian culture, Indians can know the difference. So, the mixedblood Hoey, acting for the good of the white society, has killed the evil white and is himself purged of his hatred. Meanwhile, Cole has found the bones of his brother, Attis, and wants to take them back to the ancestral home in Mississippi, where they can rest in peace.

Having finished the life cycle in California, Cole, his father, uncle, and aunt plan to return to Mississippi, their homeland. They leave on their hegira at dawn, heading east into the sunrise. On the way they pass through the Oklahoma towns of Choctaw and Shawnee, where their people had lived on their way to the West. In four days they are in Mississippi, "Where an old man and an old lady were ready to take them home" (263). It is indeed a triumphant return. Cole has grown up into knowledge of the value of the past, and has matured. Hoey has given up the world and gone back to his ancestors. They have discovered that one can and should go home again.

With a richness reminiscent of William Faulkner's works, *The Sharpest Sight* graphically details the conflict between cultures, the growth of one young man to maturity through experience. Cole "becomes comfortable with the dead. . . . He knows at last who he is" (262). But he has traveled a long road to achieve that maturity, over his own version of the Cherokee Trail of Tears forced on that nation when President Andrew Jackson relocated them in 1828 from the South to Oklahoma. Hoey, too, having been purged of the cancer of hatred can go back to Mississippi with the family. It is a return to a new beginning.

The story is rhetorically rich and filled with Choctaw lore and mysticism. It is fired with traditional Choctaw hatred of whites and the United States. Cole's father Hoey, for example, seems to get angrier and angrier "about the raw deal the Choctaws had gotten in Mississippi" (14). "You don't owe this sonofabitchin government nothing," Hoey says to his son Cole. The "Choctaws won the battle of New Orleans for them. And then that rednecked sonofabitch Jackson sent in the troops to steal the land and cattle and slaves and everything else and move them all to Oklahoma" (20). Hoey thinks he knows the whites.

But Cole had to relearn his knowledge because he did not understand the past with its rituals and their meaning. For example, he's been reading books and trying to figure out what being Indian is but he has had trouble. Hoey, his father, likewise had to relearn. "Remember when I took you to that powwow them Indians had in San Luis? It was like a circus to me. I didn't know beans about what them dancers was doing" (57), he says. All Indians were forgetting the past. Uncle Luther has to teach them virtually everything, beginning with the ABCs of Choctaw culture. But he is the library, the CD-ROM of Choctaw civilization.

Uncle Luther tells Cole about "*bohpuli* and maybe *kashenpotapalo* so's they don't surprise you in the woods. That first one, he's the little guy, about this big." He held his hand a foot above the edge of the boat. "He likes to have fun, throwing things and confusing people. Some call him a hide-behind. He ain't no danger, don't have a mean bone in his body. That second one, he's a man and a doer and he likes to scare folks when they're out at night" (77). The shadows of dead people "is very lonely and always wants to take a loved one, or anyone, with it" (164). Choctaws are not perfect people and know their imperfections. Cole, trying to figure out who he is, admits he's a mixedblood, and remembers, "All I know from books in school and those old TV movies is that a half-breed can't be trusted, is a killer, a betrayer, a breed" (10). But all he knows about Indian life is what he learned in Boy Scouts (55).

Choctaws believe that unlike themselves, whites are immature. Uncle Luther talks about cowboys-and-indians stories and other tales about kids. But "White people don't have a monopoly on ignorance, . . . Neither do red people or black people" (188). *The Sharpest Sight* is a keen reading of page one of contemporary Choctaw culture.

Bone Game, Owens's second tale, is more intentionally intellectualized, as Owens places the work on the campus of the University of California, Santa Cruz. The story follows some years after *The Sharpest Sight* with Cole McCurtain now a professor of Indian literature at that university. He is still obsessed with dreams of Indian mythology, in fact is always carried away by them. He dreams of Spanish California and the Spanish priest who was murdered in 1812. Owens prefaces the book with a brief descriptive paragraph about that event:

> October 15, 1812. Government Surgeon Manuel Ouijana, accompanied by six armed men, is dispatched from the presidio in Monterey with orders to exhume the body of Padre Andres Quintana at the mission of Santa Cruz, Exaltacion de la Santa Cruz. The priest is found to have been murdered, tortured in pudendis, and hanged.

Then for contrast but to demonstrate that mankind is just as murderous and cruel in 1993, Owens adds a sentence about today: "November 1, 1993. The dismembered body of a young woman begins washing ashore on the beaches of Santa Cruz, California." With this beginning, the novel recounts how some dozen more bodies of young girls, and one boy, will be found around the college town. While Cole dreams about earlier Choctaw culture he is called upon to help investigate these murders, and meets some weirdo colleagues and students.

One anthropology colleague is a cross-dresser, though he claims he should be called something else. His actions are attention grabbing. We meet him just after he has slaughtered a deer on campus, against rules, and is quartering it for cooking. Cole reluctantly has to work closely with the students. Some get close to him in conferences at the office and at his home. Although divorced from his wife, Cole has an eighteen-year-old daughter, named Abby, who comes to live with him and help him through his troubles. Cole is in the midst of a midlife crisis and cannot see the resolution. Realizing the magnitude of Cole's problems on campus, his relatives from Oklahoma also come to help him because the story is so big that Cole can see only a portion of it and he needs four generations to help him solve it: the grandfather tradition, the uncle (or father), Cole himself, and his daughter Abby.

Cole's problem is himself. He burns with his brother's trouble in Vietnam and the guilt of not having died in that war as his brother almost had. He is weighted down with survivor's guilt. "We just got to empty ourself of the stuff that gets in the way, and sometimes we don't know it worked till a long time later" (164), he is told by Uncle Luther. The point is continued by Onatima, his wise old aunt:

> It's not wrong to survive. I see Indians all the time who are ashamed of surviving, and they don't even know it. We have survived a five-hundred-year war in which millions of us were starved to death, burned in our homes, shot and killed with disease and alcohol. . . . Survivor's guilt is a terrible burden, and so we feel guilty if we have enough food, a good home, a man or woman who loves us. (163)

But Cole's obsession with the past is so blind that a beautiful woman who enjoys sleeping with him gives up, saying to him, "You're fucking the past" (74).

The danger of Cole's obsession when carried into violence is demonstrated by a young man named Robert, Cole's student, who turns out to be the murderer of the young females on campus. He is infatuated with Native American myth and artificiality. In a conversation with Alex, the transvestite professor, Robert says, "Native Americans have a lot to teach all of us" (119). "Like what?" Alex questions. "How to live in harmony with the world, the environment," Robert says. Alex answers graphically. "Go to a reservation sometimes, and you'll see junked cars, arroyos full of wrecked refrigerators, broken bottles, cans—all the same squalor you'll see anywhere, maybe worse. Not very harmonious." Robert reveals his problem with another statement: "I never knew what to do with my freedom" (238). So Owens demonstrates here as in other books the problems Indians and whites have in life. They envision their desires but do not know how to walk the road of life to satisfy those desires or how to cope with them once they seem to have been achieved. Cultural intelligence is at best a mere slit in the blindfold covering all our eyes.

Specifically by implication Owens is saying that whites, and Indians, don't know what to do with their freedom. One worships the myth of the Noble Savage, the other the myth of the glorious past. Perhaps both are hung-up on the myth. Californians and whites throughout the land don't like to read of their sordid past, so they bury it, but once it is uncovered they don't know how to handle it.

The cure of this navel-reading and guilt-wallowing is clear to at least one person. In a serious conversation with Cole, Uncle Luther, a wise voice from the past, tells his nephew: "They got too many stories about us. We need to write books about them now. Get even." Then recalling an 1887 interview with an Indian named Lorenzo Asisara, "the son of one of the men who killed the priest," in 1812 who had green eyes, even Cole begins to see the light, though there is "a line of low clouds or fog along the ridge, graying the morning" (226).

"How do you think the son ended up with green eyes?" Luther asks (227). The answer is, of course, sexual integration, two individuals forgetting about the differences between Indian and white. This is a message that floats through the remainder of the book—the need for leveling the differences between the two groups of people and generating a mixture of the cultures. That is the message of the title of the book *Bone Game.* The bones of the past should be buried and a new attitude toward life and society created at the graveside. It is a message that Owens carries into his next book, *Wolfsong,* though in a more tangential way. Owens will demonstrate that the commitment must be cautious and careful. Intrusions from the outside can be threatening, and wholesale uncritical acceptance of white values can be devastating to the Indian community.

Wolfsong switches to another part of the country and introduces a new character. It is an environmental degradation novel. Tom Joseph, a fullblood, has been admitted to the University of California, Berkeley, because of the Affirmative Action quota. He has returned to his home in the Cascade Mountains of western Washington because of the death of his uncle, an old-fashioned Indian who protested against the pollution of the valley by white mining and lumbering interests. Tom is urged to go back to the university and get his degree because he will be the first person from the valley, let alone the first Indian, to graduate from college. But he has had enough of white culture and decides he is going to stay in the valley and fight to save it from the onslaught of the whites, just as his uncle had. But his fight is against overwhelming odds. Combating the takeover by a man named J. D. Hill, Tom shoots into a gigantic water tank, which explodes and drowns the white man. Tom is then forced to flee north, trying to get to safety in Canada, pursued by both whites and Indians.

It is a fine Indians versus whites novel, though somewhat heavy with all the environmental baggage that Owens picked up during his years working for the forest service and his near irresistible desire to be a lifetime backpacker and fisherman.

In developing the novel, Owens uses both Indian mysticism and symbolism. The story begins in a rainy Washington state, and the rainfall continues throughout. The gods are not smiling on the Indians; in fact they are crying over realization of the Indians' fate. The traditional animals also symbolize the future of the Indians. One of the women, with whom Tom has sex, always dreams of bears—five of them. They take care of her, excite her sexually, and answer her every need. Tom believes that they are from the Cherokee ancestors about which he should have discussed with an ancestral singer like his uncle. But we understand it as the voice of the past lamenting the ugly fate of the Indians in the present and future.

The fate of the Indian land arose partly from the fact that the Native Americans had abandoned the faith of their ancestors and taken up Christianity instead. The valley, according to one of them, was filled with Jesus people. When the Indians tried to become initiated into the forgotten faith of their fathers, as one did, the result was not promising. He fasted for three days and on the fourth "he took off his clothes and smeared the stone he'd chosen with saliva the way his uncle had said he should, and then he'd waded in the water, feeling the cold cut into his groin and chest, excited and terrified. And when the water closed over his head, he held the stone and struggled to stay upright, waiting for the vision he knew would come" (87). It didn't come because he had not really believed in the faith of his uncle.

The flora and fauna suffer from declining expectations. The wolves have been replaced by taunting coyotes. Where there used to be a pair of nesting falcons, there is now only one, and it generally is only a fading speck in a distant sky.

Wolfsong is a sad book of surrender. But not all the symbolism points down. The ending, though portentous in its prediction of the Indians' fate, is at least clear and sparkling.

In Tom's flight from the group of lawmen who are out to capture him for the murder of J. D. Hill, the world opens into new vistas. Fleeing into the mountains, Tom hears his destiny. "A deep tunnel of sound welled up in the clear night and enveloped the valleys and rose up around the mountain, a howl that came out of the forests and ascended until it filled the world" (248). In the midst of this symphony of affirmation, Tom takes his knife and starts chipping steps in the glacier so he can climb up toward his heaven and paradise. Tom, though wounded twice by his pursuers, seems able to make his ascension. "The moon framed him against the glistening wall . . . and inside him the song grew louder, and the explosion of a rifle turned the night suddenly quiet. He pulled himself over the edge and stood, looking down at the three men wrestling with the rifle below him. And then he turned and started to run just as the wolf began to call again, and this time it kept growing louder and louder and spinning ever-widening circles through the thin air until it was deafening and seemed a part of the air he breathed." Tom continued his headlong dive into immortality. "He ran with long, smooth strides down the mountain, the moon hurling his shadow northward before him, listening to the rising howl of the wolf that went on and on until the night seemed ready to burst" (249).

So Tom, not broken by the inevitable fate of the Indian nation, ends his life as he would have liked. He has remained, though for a very short time, in the valley of his ancestors and he ends his adventures and this world in a shower of clarity. Owens's story, told in vernacular language, is a success. The site, the language, the symbolism, the conclusions reveal a novelist with a future.

Nightland, Owens's fourth work, is more a North American action novel than detective story. It grows naturally out of the ending of *Bone Game.* That novel had concluded with Owens's admonition that Indians should give up some of their myopic and protective views of themselves in society, their clinging to old traditions, and move out or at least face out to the larger society. *Nightland* shows that outfacing has its hazards and results.

The opening is deeply symbolic and threatening, with Owens developing the setting in great detail and explicitness. Billy Keene and Will Striker, two poor half-Cherokee farmer friends, are alone under the canopy of threatening clouds. Something looking like "a black buzzard" comes tumbling out of the western sky. Soon recognizable as a man, it impales itself on a dead tree limb that penetrates the body through "belly and back, so that the man flailed for a moment and then hung limply, black-suited fish bait against the heavy sky," the limb holding the body like a long flailing saber, "almost suspended between heaven and earth." The falling, or "descent" as Owens calls it, is accompanied by a flash of lightning. Billy says it was like "he was dropped by the Creator himself" (13). As the two men begin to talk about something that separated itself from the falling man and fell independently, there is a heavenly observance of approval, "a current of light eddied through the clouds directly overhead and a deep, conversational rumbling shook the sky," as though the gods were discussing the situation and speaking to the two men. They find the suitcase that is filled with money. Billy calls it a "gift from the Great Spirit" and the gods seemed to approve of his observation, as "the whole sky rumbled and diffuse lightning forked tentatively over mountains and plains" (7).

Striker, the more cautious and traditional of the pair, however, is not so sure that the gift was sent from heaven. He reminds Billy that Grandfather Siquani, the resident old timer and spokesman for tradition, had told them many stories about the evil and threats of buzzards and forces coming from the west.

Driven by his apprehensions, Striker examines the corpse more closely and sees supernatural implications written all over it. The corpse's face "was strangely white and detailed, almost luminescent, the eyes black and shining and the blue lips set in what looked like a light, sad smile. It was nothing like the face of a dead man" (12).

It was the face of an Indian. Groping toward earth, the body had brought evil and temptation to the people, like a demonic being, and was now glad of success in his evil mission. That evil intent is almost immediately implemented when a helicopter, again approaching silently on the winds of the exploding storm, appears overhead and someone in it starts firing at the two men. As Billy fires back, the helicopter explodes. So, though linked to earthly reality, the two seem at the moment triumphant. But one of them, Billy, is lividly marked across his face, in what we learn later is a "lightning bolt" (114). He is thus marked for extermination.

The element of evil is furthered by vengeance in the form of a sexy, cold-hearted, and utterly self-centered female named Odessa White-hawk. Her violent introduction occurs when Billy in a saloon is challenged by a drunken man named Mouse Melendez, a Mexican with whom Billy has fought dozens of times throughout the past. This time, Mouse, a large and powerful man, is about to force Billy to cringe and creep out of the saloon and compromise his dignity, not so much in fear as in the desire to avoid violence. But either motivation will demean the Indian. To interrupt this self-demeaning act, Mouse is struck on the back of the head with a pool cue swung by a large, powerful, and beautiful lady, who finally introduces herself as Odessa. Billy is alerted to the unusual atmosphere generated by this whole affair by the fact that Mouse had acted very strangely and out-of-character in forcing Billy to back down, and Billy had been saved by this total stranger who is also acting very foreign and strange. The electricity of threat and doom charges the situation.

Odessa, she explains, is a Ph.D. from the University of California, Berkeley, who majored in Indian sovereignty and what she later identifies as "genocide." She insists that all Indians are free of U.S. government control and should act independently. The danger of that attitude carried to an extreme is demonstrated by Odessa's willingness to destroy everything and everybody to achieve her selfish goals.

The two suitcases contain nearly a million dollars of drug money. Two men who have nothing to do with the money try to take it nevertheless, but it is Odessa, the real owner, who executes Billy in order to get it back. She is willing to give up all pleasure for the joy of holding that million dollars. She enjoys sex with Billy but is obsessed by her more powerful lust for wealth and the independence it can bring. She explains her extreme and atypical Indian attitude in great detail to Will as she prepares to murder him because of his part in trying to take the money from her:

> This land was the home of my ancestors. They never pretended to own it. But their bones are in the earth you call yours. You and Billy aren't supposed to be here. You're no better than the whites. You let them push you off your own land in the east and march you into the homes of other Indian people in that so-called Territory, and you became just like them. You let them fuck your women and create half-breeds like them. Westering, it's called by white historians. That's what your families did. You came here and became part of the whole pattern. You live on top of my people's bones now. (302)

When Will asserts that it's not just the money Odessa wants, she replies:

> I have a Ph.D. in genocide. . . . When I was young and innocent I thought I could get a white education and fight back. But I was stupid. Now . . . I'm going to have the American dream. Almost a million dollars. It's not that much really, but I'm taking it all south. I can live fairly well in South America with a million dollars. I'll be a rich, brown-skinned Yankee in the middle of all those poor Indians. (202)

As she prepares to murder Will, Odessa points out his strength and his ultimate triumph. Billy was executed because of the inseparable pair, Billy and Will, he was always the leader, who dragged a weak Will into whatever scheme he desired. Billy took the initiative in appropriating the suitcase filled with money. He is also the guiltier of the two men. He killed the man in the helicopter and was responsible for the death of two other men. Will was guilty of being willing to steal the money, an accomplice after the crime. With Billy's death, Will became the free and independent man he should have been as Indian all along. He shoots Odessa as she prepares to blast him a second time. In doing so he releases his own strength and becomes a leader.

But he is a leader in the Indian community. He has tried the outside world and found that it is too full of violence and threat for him and the average Indian. In this realization he turns to Grandfather Siquani again, who tells him, "Our world is still here. . . . Sometimes we forget because we got to look so hard to see it, and people get tired and forget how to look. But the animals know; they don't forget. We got to listen. I think maybe it's time to go home, Willum" (309).

Not quite believing that he must go home again, Will looks at the richness of the world around him and discovers that in fact to last against its adversaries he has to hide everything.

> The earth around him felt heavy and dark, populated by the dead, piñon and grass seeds falling to burrow and sprout in flesh, tree roots reaching and twining through the eyes of the dead, stitching them to the ageless earth. How could a person live and walk upon such earth? he wondered. He felt a desire to flee, to find a place where nothing was buried, where the surface of the earth bared all secrets. (311)

But realizing the irreversibility and unchangeability of nature, he accepts things as they are. He goes to the well in which the suitcases of money had been hidden, pries off the crumbling top and gazes down into the well that had dried up but now had mysteriously been refilled with water from the spring.

The heavens are aware of the great discovery he is going to make and the momentous decision he is going to reach as he climbs down to the water and, "Thunder muttered in the mountains behind him as he bent closer, and out of the corner of one eye he saw a delicate branch of lightning slip from sky to earth" (312). In the pool he sees his own re-birth and its approval by the Indian nation around him:

> As he stared into the water, the reflection of a man rose and hovered just below the rippling surface, the image wavering and breaking apart before merging once more. He knelt in the cold water, and in the deep-ening well a crowd of faces began to rush upward only to shatter and flutter downward and then rise again with the motion of leaves in a fall wind. (312)

Nightland is a moving story of the Indian's existence in today's world. It is rich in Cherokee-Choctaw legends and symbols. Grandfa-ther Siquani teaches Billy and Will all the Cherokee beliefs and super-stitions. Will recounts one of them his father had taught him about the growth of corn:

> He loved his father's often-told story about first man and Selu. Kanati, the hunter, was all alone upon the earth and bored to death, so he started killing too many of the little deer and other animals, just be-cause he was bored. The animals went to the Creator and complained, and the Creator said, "Oh yes, I forgot something." Then a cornstalk grew up beside Kanati, and when the hunter awakened there was a tall green stalk with a beautiful woman rising out of the top of the stalk. That was how Selu, Corn Woman, had become Kanati's wife. Will loved the image of the dark, black-haired woman rising above the golden tassels of the cornstalk. He could still see her swaying there in the breeze above the sleeping hunter. "That's why Cherokee people al-ways plant corn," his father had explained. "Corn is our mother." (147)

In other legends about Selu-Kanati there is a dark side to the corn mother, in which Selu-Corn Mother has to be slain by either her hus-band or her sons so that she can remain immortal. This sacrifice of a source of life is not uncommon in all mythologies.

Billy, who knew the magic of words and the Cherokee love of them, believed that the world around him was made up of two ways of com-municating. "To his young mind, it was as if the Indian world was al-ways new, made again and again when his father or Billy's grandpa told the stories, but that the white world had been formed long ago and lay there in books ready to assume the same each and every time the pages were opened. Like the Bible" (34). Billy had given up the Cherokee world for that of the whites: "Sure, I've heard the stories, but in case you haven't noticed it, it's damned near the twenty-first century. I don't pay a lot of attention to superstition and fairy tales" (12).

When Siquani explains to Billy that Indians and whites are two different kinds of people, whites half of the body and Indians the other half, Billy replies in a view of anatomy that serves as a warning by Owens: "I kind of think it's right down the middle, top to bottom" (62). The rationality of Billy on occasion is what makes the novel wrenching in its development. He makes sense at times, though eventually he is tempted by the lure of wealth and the boredom of being a Cherokee into betraying his heritage and destroying himself. Will is also a man of both worlds, but he manages to have the strength of character to finally resist temptation and remain a Cherokee.

The rich, highly convoluted unrolling of the worlds of the Indians and the whites symbolizes the complexity of the intercourse between the two, or the many societies, today. It is a romantic story, filled with mysticism of the Indians and the hard harsh reality of the whites. In order to appreciate it fully, the reader must wander in the mystical world where witches and other shadows actually exist, move around and participate in that life. Sometimes it requires the willing suspension of doubt and ratiocination. But the trip in this novel is surely worth that willing suspension.

Odessa, though hardly a philosopher we like to reason with, raises the question of what the Native American's world would have been like if Europeans had never come to the continent: "Think about it. Indian people are among the most adaptive on the face of the earth. If we hadn't been, we'd all have been dead a long time ago. So what would we be today if we'd been left alone?" (168). She adds, cynically: "Maybe we'd have evolved into the ecological saviors of the world" (169). She voices a question many ask today.

Perhaps the answer lies somewhere in Owens's pages in this novel. The reader is urged to make his own response. The two, sometimes conflicting, avenues of cultures developed and developing in America are presented, though with a bias by the author. The result is an interesting humanized story that calls for much speculation on the part of the reader. Owens is dead serious in his concerns, his questions and answers.

Readers, in addition to enjoying a splendid novel, are invited to ponder the solutions to the problems.

In *Dark River* Owens's latest novel, the author assumes a different stance in literature, or maybe his new position is the original and real Owens before he took up writing crime fiction. This new novel is more conventional general literature, perhaps with a capital L. Owens seems to be saying that just as one does not have to be all-Indian to write Indian works, an author does not have to be all-white to write white literature, except in this case it is an Indian story turned into literature without color. Owens is trying to write nonblooded, nonethnic, American, and world, that is, human, literature.

Owens's background and bias, however, show through in the first chapter. Here as he sets the background for the story the author cannot foreswear his love and respect for nature, for the rolling lands and towering mountains and life-giving verdure of the grasslands and rivers. It is Arizona, now cut off from its life-sustaining tie with the mighty oceans through the romantically named Sea of Cortez, not called the Gulf of California, and its life-giving vein of salmon, which in the old days brought life annually up the Colorado River and into the feeder streams and peoples on their banks. Now the rivers are denied access to the ocean and are thus deprived of their salmon and resulting culture. The clash between the past and the present must be told truthfully. As his model, strangely enough, the author uses Ernest Hemingway. "It's mostly his language," Jacob "Jake" Nashoba says:

> It's restful, you know, and honest; it doesn't require some kind of action. His people are all fucked up, just like the rest of us, but there's this sense that he's not trying to hide anything, that nothing's going to change and it's not so great but basically okay. I tried one of those Indian novels, a best-seller supposedly written by a real Indian, but it was nothing but a bunch of stupid skins drinking and beating each other to death and being funny about it. At least the writer was trying to be funny about it. (11)

Nashoba, his spokesperson in this novel, a Choctaw veteran, a drunken failure in readjusting to life after the war, has landed a job as game warden on the Black Mountain Apache Reservation in central Arizona. The life situation here demands truth, and Hemingway is the model for revelation. Owens is apparently foreswearing his past tenets and novels about literature but developing his philosophy that one does not have to be Indian in order to write about Indians, not white to write non-Indian stories. He has always felt that Indianness is attitude, not genes, and one therefore could write about Indians if he had the proper attitude. Truth demands more than genes.

Life on the reservation, as elsewhere, all flows to the Dark River of human degradation. Most whites and Indians who make up the power structure of the reservation are corrupt. They are selling to rich whites licenses to slaughter elk and deer as trophies. Then the Indians are poaching themselves and selling the trophies to whites for $10,000, and keeping the money, thereby enriching themselves. True, they give the meat of the illegally slaughtered elk to the poor, thus salving their own consciences. Interestingly, women play a dominant role and demonstrate that they are survivors, generally above the flow of corruption.

The men, on the contrary, at least the honest men, are losers. Nashoba, the fulcrum on which all action turns, is accidentally shot by fellow veterans and introduces an ambiguity about the meaning of the story.

This is not a conventional crime novel though there are two murders, one accidental, the other a deus ex machina to implement Owens's point of view that life goes on around one even when he is unable to participate in it. And Nashoba, after being the center of conversation about his recovery falls into a deep crevasse and is swallowed up by Mother Earth. Is he vanquished or triumphant? Apparently the latter: "It is said that Jacob Nashoba went home," Owens concludes as an epitaph to the dark but hopeful side of human fate.

James D. Doss

Another author rich in Indian lore and life is James D. Doss. His first novel on the subject, *The Shaman Sings,* is two parallel stories interwoven around a single theme. Doss had set out originally to write a novel about how a professor abuses and steals the work of his students, a concern of many conscientious academics. In the novel, as it works out, the student of a professor at fictional Granite Creek University has worked out a room-temperature superconductor and the professor killed her and several others so that he could announce the development as his own, acquire an international reputation, and get rich.

The other story has to do with Ute beliefs and practices about this world and the next. It is close to Louis Owens's works in interest and commitment to Ute mysticism. A *petukupf* is a dwarf that plays back and forth in daylight and darkness doing harm. Around him develops Doss's treatment of Ute culture and beliefs. As Doss describes:

[The dwarf] dressed his small body in bright green; he expected gifts from the Dreamers among the Ute. Only a Dreamer could find the dwarf's home, and only after its location was revealed in a trance. Other passersby would believe that the lair was that of a badger, but the Dreamer would see the faint wisps of smoke rising from the piñon-wood fire on the *pitukupf*'s hearth, which was usually invisible to other Utes, much less to *matukach*, the white people. (119)

Since Doss sited his stories in Ute territory he needed some Ute characters for local color. He chose a female, Clara Tavishuts, as a dispatcher of the Granite Creek police station, and Daisy Perika as a shaman, who was "a necessity because someone had to talk to the 'little man'" (interview). Charlie Moon was created because a Ute policeman had to show up at the end of the tale to rescue Scott Parris, the white police official. Doss liked Charlie so much that he became a major character in the second novel *(The Shaman Laughs)*, the third *(The Shaman's Bones)* and the fourth *(The Shaman's Game)*. With these Ute characters and the others necessarily associated with them, Doss has the personnel for rich stories of Ute life and the imagination to develop them.

Doss recognized that when you tie together stories of man's evil with belief in the spiritual you have a strong story. In *The Shaman Sings* Doss develops that strong story. It is a novel of salvation through a baptism of fire. The shaman sings because she manages to conquer evil. Doss should sing because he has authored a story of Ute culture against a background of white evil that is well told, interesting, and deals fairly with the Native Americans about whom it is written.

The Shaman Laughs is a considerably stronger story, and is especially powerful in developing both the spiritual and the physical aspects of life. Doss juxtaposes the two, sometimes abruptly, and the reader must take a moment for the transition from real world to dream world to take effect. It does, however, more easily for the mystic than for others. In his development Doss is more suggestive than revealing. His characters develop from the outside in rather than from the inside out. In him reality and mystical truly merge. And his two worlds are close and at times blend into one.

Doss's characters are strong, especially the Utes, as we would expect. Scott Parris, the Chief of Police in the university town of Granite Creek, is endowed with professionalism and real common sense. Charlie Moon, the Indian policeman, here plays a major role and obviously will continue to grow in subsequent novels. Shaman Aunt Daisy Perika, with whom Doss has fallen in love as a character, is a budding flower of ancient but indeterminate age who shows much potential growth. Other characters are not as realistically developed. Anne, an eager newspaper reporter, comes on too strongly. Described as beautiful and developed as a paparazzi who is determined to succeed, her behavior is either unnatural or unbelievable.

The Shaman Laughs, as the title suggests, is a book about laughter, and in an entirely different mode from its predecessor. Some of the laughter is devilish, some sardonic, some conventional. This second book is more complicated and more accomplished than the one before it. When dwarfs and shamans laugh, it is a grotesque world for us all, a mixture of Ute mythology and American reality that requires a foot in each world. The story begins in a reality that raises numerous questions.

On the plains a buffalo is killed, its testicles and ears cut off. Later a prize bull suffers the same mutilation. The Devil is appearing in the valley dressed in feathers, with one red eye. Shaman Daisy Perika and the other Utes know that this frightening figure forecasts death, presumably the death of the Utes. Arlo is a bad Ute who scams fellow Native Americans whenever possible, and won't pay the insurance that had been taken out on the prize bull. He is playing around with other women. His wife and her father think that Arlo has infected her with AIDS, so they kill and mutilate him. Ironically it is discovered that she does not have AIDS, so Arlo was killed for the wrong offense, though he probably deserved to die.

This *Shaman Laughs* is an unusually complicated novel. Like other authors of Native American fiction, Jean Hager for example, Doss injects a world of Ute mythology mixed in with Catholicism and Protestantism, religions and cultures. In this convoluted work, Doss creates a kaleidoscope of many changing colors and actions, looking inward. He leans heavily on atmosphere and legends.

Daisy Perika is perhaps the best instrument for delineating Doss's use of Ute mythology. Unable to sleep one night she hears approaching thunder and recognizes it as the beating of "the great buffalo-hide drum of an-in-the-Sky." Gradually she recognizes that she is being taken from the earth to the Lower-World and she assists in the flight by whispering the song her uncle had taught her:

> Carry me over the clouds
> Carry me over the great snow mountains
> I will hear the sound of your wings
> Carry me there on your shoulders

> Carry me down to Lower-World
> I will hear the sound of your songs. . . . (120)

Without any fear she feels her body plummeting from the sky into Lower-World:

> Without any sensation of landing, she was in a deep forest of vines and ferns and trees that were old beyond reckoning. She found herself in the eternal twilight of Lower-World; a trio of pockmarked orange moons cast strange, flickering patterns over the fluttering leaves and twisted vines. At first, the shaman felt rather than saw the presence above her. A shadowy form moved slowly above the mossy forest floor, floating like a kite under the branches of the trees. Fascinated, she watched the shadow transform its amorphous darkness into another shape, the form of an animal with wings. It was now a great bird, like an owl, with pitiless yellow eyes and curved yellow talons that ached for prey. The feathered creature dropped behind a mass of ferns, as if to make a kill. Daisy heard a scream. The awful shriek, which gradually fell to a low, pleading moan, left her trembling with horror. Was she the next victim? When the enormous bird arose with a ponderous flapping of wings, its talons were crimson-dripping with blood! Daisy shuddered as the great feathered creature circled under the limbs of the ancient trees. While he watched, the bird was gradually transformed. . . . It was one again a flickering shadow, without discernible form, darting to and fro like a great moth among the mossy trunks of the trees. (121)

No matter how mysterious and spooky such passages are, Doss's Ute world also looks out and is realistic. The author has much fun with it. Although at home in this mystic creation, he dances joyously in the pragmatic world, moving from the Ute mystical atmosphere to the materialistic dominant world around him.

One element in the novel that is of paramount importance is comedy, comic people, situations, and actions. One constituent of the comedy is the FBI as an institution and James E. Hoover, the local representative as an individual. Hoover, a city boy new in the neighborhood, is the butt of locals' humor. When the prize bull is killed, for example, the FBI man gets in on the case thinking the victim is a human being, mislead he thinks by the statements of the local law officers which he interrupts and misinterprets.

When it disclosed that "Big Ouray," the victim, is a valuable prized bull, Hoover, affronted and embarrassed, explodes. "Hey, it's what I should have expected out here among the mentally deprived. Country yokel plays a prank on the city boy," he blusters. Breathing in short gasps he reaches his highest insult, calling Charlie Moon, the Indian law officer, an "overgrown, inbred . . . shit-for-brains asshole!" (89). Doss demonstrates that the Ute reservation is a long way from Washington, D.C., or even Nashville, Tennessee, when Charlie's friend Parris wants to get back to the local restaurant where he can buy "a twelve-ounce R.C. Cola and a Moon Pie." Detective Moon's confrontation with these staples of American culture is one of ignorance. "Somebody name a pie after me?" he asks (144). He also does not know that the jukebox song "Maple on the Hill" is a classic country song. "Not in Ute country, it ain't," says his companion (144).

In these Native American crime novels it is imperative that the Indians come out ahead of the whites, especially the FBI and the Washington bureaucracy. In this work, since the leitmotif throughout has been mutilation of beast and man in cut-off testicles, the story can powerfully end with perhaps the ultimate joke on the FBI and its self-generated image of machismo. Hoover, in the presence of his superior, is served at the restaurant the special of the day, the only one left, which is called *sarachi cuquiana,* Ute words that cannot be translated "too good" into English. When Hoover learns that what he has pronounced "a passable dinner" is really testicles, he rushes to the toilet to vomit. This may seem too violent a reaction on Doss's part since bulls' testicles are eaten openly throughout the mountain states as "mountain oysters," with only a modicum of condescending derision elsewhere. But Hoover may be especially sensitive.

Although the situation is electric with potential disaster it ends to the satisfaction of all. Sam Parker, Hoover's superior, assures him, "Don't worry, James. The Bureau takes care of its own" (323), whatever that threat means. And the shaman, along with the rest of the Utes, "laughed until streams of joy blinded her" (324). The book is a triumph in every way: excellent story, ripping humor and self-respect for the Native Americans.

The Shaman's Bones is more intensively Indian than either of the earlier books. From the beginning it sets the stage both deep and wide for development of Ute culture, Shoshone culture, and dominant culture all radiating around and from a honky-tonk called the Pynk Garter Saloon. The saloon is the locus for a drug traffic that results in murder and a long investigation by Parris, Moon, and the FBI man Hoover.

But far more than that simple theme, the novel is in fact a garbled and danger-ridden lullaby for a Ute kid named Sarah who loses her parents and must be cared for by the shaman Aunt Daisy Perika, aided and abetted by Parris and Charlie Moon.

Again like Doss's other novels, this one is filled with magic, mysticism, and experiences beyond our cognition, as this paragraph will indicate, as the shaman summons fire from the heavens:

> Initially the old Ute was bathed in a brilliant flame of blue-white light that encompassed him like a halo. He fairly shimmered in this light, and seemed almost transparent, more like a spirit than a mortal. Then it was as if a long finger reached down to delicately touch the upraised wand in the *bugahant*'s hand. Even when the blue fire from heaven consumed him, Blue Cup did not flinch. Neither did he cry out. The Ute shaman stood like the resolute warrior that he was, his mulberry staff raised in defiance . . . or salute? And then the wooden rod burst into flame. The peal of thunder rumbled like ten thousand cannon; the blast of hot wind blew the Shoshone flat on his back.
>
> And it was over. (230)

The ending of the novel is doubly effective and must consist of the tying together of the two main plots developed in parallel throughout the work. The first is the fate of Sarah, the child whose father and mother have been murdered and she left as a ward of the tribe. But in the tradition of the Indians she has also become the battleground of a tug of war between everyday and magical forces. Before she realizes that her parents are dead, while waiting for their return, forces of the other world abduct her.

In a passage typical of Doss's easy eliding from one world to the other, he tells of her abduction. Daisy Perika, outside the house trailer in which Sarah is waiting for the return of her parents, sees a man leading a horse appear with Sarah on its back. Daisy thinks that for certain the man is Sarah's father, Provo Frank, taking his daughter away. Suspicious, however, Daisy looks into the window of the trailer and sees that Sarah has left her kitten behind, something that she finds incredible. Then Doss slips from everyday reality into magic: "The old woman hurried after the man and the horse and the child, but within a few heartbeats there was no sign of them. Only the lingering mists of morning. And these, like smoke from a great pipe, were slowly being inhaled by the mouth of the canyon. So that was where he was taking his daughter—into the depths of *Canon del Espiritu*" (200).

Daisy follows the specter into the canyon that has magically become Middle-World, meets the custodian of the place, a Navajo Guardian, and with a trick worthy of Coyote Trickster, forces the Guardian to take her to Sarah. She does this by getting him to play the oldest universal con trick in the world, known among the Navajos as the shoe game. To play it, you take off your shoes and have a black stone placed in one. The game is to guess the shoe the rock is in. Daisy outsmarted the "chucklehead" by placing the stone in her pocket and then giving him one guess as to which shoe it was in.

To get to the Middle-World, Daisy falls into a trance. When she awakes, Sarah is beside her, but with poignancy reminiscent of a Shakespearean female heroine like Desdemona or Ophelia, she has lost her ability to speak and communicate with the natural world. Unable to talk, Sarah is "picking dandelions and blowing the white fluff into the breeze" (209).

Doss himself in these books is a man who lives with one foot in each world. Sarah must be brought back to the reality of everyday existence. Doss does it pragmatically, even humorously, by having her touched with the magic of childhood and American everyday culture. The people around Sarah have prescribed all kinds of cures and magic potions to get her to speak again. But she refuses or is unable. It seems that Sarah is going to remain mute until her father returns. He had promised her a pony for her birthday, and she waited for both him and it.

Meanwhile all kinds of worldly help was tried on Sarah. The kindly *Matukach* (white) psychologist had

> talked, and cajoled and talked some more. . . . Sarah had obligingly put little round pegs into little round holes. And little square pegs into little square holes. She had, by pointing, correctly identified the pictures of dogs and cats and elephants. The child had been patient when the social worker took her to the clinic, where her throat had been examined, her ears probed with a pencil beam of light, her little knees gently tapped with a small hammer. (271)

A Ute medicine woman

> tried several Navajo tobaccos. First she used *hozhooji natoh*, the 'beauty way' smoke. Then *atsa azee*, which is eagle smoke. And *dzil natoh*, the smoke that comes from the mountains. She would light these tobaccos in her second husband's old brier pipe, suck in a lungful, and blow the smoke in the face of the child. . . . The smoke did not bother Sarah, but the child uttered not one word. (272)

Sarah, however, was cured by weakness of human flesh and by appetite for one of the most magical aspects of American culture, ice cream.

A French Canadian visitor who has brought some ice cream and sweets to the adults allows Sarah to touch the cold carton: "Sarah reached out to feel the coldness of the ice cream cartons. The child looked up at the visitor, and spoke: 'I like ice cream. Is it chocolate?'" (273).

Thus ends the first major theme in the book, care and nurture of children through the vicissitudes of life. Sarah has grown up in this magic moment and starts revealing her mature curiosity, asking Aunt Daisy where ice cream, cookies, and babies come from. Assured that at some time in the future they will talk about these adult concerns, Sarah is temporarily satisfied.

But there is a more profound major theme that must also be finished, with Charlie Moon and the mythology of the Utes. Given a sacred object to bury in some desolate place, Moon wonders if it should not be given instead to the Council. But following directions Moon steps into the magic land to which he was directed by old man Walks Sleeping. He buries the whistle, and then fearing he has misplaced it, Moon waits for a sign that he has done right. Although during the day he is "an entirely rational man," at night Moon reaches back into Ute mythology and mysticism. Moon waits for heavenly approval. Stars in the sky shoot down through the atmosphere and he gets the confirmation he desires, "a gentle, persistent whisper: *Listen . . . listen to the voices of those who sing the song eternal*" (275).

Doss's next book, *The Shaman's Game,* in its mysticism picks up where its predecessor left off. In this book Doss is far and away the most mystical writer working in Native American crime fiction today, and, aside from professional mystics, probably in all American literature. Doss begins in and writes in Native American mythology, only occasionally stepping out into the regular world. Most writers using Native American mythology and mysticism write in everyday culture and move into that of the mystical Indian world only to make points. Doss, especially in this book, on the other hand, is in the Native American spiritual world, coming out only occasionally to touch base with what we commonly call reality.

In this book, Delly Sands, a cute small woman, has returned to Granite City a sparkling dynamo who is changing the whole dynamics of the town. She is especially working magic on Charlie Moon, six-foot-six-inch policeman who can be hardnosed about everything but women. He already has an ordinary woman who is trying to bed him and who becomes very jealous over the effect Delly Sands is having on Charlie. To no one's knowledge but her own, Delly is in the advanced stages of bone cancer and is making a last fling at life before dying. To try to prolong her own life she practices Ute magic on two men and one old woman, all of whom die. Delly is contrite and plans to publish a confession in a newspaper but dies before she can. The female casualty of Delly's work is Old Popeye Woman, a Ute magician who is marked for her work by the fact that her left eye pops out and seems to look in all directions at the same time despite the fact that she is blind.

After a very emotional and touching ending of Delly's life and her burial, Charlie Moon, having been nearly convinced that all these deaths were supernatural, goes out to the burial place of Old Popeye Woman and sees the naked footprints of a woman leaving the grave but not coming back. As he stands beside the closed tomb, however, wondering if indeed Old Popeye Woman though dead is abroad doing mystical things, he hears approaching footsteps of a person like Old Popeye Woman, who was blind and club footed. The approaching footsteps are slow, hesitant, and clearly have one foot dragging behind. Maintaining his mysticism to the very last, Doss averts his eyes and has Charlie Moon walk away not wanting or not daring to discover the truth of whether the dead are abroad in life.

That would have been a strong, though perhaps unnecessarily tantalizing, ending. But it is not enough for Doss. He ends the book, instead, away from Charlie Moon, leaving him wondering if he made the right choice in walking away from a solution, to turn to religion, back to Catholicism and the Bible. The woman Delly, it seems, was calling herself a diminutive of a much more famous and powerful name from the Bible. Doss reaches his ending by sliding off Shakespeare's famous question: "What's in a name?" and ends: "This lovely young Ute woman who had attempted—perhaps even succeeded—in stealing strength from the strongest of men.

"Her name was . . . Delilah."

That ending is perhaps one small step for a novelist and one giant leap for mythology, one small biblical allusion for this work and one long leap into biblical teachings. But the leap for the reader might be a little stretching. The ending seems far-fetched.

Nevertheless, it and the conclusions to the books before it have taken us through the trails of Ute mythology in search of eternal truth and left us halfway between two worlds more positive than the British poet Matthew Arnold's vision of two worlds, one dead and the other helpless to be born.

Doss's next book, *The Night Visitor*, is less successful than his earlier works. He allows his whimsy to get out of control, and the book becomes more an exaggerated caricature than a deep and interesting mystery. Doss's characters degenerate. Charlie Moon, the leading protagonist in the earlier books, has become fleshy, generally silly, and an object of derision among his colleagues. Daisy Perika, who in the earlier novels has been a major source of power and the shaman who is the connecting link between the Indian mystical world and that of everyday reality, here is presented as near senile, crabby, and generally unappealing.

The trouble begins with Doss's choice of subject and its development. He chooses as his theme and major avenue of development the folklore about the Arkansas Traveler, who since the early nineteenth century in song and story has been a sharp dealer and con man who has influenced American tradition and development. Out to con himself into an easy life through lies and deceptions, Horace Flye, Doss's version of the Traveler, winds up on the property of Nathan McFain, the splendid remains of a gargantuan beast at least thirty thousand years old have been discovered. McFain is also a con artist who wants to establish a museum over the site of the uncovered remains. This desire leads Doss into what develops as the second weakness in this book. Apparently he has a personal vendetta, or a strong sense of humor, against established archaeologists and paleontologists, and the established professionals who are brought in to verify these remains are turned into objects of scorn and derision. One is an old man who cannot make up his mind about anything; the remains might be thirty thousand years old, but then again they might not; the scientists will say whatever he is expected to say. Another scientist called in to verify the age is an arrogant Princeton-graduate medical doctor who is interested only in brushing up his personal glory. One character is, surprisingly since Doss, as a Los Alamos National Lab employee, is a member of the University of California community, a know-little Berkeley paleontologist.

Doss further strains credulity by having a corrupt Arab working from his native land through a purchasing agent, who will invest any amount of money in artifacts that he smuggles in, but who is knife-edge sharp in having his purchasing agents murdered when they buy him bogus artifacts, as the agent in this book does. Further, Doss leers too much at sex. One of the established female archaeologists offers herself incredibly to the Arkansas Traveler in all his unpleasant character traits and physical unattractiveness. Doss handles his children ineptly. In this book he has two, Sarah with whom he has worked before to great effect, and a new one, incredibly named Butter Flye, the six-year-old daughter of the Arkansas fraud, who spends most of her time associating with her cat Zig-Zag (whose name nobody can quite get right) and her Gila monster, which though thoroughly ugly to everybody, was "not to its mama."

Doss's paleoanthropological motivation is to further demonstrate that the so-called Clovis limitation of the dinosaur age to ten thousand years ago has been demonstrably broken and proved far too recent for new finds and proper aging. This motif would certainly be interesting and worthwhile had it not been developed in caricature and with the silly characters whose attitudes and professionalism are of concern to few readers. Finally, the ending of the book, with Charlie Moon and his fellow policeman Scott Parris talking about women and food, is too undignified to be worthy of characters with their history and significance.

Doss's next book, *Grandmother Spider,* continues in this new direction, one that some readers think is perhaps not the author's strongest vein, but apparently one that he enjoys working in. It reveals an author who has found self-amusement in what seems to be his ideal in novel construction—fantasyland strengthened by a keen sense of irony and humor. This fantasyland opens Doss to new means of development. He journeys into Alice's wonderland filled with Shakespearean witches. The journey is framed in two kinds of fantasy and sparkled throughout with tall tales, jokes, and incredible happenings. There is no question here whether Doss is concerned with paying back the Indians for past injustices. He is too busy with what his serious purpose—if he has one—is, except to indulge in a lot of spider symbols, play, and fun.

The plot begins in a display of contrasts. It is the perfect physical world: "to the East, an iridescent rainbow arches shimmerlingly over misted mountains. In the West, the crimson sun descends through opalescent clouds." Into this Eden "a triad of shadowy fingers reach out . . . slipping stealthily along the piñon-studded ridge toward the isolate home. As if to grasp and crush the Ute elder's modest dwelling" (1).

Inside the home are two of our well-known characters. Sarah Frank and her hard-nosed shaman grandmother, Daisy Perika, who is cooking green chile for herself and Sarah. Sarah, hot and sweaty, makes the mistake of smashing a spider—against all Ute wisdom—and unleashes the vengeance of the Spider People, who according to Ute legend came the night following such a killing to kill a member of the family that destroyed the spider.

The apparent revenging spider makes its appearance from a nearby lake—a giant creature with eight legs and interrupted flashes of bright orange light. The giant creature steals one man and deposits him in the branches of a distant tree. Subsequently, murders follow along with rumors of sightings of the creature throughout the neighborhood. The FBI and CIA are called in to assist the local police in trying to solve the mystery. Charlie Moon and his fellow officer Scott Parris investigate the sightings and murders. It turns out that the giant spider was in reality a balloon in the shape of an octopus that was in the neighborhood to be used as an advertising scheme by the Ozzie Corporation whose restaurant chain, specializing in seafood, used Ozzie Octopus as their advertising logo. The story ends with the murders and mystery explained and with Charlie rewarded by one of the terrible old ladies in the plot with a large idyllic ranch. Charlie takes his friend Scott Parris with him for an extended vacation on his new ranch. He plans to retire there and do nothing but fish and loaf for the rest of his life. But he is tracked down by the luscious female Camilla, who promises him all kinds of pleasures—but with of course accompanying troubles. With Charlie and Scott new adventures await the coming of a new day.

These new adventures come with Doss's latest novel, *White Shell Woman,* which is more than usually effective in developing new materials in new ways. At the end of the preceding novel Charlie Moon has grown tired of being a Native American policeman, has inherited a large ranch with a fortune to support it, and has decided to take his girlfriend(s) and others who might show up and retire to paradise to lounge in the sun and to fish. He is dragged back into detective work but the ranch provides new territory, new personnel, and new tensions in which Doss can work out a very entertaining crime novel. This is, in fact, by far Doss's most comical and amusing. It a sustained comic novel held together on the bones of crime.

White Shell Woman is based on and developed on a myth collected from the Navajo about White Shell Woman who is in effect the four directions of the compass and four ages of mankind: when she walks toward the North she returns a young girl, to the South she returns a young woman, to the West a maid, and to the East a middle-aged woman. She is called White Bead Woman. As White Shell Woman in this novel she is heavenly rain that falls on the desert of the Navajos. She is timeless womankind, and ever-returning beauty. Sandoval, Hastin Tlo'tsi hee (Old Man Buffalo Grass), who told the myth to a white woman says that although he looks ugly inside he is beautiful. It is the theme of timelessness and beauty-under-ugliness that informs and energizes this book. Doss begins each chapter with a quote from the myth and develops that chapter in one way or another to one degree or another along the line of that segment of the myth.

As is becoming increasingly common today in Indian crime fiction the story develops along the line of archaeology, paleontology, paleoastronomy, theft of Indian artifacts, and the efforts of Indians to save their heritage, which is controlled by NAGPRA (Native American Graves Protection and Repatriation Act). Throughout the story, a subtheme is White Shell Woman who is supplicated for rain that will come in the form of big tears forming in the eyes of the residents.

An anthropologist and several graduate students from Rocky Mountain University Department of Anthropology and Archaeology are at the Chimney Rock Ruins and nearby associated Indian ruins with a tour of Native Americans. One little Indian girl wanders off to a cliff and nearly falls but is rescued by Charlie Moon. "It was a perfect time for Native American Day at Chimney Rock" (31) and there are several kinds of archaeologists working the *Canon del Esperitu.* There is a straightback honest professor of archaeology who is something of a stuffed shirt, the ambitious Amanda Silk, and several female students. Amanda, a faculty member, has discovered some relics in the Indian ruins that she wants to steal so she can write an article and make a name for herself. She goes to the ruins at night by herself and starts digging. But another graduate student, the April Tavishutz we have known in earlier novels, discovers her. Silk must kill Tavishutz and bury her in the ruins. The murder is laid on the shoulders of Tavishutz's stepfather, Alvah Yazzi, who has to be hidden by Moon's aunt, Daisy Perika, at Charlie's huge ranch.

As the pressure on the perpetrator of the first murder increases, she is forced to kill another graduate student who had half-witnessed the earlier murder. The FBI and CIA are called in because the federal government controls the Indian reservation. But the local sheriff, Scott Parris, whom we know from earlier books, and Moon the special investigator, manage to work their way in. Although the circumstances area similar to other Native American crime stories, this one is far different and in many ways superior.

Aunt Daisy Perika, though still wrapped up in her never-ending affair with *Piraka,* the dwarf from the Underworld, is given a much deeper role, and in fact helps solve the mystery. Parris, Moon's long-time friend and helpmate, is given a reduced role, serving mainly as an earpiece for Moon's confessions and development. The Indians are more thoroughly developed, and Charlie Moon's role is much developed; all the young women are constantly begging him to play with them sexually. He associates with his three ranch hands as ordinary folk more than in the past and actually depends on his foreman for assistance.

While associating with the ordinary folk Moon digs more deeply in the shadows of Ute mythology than before. Doss's entry-door is hallucinations. Aunt Daisy's adventures with the dwarf—and both she and Moon reaching out to other characters—have been surreal. In *White Shell Woman* Doss investigates more deeply the implications of hallucinatory associations with reality.

Moon and Amanda Silk are at the Indian ruins investigating Havistutz's murder. Moon is investigating and Silk, it turns out, is keeping an eye on what Moon discovers. Moon is attacked by some unidentifiable force or monster, "a dark, amorphous shadow between his grave and the starry sky. In the center of this singular darkness, a Cyclops eye appeared . . . flicking in the fire." Moon is more seriously threatened. "The shadowy thing leaned toward him. The fluttering flame grew larger. Then, simultaneously, a guttural garaowl, a snapping of teeth—a gut-ripping shriek" (200). Moon is knocked unconscious and while insensate takes a fantastic journey through Indian immediate history on a train where he meets kindly old Nahum Yaciiti, now dead, who explains that Moon is on a train "headed for a destination" (202) and begins to explain the future.

Moon wakes in a hospital with a concussion and learns that everybody had expected him to die. The attending physician asks Moon how he feels and when Moon replies that he sometimes feels strange and as if he had been shot, like "a big hairy" animal, the physician explains that this is usual "post-concussive disassociation." In other words the monster that attacked him in the Indian ruins was a heavy blow by Amanda Silk that knocked him unconscious. In fact, of course, all the supernatural or Indian mythological happenings had been man- or woman-made.

In future books perhaps Doss will return to the tradition of his earlier novels and with their effectiveness demonstrate that of his two worlds—the real and the mystical—both are present but maybe one is preferable.

Dana Stabenow

The authors John Straley, and his private investigator character Cecil Younger working out of Sitka, and Sue Henry who lives in Anchorage and writes about Alaska State Trooper Alex Jensen and his musher friend Jessie Arnold, use Alaska as background for conventional crime fiction. Henry's first novel involving Jensen and Arnold was *Murder on the Iditarod Trail,* which graphically describes what that grueling contest can contribute to crime.

John Straley's five novels to date feature an alcoholic, cynical ex-schoolteacher who just manages to cling to life with jobs that slide his way through little effort on his part. Straley himself works as a private detective, sometimes with time on his hands, so he writes of Younger, his private eye, who like private eyes everywhere, is bored, poor, and cynical. Straley's first novel, *The Woman Who Married a Bear,* sets the stage for the author's style of development. A Tlingit woman told Straley the legend about such a woman. It and a similar one about a man who married a bear may constitute his strongest contribution to crime fiction so far.

The story about a man marrying a bear is common in Indian legend and develops around belief in the supernatural life-creating power of the bear, perhaps because of its anthropomorphic appearance and behavior, at times seeming to change into human form and act like a human being.

A Hopi legend about a gambling boy who married a bear will serve to illustrate the type. A young man obsessed with gambling loses his parents' valuable dancing costumes in the game and as a consequence is forced out of their house. Compelled to wander in the forest with no destination, he is approached by a female bear that takes him to her kiva. There she transforms herself into a beautiful girl in the midst of other bears who change into human form. He sleeps with the girl and a year passes magically. He decides it is time for him to go back and see his family. The bears get the young man to promise to supply them with prayer feathers and *tagvahos* because they are short of these necessities. But back with his family the man resumes his gambling and forgets his promise. He plants corn, apparently unconsciously for his bear wife and two children, since they start gathering it. The man's friends pursue the marauding beasts and the bear wife kills her husband. But he is not really dead. He returns to life and is taught by his bear wife to be a medicine man. He brings curative magic to his real people, then goes to live with his bear family. And that is how medicinal power was brought to the Hopis (Malotki, *Hopi Animal Tales* 357).

In Alaska crime fiction today one of the stronger voices is that of Dana Stabenow. As we have seen previously, she was raised in a half-Aleut half-Filipino family in Seldovia, Alaska. From childhood on she wanted to write, and though she tried her hand at several jobs she always gazed lovingly at the computer and determined to get back to it as soon as possible. Stabenow's fiction is strong on action but has the activity carried on the shoulders of two or three of the more powerful characters in crime fiction.

She began her series, *A Cold Day for Murder,* with real flair. A national park ranger disappears when sent into the wilderness to investigate a group of rabid Alaska-firsters who resent all efforts of outsiders to integrate their state in the national conditions of the rest of the United States. A man who went to learn the truth of the ranger's disappearance was apparently also killed. In the midst of Arctic weather hazards, Kate, who is hard as nails though humanly warm, fights against her family and other opposing forces to go in and locate the guilty. Kate's grandmother, Emaa, appears as a fully developed well-drawn character who is torn between protecting her family and being an accessory after murder and helping Kate identify the killer. The drama of investigation and discovery is placed in and against the power and charm of Alaska.

In *A Cold Day for Murder,* Stabenow develops her characters and plot with skill and definiteness. Kate is fully described. She is "twenty-nine or thirty. . . . Five feet tall, no more, maybe a hundred and ten pounds. She had the burnished bronze skin and high, flat cheekbones of her race, with curiously light brown eyes tilted up at her temples, all of it framed by a shining fall of utterly straight hair. . . . She moved like a cat, all controlled muscle and natural grace, wary but assured" (9-10).

Her voice, we are immediately informed, "was odd, too loud for a whisper, not low enough for a growl, and painfully rough, like a dull saw ripping through old cement" (9). The cause of this unpleasant though distinctive trait is soon revealed, as one man saw it: "For a moment her collar had fallen away and he had seen the scar, twisted and ugly and still angry in color. It crossed her throat almost from ear to ear. That explains the voice, he thought, shaken. Why hadn't she gone to a plastic surgeon and had that fixed, or at least had the scar tissue trimmed and reduced in size?" (10).

The adventures of this diminutive dynamo when confronting the bad men and women and ugly weather of Alaska are entirely successful. The book shows great promise for a new series, with a fascinating background and locale and a cast of strong, appealing characters.

Dead in the Water, Stabenow's second novel in the series, demonstrates power of another kind, that of nature nearly overwhelming the characters. It is almost as though the author wrote the novel with a gazetteer and weather chart open before her. Stabenow spends a whole page, for example, describing the Bering Sea and the two islands, and the villages of Unalaska and Amaknak, which rise through the fog above them. But, as Stabenow says, "Kate always felt better when she knew exactly where she was" (26), and the author obviously feels that the reader too must know the setting for the adventure.

She describes Dutch Harbor in some detail, "a sheltered piece of Iliuluk Bay, nuzzled up against Amaknak Island behind a mile-long spit of sand and gravel and grass" (25). She also recounts for us how during World War II the Japanese invaded Attu and Kiska, and how the U.S. government "bundled every last Aleut from the Rat Islands north and settled them in villages in south-central Alaska. After the war, almost none of them were resettled in their original villages, and the soldiers trashed what little housing was left standing. They'd burned or bull-dozed most of it anyway, either to keep the Japs from using it or to make way for their own construction" (67).

In Kate's Dutch Harbor, there was one woman for every twelve men, most of them Russians who could not speak any English. There is much sex going on all the time. She is graphic in describing one of the honky-tonks, The Shipwreck Bar, which had been "a Dutch watering hole from time immemorial":

> A cargo ship for Alaska Steam, she'd been conscripted for General Samuel Buckner to supply troops rushed to the Aleutians following Pearl Harbor. A gale drove her ashore during her first year of service. The Seabees restored her to an upright position, filled her hold with concrete for ballast, reconditioned her generator and used her for a barracks during the war. Abandoned for two decades, when the crab fishing picked up in the sixties a local businessman acquired her as government surplus and remodeled her into a restaurant, hotel and bar.

Strange behavior was enacted within her restored hull, as Kate discov-ered. "Double doors were cut into the side of her hull. Kate entered first, only to dodge back out of the way of a fisherman dancing with a bar stool, eyes closed and cheek to seat" (31–32).

Although perhaps overly detailed in geography, cultural artifacts, and details of crabbing, *Dead in the Water* is very much alive in further-ing the general course of Stabenow's effective treatment of the cultural crime involving Kate and her associates. And it very much demonstrates how the diminutive Kate can hold her own against any man, whether working a crabbing boat in a hard Alaskan sea winters' blow or contest-ing the right of drunks in a bar. To the doubtful seeing is believing.

In *A Fatal Thaw*, Stabenow's next work, the author manages to parallel nine ghastly murders with a quiet bucolic Alaska setting. Both performances are impressive.

One bright sun-drenched day, on the first day of spring in Alaska, a man deliberately takes his soft-nosed bullets and coldly murders eight of his neighbors. But when the bodies are counted there are nine corpses present. After the killer of the eight has been determined it is Kate's task to find out who killed the ninth. Kate lives in an Alaska rich in flora and fauna, life and culture. Stabenow is especially ample in her description of a potlatch, thrown by her aunt Emaa, not for a marriage or any other customary reason and not exclusively for members of her clan, but for everybody in honor of the eight white people killed by the serial gunman.

Stabenow describes at great length one of the dances, performed while the women might be dressed in all kinds of nonethnic paraphernalia. Kate participates:

> The dance began to slow and ease in volume, and Kate's movements slowed and eased with them. The song ended on a long fade. Kate's dance with a last, graceful flight of eagle feather through the air. The music stopped as she came to a halt before Chief William. She reached for his gnarled, twisted old hand and, bending forward from the waist, held it for a moment to her forehead. She returned the finger mask to the Koniag dancer and held both hands out, palms up and eagle feather lying across them. (144)

The scene is spiritual and sufficiently evocative to cause a nonbeliever viewing the dance and the "spirit it invoked," to remark, "That was the most beautiful thing I've ever seen in my life" (144).

But in the midst of this beauty celebrating life, Stabenow reminds us that there is violent death. As it turns out the death of the ninth person develops a motif as old in folklore as time and sisters. Lisa Getty is blonde and beautiful and the neighborhood sex machine. Her sister, Lotte, is huge and ugly. "Next to Lotte Getty Sasquatch would have felt dainty" (57). In addition to nurturing her hatred of her sister because she was popular and enjoying all the sensual pleasures she would like to experience, Lotte also is growing and selling marijuana. A misfit in her community, she is still basically Alaskan. When she is confronted with the knowledge that Kate realizes she is the murderer, Lotte goes up the mountainside and jumps off. Like all Alaskans she can't stand the thought of being jailed.

Stabenow's ending is melodramatic, perhaps better suited to myth and folktale than reality. But it successfully reminds us that life in

Alaska is indeed different from that in the lower forty-eight states, and as such it is to be respected.

In *A Cold-Blooded Business,* her next novel, Stabenow returns to frontier Alaska with all its physical and meteorological difficulties to tell a story with a definite moral. Somebody is selling cocaine to the crew-people and managerial staff on an oil company's rig north of the Arctic Circle. Kate is hired to infiltrate and discover the dealer. What she discovers is more than cocaine up for sale.

It's an in-and-out business. The same people who are importing the cocaine are exporting all kinds of priceless artifacts derived from grave and site robbing and any other kind of seizure possible. Kate, after much suffering and buffeting around by both people and weather, discovers that the head of the smuggling pipeline is Toni Hartzler, the public relations woman, who is beautiful, large, and cold as ice.

In Alaskan situations, particularly in snowstorms, Stabenow is unexcelled in describing a fight to the death. This time it is between Shugak, on the side of freedom and life, and Toni Hartzler, graverobber, desecrator of Alaska culture and importer of cocaine, on the other.

The battle began when Kate "took three giant steps and came down on her with all talons extended." Back and forth they tumble, one gaining superiority for a minute then losing it as the other opponent grasps a new hold. Finally, after much brutality and profanity, Kate overcomes her opponent and makes her cry wolf, or whatever Alaskans cry when defeated. Then Kate, finally prevented from killing Toni, subjects her to a cruel punishment never before recorded in literature. She makes Toni stick her tongue to a metal pipe: "It flattened out against the pipe and in the freezing temperature instantly froze to the metal," and Toni was held more securely than if she had been bound hand and foot (218).

This crime novel is far more than mere fiction on the subject. Throughout it is a protest against environmental degradation and misuse. It also is a general comment on human actions. And the picture the author draws should make all of us more cautious in our behavior. Of society in general she has only a modified respect. "The reverence one is likely to have for their ancestors decreases in direct proportion to how hungry their children are at the time," one of the graverobbers suggests (160). It is a chilling worldview Stabenow has but she recognizes that the bitter pill goes down a little more easily with a bit of humor as sugar. And the pill is worth taking. The only thing at stake is human culture and a future.

The lack of sunshine evidenced in Stabelow's view of life in *A Cold-Blooded Business* persists in her next book, *Play with Fire*. This novel is about the pollution of Eden—Alaska—by fanatics who misread the Bible and fight for the triumph of their extreme point of view. One fanatical religious sect headed by a crazed patriarch has taken over a community, significantly close to the site of a proposed community college, which should provide some enlightenment, and is determined to keep out of their public schools—and by extension all the schools of Alaska—all modern "atheistical" matters, such as evolution. Because the instructor in the public school teaches evolution, dinosaurs, and that kind of thing, he is murdered and ritualistically mutilated. Kate, against her will, must ferret out the murderer. The assignment—and the action driving it—is unpleasant.

The book is about all kinds of growth, especially in Alaska. It is about the state as the rich ground for growing mushrooms, and other crops, as agricultural advancement. Stabenow prefaces each chapter with a quote from a classical author such as Pliny. But as we all know mushrooms grow in shade, and Stabenow parallels the development of one benefit of shade growth with that of an evil product, the dark side of religious practice and the potential resulting evil.

Play with Fire is also about development in education. Stabenow is more literary in this book than in any other. She demonstrates her interest by quotations and references to an extensive knowledge of the Bible and numerous English and American poets. Most important in the growth line, Kate is taken back to the University of Alaska, Fairbanks, and talks extensively with her English professor who taught her to love literature. We see a literary side to Kate that we have not seen before.

One other side of Kate's development is demonstrated in the diminished role that Jack Morgan, head of Special Investigation of the Anchorage Police Department and Kate's sometime lover, plays in the book. He is not needed for the plot and is brought in only for a short period to serve as Kate's understudy and satisfier of her lust. So Kate has matured. Most of her fans, however, probably hope that Jack is not being phased out of the series.

One element common to all the novels to the time of this work is the overwhelming presence of Grandmother Ekaterina, Emaa, as Kate calls her. She symbolizes Kate's tie with the past. Emaa is tradition, a pillar of strength to Kate when her present and future become clouded and insecure, though the tie with what Emaa represents is under constant strain and painful readjustment. Emaa is like an Aleut myth. She is known by all, is a constant point of reference by everyone. Stabenow is more than usually descriptive of Ekaterina in this book:

> A massive figure, square-shouldered and big-bellied, clad in a dark blue house dress Kate would have sworn she'd seen her wearing when Kate was in kindergarten, stood planted in front of her as if she'd grown there. . . . [With] calm brown eyes, her brown face seamed with wrinkles, her black hair pulled back into a neat bun at the nape of her neck. (31–32)

Despite the splendid new aspects of Kate's life presented here, however, *Play with Fire* is less effective than Stabenow's earlier books. This is a novel burning with acid hate, and Stabenow fights it with undiluted venom. She is more concerned with combating hate than with depicting life artfully. Kate never smiles at her adversaries. Stabenow is never relieved from her detestation of the religious fanatic.

Yet the book is not one of insurmountable clouds of despair. After the mystery of murder and mutilation has been solved, Kate, like the good person she is, agrees with the Scriptures that all evil will pass away. Maybe religious zealots and naive tourists can be excluded from Alaska, or at least kept under control. Alaska will continue to be the pristine wilderness that she calls home, and for which she hungers. As the sun "was teasing the horizon, just brushing the tops of the trees with pale fingers," Shugak is overwhelmed with the homing instinct. "She knew a sudden, intense longing for her own roof, her own trees, her own creek, her own mountains, her own sky" (282). She is ready to continue her growth in her garden. We are delighted to see that garden bloom.

In *Blood Will Tell*, her next work, Stabenow is in complete control of all aspects of her subject and therefore writes a Native Alaskan triumph. A group of Anchorage business moguls is trying to get a large section of Alaskan wilderness belonging to the Aleut declared a National Wilderness so that they can clear-cut the forests. Subtly they infiltrate the Aleut's Native American Association, kill off two members of a board of five and expect to get the Aleut's approval of the proposal and then the government's. Because her uncle is killed, Kate gets interested in the process and chases down the whites guilty of the attempted murderous coup. In fighting against the powerful white interests and for the Aleut's rights, Kate discovers how strongly native she is, and the reader witnesses another right of these Native Americans being threatened by the dominant society but being saved from their greed. Rounds of applause go from reader to the victors.

This book is different from Stabenow's others in two ways. First, the author is so comfortably in control of Kate and the whole situation that she has a lot of fun. The novel is a comic triumph. Kate is given a side to her character that in the past we have seen only glancingly. Because Kate and Jack are going out to spend an evening in high society, Jack thinks Kate must have a new appropriate wardrobe and be dolled up. They go to an Anchorage store for the dolling. Kate profanely protests every idea, suggestion, and move made by her advisors. She thinks clothes are merely first steps to women unzipping their flys. When the saleswoman asks Kate if she has had her "palette done" Kate explodes: *"My what?"*

"'Your palette,' Alana said, irritatingly patient. 'Your colors. Are you winter, summer, spring or fall? Khaki is a good color for you, yes, I can see it setting off your skin and hair, but I think a warm peach, or even a red, yes, a red might just bring out even more highlights. In fact, there's a little dress on this rack—'

"'I don't wear dresses,' Kate stated in reply," and the contest between fashion designers and the independent backwoods woman gives strength and hope to such people throughout the world (102–4).

Breakup is of a flush in nature and human society. When spring breaks in Alaska, all hell moves. Snow melts, rivers rise, bears come out of hibernation hungry and ill-tempered, people emerge from their cabins horny and hungry for human companionship. In this latest novel of crime among the Aleut and other Alaskans, Stabenow develops along new lines and toward different goals. In effect this novel is a Golden Age crime story with the closed room being the entire state of Alaska.

Kate Shugak's world is threatened by both implosion and explosion. First Kate has the engine of a 747 flying overhead drop on and destroy her truck, her only means of transportation; a mother grizzly, just out of hibernation with her two cubs, attacks her; flying bullets from angry wives zoom all around her and through her; murderers come to her for alibis and protection. Breakup in Alaska means temporary near destruction of civilization. But under the insistence of all citizens, Kate rises to the occasion and leadership in the community, consisting of the extended community, which is in fact the whole state.

This adventure with the redoubtable Kate Shugak is different from its predecessors. Even the language takes on a new tone. Although it is a male language in which Stabenow writes, and the whole book seems to consist of one long, interrupted, moveable dialogue, the words are less explosive, less violent. Further, the context seems to be a heightened comedy, with many flashes of unusual humor.

Of the changes, however, the story and the cast of characters are the major difference. Kate and Mutt, her half-wolf half-husky constant companion, and the secondary cast of characters are present. But though Kate is horny after a winter of loneliness and dreams of Jack, her some-time lover, Stabenow manages to keep him in Anchorage, apparently busy and nearly forgotten. Without Jack in the cast of characters, Kate is bound to behave differently and the story to develop on a different turn. Kate is busier than usual doing her own thing.

In an interview with me, Stabenow said that, "Kate is a strong char-acter, with a low tolerance for fools and a willingness to take action when it is necessary. She is also a loner by preference, an echo of the independent and nomadic existence of her ancestors. In future, I see her being dragged kicking and screaming into a leadership role in her tribe. There is a movement toward Native sovereignty up here, much analyzed and debated and which naturally terrifies the state government into idiocies such as appropriating $500,000 to fight it in court. There is also the issue of subsistence, or who gets to catch what fish there were, that is vital to Alaska Native concerns, in particular in the Bush communities. Both issues generate a tremendous amount of passion and conflict on every side, the stuff of drama. My stuff. Kate will definitely be con-cerned with both."

This novel is Stabenow's determined drive toward having Kate break out into a larger role, self-sufficient and successful. She is too powerful a figure not to have her personality dominate her community. Here she dominates. She forces her will on a group of reluctant council members to establish a clinic to provide counseling because the people lived by the gun and needed that counseling to soothe the resulting ten-dency toward violence. So Kate is forced into the leadership role. The new role is not a fur that fits easily without scratching: she is now not merely a "private investigator," and might in fact never have been one. She has taken on a much broader and more compelling role:

> There was the acute personal frustration of being thrust into a position
> of responsibility for the tribe, of shouldering duties and assuming obli-
> gations she had never sought and had certainly never wanted. It wasn't
> just the tribe, either. It was the whole goddam park, Native and white,
> cheechako and sourdough, ranger and miner and homesteader, fisher

folk and fish hawk. Predicaments RUs, You Bring 'Em, We Fix 'Em, K. Shugak, Proprietor. Meetings Mediated, Marriages Counselled, Murders Solved. She didn't even have to advertise, they came, bringing their baggage with them, whether she wanted them to or not. (24)

But though Jack was not around, another more powerful force was with her, the tribal flood of her ancestors. Earlier in *Blood Will Tell*, Grandmother Ekaterina was allowed to die without any cause in the plot. This powerful woman, Emaa, had been Kate's source of wisdom and strength, her tie to the Aleut's roots. But now she is gone. In order for Kate to come to her full strength and independence Emaa had to be removed from the stories. So she died. Kate is on her own. In this book even Jack is not around in body and spirit. Just Kate and Mutt, and even Mutt is less important than she was in earlier books.

Kate is emerging as a five-foot, 120 pound (she has now gained ten pounds) giant able to take on all the troubles of Alaska and all the evil of human kind. She does not stand fully straight upright just yet. She is emerging, perhaps like a bear that has hibernated too long in the cave of her traditions. But her head is out and the body will follow.

Stabenow uses the emergence of spring, with its symbolism and physical happenings as statements about which she develops Kate's growth. In Alaska, spring means a return of life, the promise of development and growth. In an earlier book, *Play with Fire*, Stabenow had used spring as the symbol of peaceful hope. Kate had stepped into the river to wash herself and her clothes. She had heard a bird sing and knew that spring had come.

Now in *Breakup* with an entirely different goal in mind, Stabenow uses the same symbols but with different purposes. Again Kate sings, "Spring is here." Again a bird perches on a twig close to Kate and sings three notes in a descending scale. They remind her of Grandmother Emaa, now dead. Kate sees Emaa in nature and confesses how much she loves, misses, and needs her grandmother. Finally, Stabenow's concluding lines make clear how much Kate has developed in this novel.

Breakup is a coming-of-age novel, an Aleut Bildungsroman, an account of the coming of maturity, a type common in American literature and the literature of any nation that is dynamic. Kate's head continues to rise above the community in the leadership role that Stabenow says her hero must assume. *Breakup* is Kate's breaking from the chrysalis into her full winged strength. In many ways *Breakup* is Shugak *agonistes*. We all will be the benefactors of the new hero.

Killing Grounds (1998) is a different kind of accomplishment. For subject matter Stabenow returns to the sea, this time to the salmon fishing bay in the summer when millions of salmon are trying to get back to the sands of their birth. It is the Fourth of July week and hundreds of fishermen and women are on the bay with their nets. The price of salmon has dropped to fifty cents a pound and the fisherfolks are angry enough to go on strike. There is deep irony in the fact that on the Fourth of July fishermen have to go on strike to try to force the capitalist powers to pay them a living wage.

One of those capitalists is the meanest fisherman on the bay—Calvin Meany—who fishes on through the strike, angering the whole fishing community. The next morning he is found floating in the bay, dead of several mortal wounds. In an effort to cover his crime, Calvin's brother, the killer, murders his niece and attacks Kate, who is somewhat on his trail. The brother, who is, as we say, pursuing a Ph.D. in William Butler Yeats at the University of Cincinnati, kills his brother because he will not pay for his schooling and is otherwise so desperately evil.

Kate's boyfriend Jack turns up for a while, trying to have sex with the horny Kate but who is forced to postpone the encounter because of different circumstances. Kate admits that she misses Emaa, whom Stabenow killed off two books earlier, and is resisting being forced to become one of the tribal leaders. And Stabenow does a fine job in developing the characters of four of Kate's aunts, who are illegally fishing for salmon, drying them, and selling them to a local cafe manager.

All in all *Killing Grounds* is more successful as an environmental study than as a gripping crime novel. Kate is somewhat incidentally developed and not as interesting as in the former books, and Stabenow allows the environment to overwhelm her. But for those readers wanting atmosphere and a detailed chapter on salmon fishing in Alaska, this is an interesting book.

In her latest Shugak novel, Stabenow achieves much more. She has wandered onto a new path and purpose in the development of her heroine. In this work, *Hunter's Moon*, Stabenow downplays Kate's past and her use of her heritage in her growth as a major voice in Alaskan culture. Kate is only slightly interested in the fact that she is Aleut and has grown in and out of that culture. Instead Kate is faced with a very modern situation and threat to the future, and her hostility hangs out all over.

A troop of ten very successful and wealthy German computer manufacturers, having exhausted all other adventures, are looking for the ultimate thrill in hunting moose and grizzlies, with the finest and most expensive guns available, in Alaska. There are nine very blond men and one tall, muscular and sexy blonde who is bisexual or all-sexual, and dedicated to employing sex for any desired end. Senta looks like a Wagnerian Valkyrie and plays the role well. All of Kate's dislikes show her contempt for the Germans and for all off-center females. All the men act guilty but the monster in the German tribe of Valkyries is Senta, a beautiful, statuesque blonde who fairly drips and shines with sex.

In this new novel, which is more crime fiction than detective story, we meet a new Kate, driven by an author with a different purpose. In the past Kate has stood with one foot in her heritage and one in the hard world over which she had to triumph. She was self-conscious over the ropelike scar that marked her throat from ear to ear, marking an encounter with a powerful man. Very conscious of her past, Kate consulted with her Aleut sage grandmother, Emaa, and tried to behave as she had taught her. Kate sought to fit into the modernized way of life of her ancestors, to be a twentieth-century and capable Aleut.

Here both author and character head in a new direction. *Hunter's Moon* is a feminist novel in both the narrow and broad sense. Kate wants to prove female equality in all the world. In what is the fastest, most direct, concise, and intense beginning of all her novels, Stabenow sets the stage development. Jack Morgan, Kate's forty-five-year-old lover from the Anchorage police department, asks in the first sentence of the book, "What's the Bush word for Renaissance woman?" He asks because in his admiration for Kate he delights in enumerating all her qualities of superiority. Kate assures him that her superior skills are "just geography." "It's where I live. I'm not special or different. Not from anybody who lives like me. When you live in the Bush, you do what you have to to get by." Jack's admiration is not lowered in the least. He is still brimful of praise and says, "And that's probably what is most amazing. You actually believe that." Kate universalizes herself as woman and as human being in answering: "She cast a baffled glimpse his way. 'What else would I believe'?" (1).

But Stabenow has Kate prove her superiority by doing more than others and triumphing when others fail. In this book her ultimate triumph is over her very powerful sexual needs and sense of community in her determination not to sacrifice her personality and total self to their drives. Jack, her badly needed and thoroughly enjoyed sex partner in the previous books, is acting as one of the guides handling the German hunters. He and Kate are therefore constantly thrown into close physical and emotional contact. Both are supercharged with sexual drive. They cannot be near each other without fondling and not alone without undressing. Jack, though only forty-five, has decided to retire and live full-time with Kate if he can get her approval. Again and again he pleads his case, trying to point out the pleasures of permanent cohabitation. Again and again Kate responds that she is a loner, prefers her private space, does not want Jack with her full-time. Finally, however, Kate gives in to his urging and promises he can move in with her permanently. But immediately she regrets her acquiescence and knows that she cannot follow Jack's desires. At this point Stabenow has driven herself into a corner from which there is no easy satisfactory escape. If Kate is a modern Renaissance woman, an accomplished female equal if not superior to any man and must do everything alone, she cannot sacrifice herself for the urging of a dependent and deeply loved male.

Kate proves her superiority by conquering the Germans. Stabenow has the group separate into three smaller contingents and go off on separate missions. They immediately start killing off one another until finally the battle devolves into the struggle for supremacy between two women, Kate and Senta—Senta the giant Valkyrie of the past whose strengths lay in sex and the manipulation of men, and the miniature Kate, the Renaissance woman of today who had love and empathy in her quiver of power. Against Senta, Kate triumphs. Stabenow is still faced with a still larger problem, that of the Renaissance Kate, independent and role-modeling for women in general.

She is determined not to give up her individual freedom as a woman. So Jack Morgan, the necessary component of at least half of Kate's existence, must be killed off. He dies in Kate's arms. Mutt, Kate's half-wolf companion for years, is badly wounded but will probably survive, and will accompany Kate in the future. Jack had to go, but his passing creates a furor among the elements. Nature acknowledges the passing of Jack and the old Kate and the birth of the new woman.

One of the surviving men tries to talk about how Jack though wounded will recover, but Old Sam, Kate's cousin, orders him to be quiet because he knows that Jack is dead. Then Stabenow raises her eyes and ears upward to the expanding universe and hears a tuneless lament. Nobody could ever forget.

But the changing scene is for the man. The woman will continue to hear it though through a different ear. The feministic drive of the book is overwhelming. The question is, now that Kate has proved herself superior to men and to other women who rely on and use men—and are therefore not true women living up to their potential—can Kate be faced with sufficiently strong men to make a novel about man-woman relationships convincing? If Kate is "not special, or different," as she insists, and her self-sufficiency is "just . . . geography" and therefore represents all true women, what can be the subject of Kate's next adventure? Stabenow is faced with a strong challenge. Only time will tell whether she is woman enough for the task. Meanwhile, *Hunter's Moon* stands high on the shelf of feminist literature.

After this novel Stabenow contracted to write a series of novels about airplanes in Alaska. Because she is interested in making money and knows a great deal about airplanes and air travel she assumed that the work would be successful. In most ways it is. But she made a bigger turn than she realized. In her former novels she wrote about universal human nature *in* though not *of* Alaska. She writes of people, especially natives, as people, members of the human family, and because she writes from the heart and soul of those natives and their traditions she writes with conviction and power. When she turns to writing of airplanes in Alaska she has taken on an entirely different task in touching human nature in its deepest roots. She flies over it, writing with power and entertainment. But in her first book she does not manage to get below the permafrost of human behavior.

Fire and Ice, her first in the new series, begins with so much strength and power that it almost gets out of hand. The opening paragraphs vibrate with raw murder. A pilot apparently walks into the propeller of a Cub and is decapitated. The investigation that ensues is done in a decibel count of ten on a scale of nine.

The novel opens with a menagerie of characters that would out-John Wayne in cast of his most violent movie. There's an "old Fart, short, dark, a grin one part mean to two parts evil," a "Moccasin Man, tall, loping, clad in fatigues and matching buckskin moccasins with matching belt patch," The Flirt, "who should have been arrested for incitement to riot the second after she'd stepped out in public that morning: she wore a red shirt with no bra beneath it and a long skirt that accentuated the deliberate sway of her very nice ass" (1). Later on we meet the native philosopher who converses with ravens, and Linda Billington, owner of the local restaurant, is magistrate and insists on being called Bill.

Into this pen walks Liam Campbell, Alaska State Trooper who has been demoted because his colleagues failed to prevent the murder of a car full of Alaskan natives. For his failure, Liam has been exiled into the Alaska boonies, where he meets his sometime love the powerful small aircraft pilot Wyanet Chouinard.

The novel is full and detailed in plane lore and Alaska life. Stabenow knows her airplanes and tells us about them in great detail. By the time we finish the book we know many details of herring fishing and the fortunes that can be made or lost, the loose human actions that circulate in a loose society that is rapidly destroying the sense of close community that has always blessed the fishing village, and the feeling of needed adherence to biblical morality that suffuses the society.

Two opposing philosophical points of view drive the community. Philosopher Moses lives by the Darwinian thesis of the law of tooth and claw, or rather, the strongest man gets the biggest fish. "We're not culling the human herd the way we oughtta. We're saving the weakest. . . . We're gonna rescue 'em all, and wipe out the human race doing it," he says (38).

The humanitarian, empathic point of view is almost invisibly absent. This is a society where the big fish get caught and the big catchers get rich, and the remainder sometimes get murdered if they get in the way.

Two people are killed, naturally for the money the fish bring in. Liam Campbell, representing the Alaska law, tries to find the guilty parties though at times he at least pretends that he is not committed to punishing them. As the story winds down, Moses again comes to the forefront and voices his philosophy: Two persons dead, he says, "We won't miss 'em, either one of them" (289). Then he congratulates Liam on his not having executed the man who wrecked the Troop's automobile earlier, killing his only son and paralyzing his wife, saying he had done the right thing. "You did what was right," Moses says, seemingly summing up the philosophy of the book and restating that Alaska is a big country and demands strong individualistic people to develop it.

Then he ties his Darwinian philosophy in with a kinder more human love that has tied frontier communities together for ages, by warning Liam that supernatural forces that aim to steal and divide will rob him when they can. "Raven'll steal your woman and everything else that matters along with her, but only if you let him," he says (286). Raven has been a creature of supernatural wisdom and devilish deeds throughout primitive folk cultures for ages.

Stabenow ends the book not on a positive note but on a question of what can one do in a pioneering land but pioneer for one's own aggrandizement. Liam Campbell, the law-abiding and law-promoting good man does not know where to turn or what to do. So he looks at Raven and trusts his wisdom. "Mind telling me what I do now," he rather simply asks his bird friend. Stabenow knows no more than her character of what he should do. "It croaked at him," she concludes.

In this new series of books Stabenow, having changed her venue and subject, has not yet learned how to reconcile frontier individualism with humanitarianism and empathy. She has lost the warm anchor of the grandmother, which flooded her books about tribal lives and customs. Here in a thinner more competitive capitalistic tradition she has not quite been able to become master. But she is a quick learner, and she will have found her footing and her heart in the second book in the series.

In *So Sure of Death,* the second book in her new series of five about airplanes and airpeople, Stabenow is primarily concerned with authoring a sure-fire adventure book that circles around murder. This one does—about aircraft, fishing, boating, sex, and all aspects of outdoor life in Alaska. But she has learned much in writing the first in the series, and her methods of handling the situations and the conclusions she draws are much more positive and humanistic.

Her hero again is the nonheroic figure Liam Campbell, whose origins are unknown and undistinguished and whose future is unstable as he seems to be succeeding in being an Alaska State Trooper; he loves it, yet is afraid to fly in a state and occupation where wings are an absolute necessity. Although he vomits at the mere thought of getting into the air, his nerves are steel on all other threats of danger. Luckily his airtime is guaranteed by the able pilot Wyanet Chouinard, who has come off a disappointing love affair but really wants more from him than companionship in a cockpit.

This adventure is built around personal and professional life in the fishing industry in Alaska, the murder of eight or nine individuals, marital infidelity all around, the evil of obsession with one's occupation, and loneliness.

Loneliness and greed flip the switch on both. Being alone in Alaska is more serious than it is elsewhere, and can trigger all kinds of neurotic responses. It does in this book and causes a rapid-action and rapid-fire adventure that leaves the reader almost breathless and drives the burning of overnight electricity.

At telling this fast-flying adventure, few if any are better than Stabenow. The long novel is almost as smooth as one long continuous sentence. The account is crammed with Alaskan lore of all kinds—meteorological, archaeological, fishing, guns, emotional, sexual. Her characters are alive and vernacular. She tells it like it is, even down to punning, as when she sinks to the double entendre or use of truisms, as in "You can run but you can't hide" (129).

In this book—as in the series apparently—Stabenow is primarily concerned with her dedication to being just entertaining. But in writing about life in a country like Alaska where there are numerous tribes, varying shades of whiteness and darkness with the consequent racial injustices, it is impossible to picture society without bringing a causes and effects of pure and mixed races and cultural reactions.

Alaska is a hard country in which to live. You either love it or leave it—if you can. Many non-natives come to the state because they love it, many natives leave it as soon as possible because they want more of the opportunity offered elsewhere. Thus the heavy traffic in human migration north and south.

Without making the subject a heavy theme in the book, Stabenow mixes her entertainment with the heavy reality of Native American against whites, as when she has one of the white female characters explain her natural advantages in the society: "First off, before everything else, I'm white. I'm as white as you can get without bleach. Before I'm a bartender, before I'm a magistrate, before I'm a goddamn Alaskan, I'm white. And because I'm white, I was *born* at go. I don't have to work my ass off just to get that far" (194).

The language, the style of writing, and its directness and reflection of Stabenow's indirect expression of her attitude toward cultural injustices energize the novel and make it serve the double purpose of keeping the reader entertained while at the same time having him drink the mickey of realization of cultural injustices. These injustices are less directly catalogued and some readers will say less effectively presented here than in Stabenow's stories of Grandmother Emaa and the tradition she represents. Stabenow gained much strength in standing at the end of the line and writing about a rich tradition of folklore and custom, which like a full river flowed rich in life-giving sustenance.

In turning to the technological world of Piper Cubs and 737s (the favorite Alaskan airplane) Stabenow faces away from her tradition except as it immediately impinges on the present. In so doing she weakens Alaskan life in one way but brings it up to the present and in so doing enriches it in another way. It is a mixed bag of great strength and lesser accomplishment.

With her limited success, however, Stabenow's novel about aircraft life in Alaska is superior to most others. Such pilot poets as Antoine de Saint-Exupéry ordinarily put their imagination on subjects other than crime fiction. So not all mysteries about aircraft life in Alaska fly at the same altitude and speed. *Coffin Corner,* by Megan Mallory Rust, an Alaskan native and professional pilot, concerns a female pilot, Taylor

Morgan, who is forced to become investigator when a friend is murdered. Rust's account is filled with authentic pilot talk as her heroine island hops in her Lear, drumming up but avoiding sex. But the actions, like the talk, are only uniform deep, not opening rich human passions the way Stabenow's novels do. Stabenow's pilot flies her Cub higher and faster, loaded with far more interesting people and depths of human emotion.

Stabenow, like most popular authors, usually keeps more than one manuscript on the writing desk. While writing these airplane stories she was also writing another Kate Shugak novel, *Midnight Come Again*. But it is different from her earlier stories in the series and is in essence a standard adventure search-and-find novel set in Alaska.

It begins just after the funeral of her boss-lover Jack, and we meet not only a new set of characters but a changed Kate. Kate, overly stuffed with the filth of civilization wants to go back to the bush and live the primitive life. But an armored money truck in Russia has been hijacked and the authorities suspect it has been brought by fishing ship to Alaska to be laundered and they want to enlist Kate's assistance in locating it. They cannot understand why Kate has run away and where she has gone to. So, in effect, an all-out bulletin is issued for information leading to her location.

But Kate has changed in more ways than one, and the circumstances of her life have been altered. With the death of Jack, Kate has suppressed her sexual drive and decided to live only with Mutt, her protective dog. As we look back on the changed years of her life as she recounts them we see the origin of the new Kate. Instead of the loving grandmother Ekaterina Shugak we know from the earlier books, who was the epitome of native mythology, love, and tribal strength, we discover that she had been a mean-spirited, weak character who could not control the strong-willed Kate, who lived with her off-and-on and at age ten declared her independence and moved into her own way of life. Kate is rather proud in displaying the deep scar on her throat that she received while killing a man who had raped a child. So she still has her fierce contempt for humankind but she wants to express it at a distance.

Yet Shugak is not the deep, humanitarian person we know from earlier books. Stabenow seems to have wandered too far afield in her Russian background, or, more likely, in writing her airplane stories for what she and the publisher felt would be a wider audience. She has slipped away from the basis of her strength, the mythological-folkloristic roots of Alaskan native culture, which she knows so well. Earlier she worked in native culture, which she could control, but with the larger one she seems not to have her characters—especially Kate Shugak—under psychological and humanitarian control.

But Stabenow is the compulsive novelist who is not happy unless her fingers are on the computer keyboard. *Nothing Gold Can Stay* is built around a Yupik story told her by a friend who got it from oral tradition as recounted by a great storyteller named Simeon Bartman. It is the story of a man who, as a result of a twisted uprearing, became obsessed with women named Elaine, or who looked enough like the Elaine of Arthurian legend to allow him to associate them with the beauty of the classic story. So women start disappearing and Wy Chouinard and Alaska State Trooper Liam Campbell are assigned the job of locating them and revealing the person responsible for their disappearance. They finally unveil the serial killer and the graves of the thirteen women he has murdered and buried with the hint of a gravestone for each marked only with the name "Elaine." The murderer almost wears the identification of Unabomber Ted Kaczynski with Alaskan overdress but he is clearly Alaskan, and the author of the book is clearly Stabenow. Pilot Wy Chouinard has come to devote herself more to revealing and rewarding her physical and sexual feelings. Liam now sleeps nearly every night in her bed, but she has not decided to marry him because she needs the comfort of her single life and the joy of the plane under her. Further, the futures of both are too uncertain, for Liam, it is suggested, will be promoted to a position in Anchorage as payment for solving the murder of the thirteen "Elaines." Stabenow, as though not altogether comfortable with having abandoned working with legends and myths, reaches back here to a folktale and may continue to work with them. Regardless, this is a hard-hitting, bloodletting novel in a land that shows no compromise for anybody, and is another of Stabenow's minor triumphs in her new genre.

The next novel, *A Fine and Bitter Snow*, succeeds because Stabenow returns to Kate Shugak for another study of the conflicts of the Alaskan wilderness. This time, however, one conflict is between office and outback. The oil interests are trying to get permission to drill for oil in Alaska in the Arctic National Wildlife Refuge (ANWR) and most of the (poor) locals are fighting back. Another conflict on a more personal basis is the fact that a park ranger, after years on the job is being forced by new management to retire in the budget squeeze they are experiencing. These two conflicts are tied together in what is really Stabenow's strength in this series of novels and all her others, the beauty and strength of the traditional Alaskan landscape and culture-scape. Here Stabenow reaches back into this timeless river through her aunts, contemporaries of her favorite Emaa. Life and death are always cold and violent in Stabenow's Alaska, though the former is always brought to the sweaty stage through sex.

So this latest Shugak novel is enacted on familiar land by some characters we know in ways that are familiar. The work suffers somewhat from being tossed by the wash from the propellers of her Liam Campbell/Wy Chouinard series, but it flashes the same style, goals and accomplishments of the typical Stabenow novel so far.

Thomas Perry

The works of Thomas Perry introduce another powerful heroine into Native American crime fiction. He learned his trade with the books *The Butcher's Boy, Metzger's Dog, Island* (1987), and *Sleeping Dogs,* all fast action novels in the tradition of Frederick Forsyth, Tom Clancy, and Robert Ludlum. *Sleeping Dogs,* for example, tells the story of a mob hit man who goes to England to get away from the mobsters who are out to kill him. They follow and find him, start killing people all around and chase him back to the United States, where everybody, mob hit men and all law officials, is on his tail. He is fast on his feet and with his gun.

This kind of protagonist feeds popular fiction. It is also found, though in another gender, in Perry's protagonist in his Jane Whitefield series. Whitefield is in the "research and consulting" business, which means that she makes people disappear when they are in danger. Sometimes she tries to meld them into the Seneca tribe, of which she is a member of the Wolf Clan. She is half-Seneca. Whitefield finds that she must accompany her disappearees and thus becomes a target for murderers. Her living arrangements, though nominally located in Tonawanda, New York, homeland of the Seneca, necessarily have to be secretive and mobile. Although she charges nothing for her work, she expects "presents" from grateful survivors and each year receives checks from secret locations amounting to hundreds of thousands of dollars. So her work, though hazardous, is lucrative.

More than other protagonists of Native American crime fiction we have examined, Whitefield is an outsider in society who works from the outside in, at least a semiprofessional position of one who works *for* and *through* the Indians though with a great personal interest.

Jane got into this work in the way most college graduates do. In her last year in college she had joined the "Tecumseh Society," "a student group formed on the theory that the Shawnee leader who traveled from tribe to tribe in the early 1800s to unite the Indians might not have been entirely misguided" (*Vanishing Act* 38). Her assignment was "to travel with a Jicarilla Apache named Ilona Tazeh through the northern plains to establish a voter-registration program on the festival circuit: the northern Cheyenne Fourth of July Powwow and the Crow Fair in Montana, the Ogallala Nation Powwow and the Standing Rock Pow-wow in South Dakota" (38). These activities eventually got her into the assignment of saving a "piece of scum" named Alfred Strongbear simply because he was the last Beothuk alive, when it was commonly believed that the last Beothuk had been eliminated in 1820. They had never grasped the European concept of private property, so the Beothuk had been forced to become "a nation of thieves" (39), and as such had been eliminated. To save Strongbear, Whitefield had to drive him off the res-ervation in the trunk of her car and see that he got to Venezuela.

In *Vanishing Act,* she has another person pursued by death who needs her assistance. Before that client can get her help, however, he must undergo the usual check-up. Whitefield's clientele are so notori-ous and so dangerously connected that she never knows whom to trust. She works only by referral, and when somebody is sent or comes to her, she subjects that person to an intimately detailed account of the individ-ual who made the referral and other particulars so that she does not take into her confidence somebody who is trying to eliminate her. In this story, she takes on John Felker, an ex-cop who has been declared an em-bezzler but actually was set up by a gang who wanted to take over gam-bling from the Seneca, a deal which would result in multiple fortunes. The plot is to have Felker sentenced to prison, where he will be killed by one of the inmates. Whitefield can save him but so intense are the as-sassins who are determined to eliminate him that he and Jane are con-stantly pursued and just one leap ahead of the fatal bullet.

In detailing the strength of the Seneca, Perry often gives in consid-erable detail their customs. One powerful example is their Buffalo Dance, which he describes in detail:

> The door on the east end of the building flew open and ten men danced
> into the room wearing dark blue carved wooden masks with pointed
> leather ears and tufts of fur on top, huge eyes and big teeth. They grum-
> bled and grunted, bent over and glared at the people gathered around
> the walls. . . . Some of the women wore Indian skirts with elaborate

embroidered pictures on them and a loose red tunic above, dangling earrings, and big silver brooches like plates. (142)

The Seneca are great believers in mysterious ritual, and Jane follows their example on numerous occasions. When she is coming home from having been out in the world, for example, she remembers that the Indians who did not call themselves Seneca but Nundawaono, the People of the Hill, are all gone now, but the Jo-Ge-Oh, the Little People, who are about as tall as one's hands, are still around.

These little people especially were "hopelessly addicted to tobacco." To satisfy their longing, Jane has brought them some, properly prepared in the old Seneca way. In that preparation she "held the pouch at arm's length and poured the rest of the tobacco down into the gorge, watching the shreds sprinkle and spread out in the breeze to become invisible" (19).

Later, in a time of utmost trial for Jane, trying to save her life, in desperation she remembers the Seneca lore her grandfather had taught her about old Nundawaono stories concerning the Naked Bear. She runs through the forest and across the lakes. Then chased by a mysterious being that was at least half-supernatural, she resorts to the Indian custom of making a bow and arrow, and guides the arrows with magic raven feathers. As the being chases her she shoots him with two arrows but they do not stop him. Then, remembering how the Seneca braves had always insulted woman about their weakness, Jane summons forth superwoman strength, fires one more arrow into the being's back, then rushes him and with two blows crushes the back of his head. Then she resorts to the sound of triumph of the warrior, male or female, perhaps most commonly seen and heard in the old movies of Johnny Weissmuller's Tarzan: "Jane drew a deep breath and threw her head back so far that the feathers in her hair brushed her spine and her painted face glared up through the leaves at the sky. Then she let out a piercing whoop of triumph and gladness" (314).

Vanishing Act is a powerful novel, filled with Seneca lore and mysticism and flirting between the two cultures, insinuating the faults of the white society and emphasizing the strengths of the Seneca. The next book, *Dance for the Dead,* goes on a different tack and is less powerful. It concentrates on a child's life and vicissitudes and is overly sentimentalized.

Here Jane is trying to save a child named Timmy and his $80 million estate from people who want to take it away from him. Without parents, he is kept in homes for orphans with no custodians. Mary Perkins—sounds too close to Mary Poppins, of dancing umbrella fame—under several names has stolen millions through various schemes. Now she is sticking close to Jane for safety. Jane's task—and culturally she cannot refuse it—is to save Mary and Timmy. Working in California, where the story begins, and in Detroit, where the chase drives her, Jane does not have much to do with the Seneca or any other Indians except in recounting several of their rituals. Perry ends the novel with Timmy safely adopted by loving parents, Mary Perkins converted from her stealing ways, and Jane participating in the activities of her ancestors, singing the Ogiwe, the Dance for the Dead. "The women sang the Ogiwe and danced together as their grandmothers had, for the brave and the unselfish, for their protectors. They sang until dawn, when the spirits of the dead were satisfied and returned to their rest, where they would not be tempted to disturb the dreams of the living" (400). From this immersion into Seneca life, Jane derives her strength to venture out into white society for her rescue work.

In *Shadow Woman*, his next book, Perry comes back fundamentally to a mature world and writes his strongest book to date. Like his others, this one plays to one degree or another with spirits. In an introductory page, Perry quotes at length from Lewis Henry Morgan's *League of the Iroquois* (1851): "Any person, whether old or young, male or female, might become possessed of an evil spirit, and be transformed into a witch. A person thus possessed could assume, at pleasure, the form of any animal, bird or reptile, and having executed his nefarious purpose, could resume his original form, or, if necessary to escape pursuit, could transmute himself into an inanimate object."

Shadow Woman is about pursuit, in fact, multiple pursuits. The book begins dramatically. A Las Vegas show-woman named Miranda makes a man called Pete Hatcher disappear from the stage by magic. This act is necessary because Hatcher is being chased by a hit squad from Pleasure, Inc., a group that wants to establish a casino gambling joint on the Seneca reservation but in order to do that they feel Hatcher, one of their former associates, must be killed. Jane has asked Miranda to perform the magic of Hatcher's disappearance to help her get him out of town.

The disappearing act is only the beginning of a hasty escape. Jane has a car parked just outside the nightclub. In it Hatcher begins a chase that will take him across the United States. When the original two hit men fail to kill Hatcher, they are replaced by Earl and Linda—professional hit people who love to hit. Smart and relentless, they chase Hatcher and Jane from Las Vegas to upstate New York and back to the Rockies, so close to their quarry that they can smell them. The absolute finest ingenuity is required of Jane to save her man and herself. And the absolute finest in action writing is required of Perry to pull off this latest adventure.

In this escapade, as in her others, to combat the evil of the white world Jane immediately summons up the gods of the past through ritual. As she comes to Dayadehokto, her first stop among the protective Seneca, Jane brings special tobacco and her nail clippings for the Jo-Ge-Oh, the Little People, who as we have seen before use these artifacts for their own addiction and protection. In this practice, Jane was acting as Seneca women had for a thousand years. The religious rites, "no religion practiced for supplication" (24), are practiced only for giving thanks. Perry keeps Jane close to the Seneca. For example he has her use the phrase "taste the strawberries," which means "you come so close that you already taste the wild strawberries that grow by the path to the other world" (31). Later, building on the magic, and the ecstasy of the strawberry in Seneca lore, Jane and her friend have sex in the wild strawberry field.

After the escape has succeeded, Jane marries Carey, her physician friend whom in the latest book she had promised to wed. But she sets up conditions for the union. She wants to give up her activities and says she will cook for Carey and be happy as a housewife. She realizes that her past has been "full of wolves." But she cannot remain a mere observer of the drama of the role of the Seneca in the world today. She says she's a "left over Indian Rights radical from ten years ago. A lot of what I know comes from the Old People" (91). Jane is so set in the old ways that one person feels she is his "Grandmother's grandmother," ninety-five years or older at least.

The Face-Changers, the latest in the series featuring Jane Whitefield, is more one of his live-action novels of early writing than a typical Whitefield crime novel. The work develops around such rapid-fire action that Perry hardly has a chance to develop any personality for the main character. Jane is generally referred to as "a pretty brunette" or a "beautiful large brunette" without much further character description. The story differs from its predecessors in a couple of other ways. Jane is so busy trying to save lives by making people disappear that she does not have a chance to thoroughly check the references of the people who claim they have been sent to her. Further, Carey McKinnon, the man she married in the preceding novel, is more prominently working with and for her than in previous works. Jane says that she is not interested in people who want justice or revenge; her business and concern only is in making people disappear so that their lives can be saved. Here also she is not interested in weak women or "stupid men."

The story concerns an elderly surgeon who has been experimenting with rapid cell replication in malignancies and based on some experiments thinks he has finally found the miracle for saving people's lives. But he has become mixed up with extralegal machinations of people who want to prevent his success. Wounded in a scrape with them, he has had to see his former student McKinnon, who is forced to call in his wife Jane in order to make the surgeon disappear and thus continue to live.

This work, as pointed out earlier, is more the adventure story than a Native American crime story. It is, however, framed in Seneca lore. It begins with a quotation from an 1851 report about how a person became a False-face, or got out of the fraternity of Falsefacers in Iroquois society a hundred years ago. Then after Jane's many rapid adventures she enters her debriefing, quietening period by references to her standard gifts to the Seneca "Little People." she brings them tobacco, fingernail clippings, and other "usual presents," and she thanks them for "keeping [her] husband safe" (367).

Although this latest effort is somewhat off track in the Native American crime fiction it still gives some Indian lore and custom for our benefit. The whole exercise informs us or confirms what we know about the Seneca.

So if not our grandmother, Jane or Perry is one of our teachers of Seneca, and Indian, ways in the world of today. We are well taught. Perry recounts many interesting and informative myths and legends of Seneca culture and uses those, as well as Jane's actions, to demonstrate, among other things, the injustices the whites perpetrated against the Indians. The whites were the aggressors, the Five Nations the victims. So in Perry, as in the other authors of Native American crime fiction, the reader benefits from excellent novels and useful history outlining the mistreatment of Indians by whites.

Margaret Coel

With Margaret Coel, as with many other authors, interest in Native Americans came when, for other reasons than crime fiction, she began investigating their cultures, and the more she learned about the Native Americans the more she became bewitched by their way of life. She therefore turned to the Arapaho of Wyoming and has written six novels about them and their way of life. All are first-class works.

The Arapaho are divided into three groups, Northern Arapaho (considered the parent group), Southern Arapaho, and the Gros Ventre Indians. All are essentially an agricultural people who, as mentioned previously, supplement their income by leasing land for oil and gas development. They are closely tied in and to their past and their rituals. Coel captures these aspects very well.

In *The Eagle Catcher*, her first, she introduces us to her main characters, Father John O'Malley, head pastor of St. Francis Mission and reformed drunk from Boston, and Vicky Holden, Arapaho lawyer who has practiced law in Los Angeles and has come back to the reservation, leaving her two children with her abusive ex-husband in Los Angeles.

The complicated story involves Indian life and conflict between whites and Arapaho. A powerful white family, Ned Cooley's, has owned a large ranch on the Wind River Reservation for a hundred years. His ancestors acquired the land through fraudulent manipulation, stealing it, in effect, from the Indians. Ned hates Indians though he never shows his animosity openly. He wants to be elected governor of the state, and needing the money wants to sell the ranch to the Indians. His oil company will then close the oil wells in order to quit paying royalties to the Indians for the pumped oil, then pump it out in slant drilling, a process known as doglegging.

Old man Harvey, on the council, at first agrees with the Indian council to buy the ranch but he is murdered, probably because word has got out that he has changed his mind and will vote against the deal with Cooley. O'Malley and Holden take it upon themselves to discover the murderer. They do, of course, but after having waded through all kinds of Indian lore and happenings.

Anthony, the nephew of murdered Harvey, is at first accused of the murder because he and his uncle had had a violent argument the night Harvey was murdered. In trying to establish Anthony's innocence, Father O'Malley and Vicky uncover old documents that prove the original theft of the ranch and the fact that Cooley is the murderer.

The book climaxes in a setting and atmosphere revealing celestial interest. Cooley has captured Vicky and taken her up a mountainside. Father John follows and is also apprehended. They escape, however, and hide in an eagle catch on the mountain. Anthony as a boy had been an eagle catcher and had told Vicky and John that "when an eagle catcher dies, he turns into an eagle and flies straight to god" (188). When John and Vicky, spurred by the momentum of this mythology, emerge from the catch they see Cooley, armed to the teeth and spraying everything around with rifle shots. But he slips and falls down the mountainside. They are saved, Anthony is proved innocent, and reservation life can return to normal. John and Vicky, though they have momentarily left town, will come back, and Anthony will be free to marry Melissa, who at the moment she is traveling in Italy.

The bucolic ending in tranquility generates a lot of sympathy for the Arapaho, though Coel insists that she is not trying to write a pro-Arapaho novel. There is the conflict between Indian and Anglo cultures as evidenced in the Anthony-Melissa love affair. Melissa is Cooley's stepdaughter, and considered far too superior to have a relationship with a Native American. Such affairs are, of course, common in Native American crime fiction, and one of the salient causes of conflict. It reminds those readers with long memories of Helen Hunt Jackson's classic *Ramona* (1884) and her story of the mixedblood adopted daughter of a haughty Spaniard named Moreno who falls in love with Alessandro, a fullblooded Indian, but they are not allowed to pursue their romantic interests. Coel's story is, obviously, an Arapaho *Romeo and Juliet,* and as such nurtures our sympathy for all star-crossed lovers. Here the stars are uncrossed and this story is solemnized—or witnessed approvingly—by God Himself, by participating in the downfall of the murderous white man and the destruction of the people who prey on the innocent.

The Ghost Walker, Coel's second work, is less complicated than the earlier book but perhaps evidences more the conflict between Arapaho and white societies. The white world is unsafe, whereas the Arapaho world is secure. In this story, Father John, up early because he has a long way to drive through the snow, experiences car troubles on the highway and is forced to walk to the nearest garage for help. On his way he sees a corpse lying alongside the road. A fast-driving white person picks him up, and O'Malley tells him of seeing the corpse. When O'Malley returns with the police to get the body, it is gone. The murder and disappearance are tied in with a gang of dope runners from Los Angeles who have with them Vicky's daughter Susan. They rent the old farm that Vicky and her husband lived in when they were married. From there they manufacture and ship drugs to nearby towns.

The invasion of the dope peddlers only demonstrates the evil of the white world. The Indians live on the periphery. "We are edge people. We live at the edge of two worlds, white and Arapaho. It is hard to remember who we are when we dwell in the edge space" (106), one says. In solving the mystery of the murdered man and in rescuing Susan from the dopesters, Father John and Vicky work more closely together, and the reader is made very much aware of the growing sexual tension between the two.

The Dream Stalker, Coel's third novel, takes the author into another dimension though she remains on the Wind River Reservation. A group of respectable white ranchers near the reservation want to rent their property for a nuclear waste storage site. Most of the Indians are against the project except those who will profit from the deal, in jobs and spin-off incomes. The Tribal Council is split and is going to vote. One man is reportedly changing his mind and will vote against the deal. He is murdered, as is a white man. The property is especially dangerous for a storage site because it used to be on a large oil deposit. When the oil was depleted, millions of gallons of water, as usual, were forced into the old oil basin. It could explode and scatter nuclear waste everywhere and destroy the Reservation and all the sacred places of the Arapaho.

Vicky Holden, instead of solving other people's problems this time, takes on the powerful vested interests and the Arapaho allied with them. She is strongly motivated. "Nothing is worth the risk of destroying a sacred place," she tells Father John (98). Others, however, are not concerned with the possible destruction or are greedily interested in their own temporary gain. In several ways and on several occasions they try to kill Vicky. She often feels that she stands alone against irresistible forces, but at the time of her greatest threat an old Arapaho ritual strengthens her determination. She asks the *Hehotti* for assistance. He goes through the regular movements. Approaching a huge bundle wrapped in buffalo hide, Grandfather Hedly, undertaking the ritual, prays softly:

> *"In a sacred manner, I am walking,"* he says. He set cans of food in front of the bundle, tobacco on the left, fabric on the right. Hadley steps back and reappears with a large pan hot with coals of cottonwood and chips of cedar. He allows the smoke to rise into the air, purifying it. He removed the sacred red bundle from its place and lifted this sacred wheel, circling it above his head, like the movement of the sun.
>
> [Vicky] heard herself gasp. She'd seen the sacred wheel many times at the Sun Dance. It filled her with a wordless awe. It was round, formed of a single branch, with ends shaped like the head and tail of a snake—a harmless water snake, meek and gentle, like the snakes that lived in the buffalo wallows. Blue beads were wrapped around the top, and eagle feathers hung from four points around the wheel. Carved into the word were the symbols of the Thunderbird, which represented the spirit guardians of creation: *Nahax,* the morning star; *He thon*

natha, the Lone-Star of the evening, and the chain of stars, the Milky Way. All of creation, all of its harmony, was contained in the sacred wheel—a reminder through time to her people that *Nih'a ca* was always with them. (146)

Witnessing the ritual reinvigorated Vicky:

She felt calm, refreshed. Whatever happened to her, she knew she would have the strength to do what she must. She felt like a warrior in the Old Time, riding into battle with the *Hiiteni*—the symbol of the power given in a dream painted on a battle shield. Confident in the dream power. Supremely confident, even as the warrior galloped toward death. (147)

The Dream Stalker pulsates with the life-giving culture of the Indians. But it vibrates with another kind of life-giving force. The sexual tension that has been building through the earlier novels between Father John and Vicky almost erupts. John prays that he can withstand temptation. Once before he succumbed to the weakness of the flesh. Now he hopes he can resist it. Vicky, more a worldly person, throbs with desire every time she is around Father O'Malley. They talk about the temptation, what they must do. We readers also wonder what they must do to withstand it. But do something they must. Otherwise the nature of the series is bound to take a turn up another road. The problem is Coel's, the anticipation of the outcome ours.

The Story Teller, Coel's fourth book, is more contrived and not as effective as its predecessors. It is more external to the essence of Indian culture despite the fact that it centers on an Arapaho artifact and little else. It is framed by an event that is necessary only if the book is dedicated to being anti-academic, as many Indian novels are.

Vicky is summoned to the side of Charlie Redman, one of the tribal elders, to hear him tell a story. The account is that a museum, in giving the Indians an inventory of the Native American artifacts they hold and have to return, fails to report owning an old ledger, which many Indians kept of their daily activities in the past. This one is worth $1.3 million, and the Arapaho want it returned. Vicky reminds them that since it is dated 1902 it is not covered by the law that says all such artifacts must be returned. Nevertheless she begins to investigate and the more she learns the more determined she is to get it back. A young Arapaho doing research in Arapaho folklore and history first stumbled upon the ledger but was killed before he could report it though he did have time to hide it. Considerable investigation on Vicky's part aided by her friend Father

John finally reveals that the Arapaho graduate student's academic advisor committed the murders because he wanted to sell the ledger for its great worth.

The novel is not as strong as Coel's earlier works for a couple of reasons. In the first place the author does not manage to make recovery of the ledger as important as it might have been, though she tries. It seems to be merely a commercial venture, not as important as if it had been a religious artifact. Second, the story is told, as it were, externally, something like a box in which the action takes place. Because of this treatment it lacks the intensity of Coel's other books. Coel says she gets the idea for her novels from local events as reported in newspapers and the like. If the origin of this story was some local event it did not provide enough élan, enough drive, to make it an intense accomplishment of Indian life and conflict.

The Lost Bird, is a study of how the Arapaho can be exploited by white society or at least the evil elements in that society. In 1964 the medical community on the Reservation circulated the medical bulletin that the drinking water used by the Arapaho was so polluted that it could not be cleaned by boiling and that newborn babies were particularly susceptible to the poison. Most newborns, especially those born in hospitals and one clinic in particular were pronounced dead. So contagious was the disease causing the deaths that the coroner had the corpses buried in sealed coffins, without anyone witnessing the presence of the corpse.

Two adults associated with the clinic had committed suicide in 1964, and an old and frail priest returns to the reservation after thirty-five years and is immediately murdered. A famous Hollywood actress returns to the Reservation in search of her birth parents and asks Vicky Holden to locate them for her. In searching out this birthing event, Vicky unearths unopened coffins from 1964 that contained only rocks, while the perfectly healthy babies that were purportedly in the coffins had been sold to outside whites. The villain is a group led by a white doctor who wanted to raise a huge bankroll in order to move his clinic to Los Angeles. He was willing to exploit the Arapaho, even murdering adults, in order to achieve his selfish and greedy goal.

The novel is a study of the injustices some whites do to the Indians. Not all whites, for the Catholic Church is nearly always there to lend a helping hand. Most white authorities and citizens want nothing to do with exploiting the Arapaho of their future in the form of the next generation. It is the evil in society that needs to be rooted out. Even the Arapaho have evil in their society, for a rabid white-hater is trying to build up political support to push all whites, and the BIA and U.S. government, off the reservation.

But the novel is more than that. It is a study in whether or not individuals and nations can return to the past, to yesteryear. The Arapaho want to go back to the good old days when their babies, and through them themselves, were safe. Vicky toys with the notion that she can return to her husband, Ben, whom she divorced years ago because of his drunkenness. Now he has returned from Los Angeles (the symbol of the Outside), says he has reformed, and begs her for a second chance. Vicky relents at least for a moment, spends the night in his arms and wonders if she should give up Father O'Malley as a lost cause and return to Ben. The Mocassin telegraph is broadcasting that Vicky and Ben might be getting back together and Vicky allows the rumors to spread. If she does return, then the message clearly is that the immutable past can be changed and one *can* go home again.

Coel's latest novel, *The Spirit Woman,* may be her finest novel to date. It is surely her most intense. It develops in and from two stories that, like Siamese twins, are joined at the passion point.

A journal that reputedly Sacajawea, the young Indian who guided Lewis and Clark on their trip to the West Coast, kept has been discovered and female historians at the University of Colorado want to publish it. One, in conducting the research, disappeared twenty years ago and her corpse has just been found. Another, not knowing of the death of the earlier historian, has just come to the reservation to continue the needed research. A male historian at the University of Colorado wants to take the journal from the women, and publish it for his own advancement.

The novel is about abused women. Sacajawea had been abused by her French-Indian husband before she supposedly died in 1812; certainly some squaw died at that time and her death was recorded as being that of Sacajawea. But evidence points to the conclusion that another abused Indian, not Sacajawea, had died at that time.

The theme of abuse extends out of the Sacajawea history and parallels in the lives of two other Indian women. Vicky Holden has partially reconciled with her abusive husband Ben. The new historian, Laura, is married to a creative writer who abuses her.

The story throbs with passion and sexual desire. Both Vicky and Laura see physical attraction in the men with whom they associate. Even Father O'Malley takes on a physical attraction which neither he nor Vicky can resist. The attraction is intensified by the fact that Father O'Malley has been told by the Church that he is going to leave the reservation in two days and go back to Marquette University to teach history and finish the work on his Ph.D. degree. He is to be replaced by a young, half-thoughtless blond anthropologist who shoots around the reservation on his motorcycle and breaks Indian tradition by insisting that they tell him of their customs and habits. Vicky too has decided that she must leave her job and go back to the law firm in Denver from which she departed some years ago and reassume a position they have offered her.

The passions have intensified to the breaking point. Vicky shoots and kills the male history professor from the University of Colorado who had slain the two female historians. Being driven home by O'Malley Vicky invites him in to spend the night. Gripping John's hand "so hard he could feel the tiny pinch of her nails against his palm" she says, "I don't want to be alone tonight, John." Deeply attracted he sees the world as a land in which only the two of them matter: "He let his hand remain in hers. He didn't say anything for a long time, guiding the Bronco with his other hand into the vastness of the plains. The mountains rose ahead, massive black shadows. They might have been the only people in the world, he thought, except for the headlights dancing intermittently in the rearview mirror. Several minutes passed. 'I'm going to take you to Aunt Rose,' he said" (247).

Throughout the earlier stories the sexual tension between Vicky and Father O'Malley had been building almost to the searing point. Here it has passed that divide. The story ends with Vicky leaving for Denver to rejoin the legal firm. Ironically, Father O'Malley has been granted a reprieve and will stay on at the reservation because the Indians have written the home office that he is indispensable. In future stories, Coel will have to find some excuse to get Vicky back to the reservation because the two must work together. She will also be faced with the opened secret that their physical attraction is virtually irresistible. A new wrinkle has been added to the series.

Coel's works then, though few in number, are the very essence of Arapaho culture and life. Readers of the series can only look forward to a continuation of the adventures of Father O'Malley and the equally fascinating Vicky Holden working in a fascinating Indian culture faithfully presented.

Mardi Oakley Medawar

Mardi Oakley Medawar writes Native American historical mysteries about the Kiowa of the plains of Texas in what must be called gentle, internal, psychological revelation of crime and investigation among generally peaceful Indians. Her approach and accomplishments are new and considerable. She uses all the ingredients of a crime novel—the crime, the investigation, and the final expose of the guilty person—in a locality not unlike the conventional Golden Age crime novel, but in an Indian setting. There is a side to the novels that is most unusual. Medawar's style is fluid and edge-rounded. Even the scenes of violence lack the usual sharp graphics of such behavior. Hers is a feminine prose that makes for gentle reading, something like strolling through a flower garden that is speckled with some weeds, and touched by a poetic and soft wind that removes the slings and arrows of life. Yet the action she describes flows through the Kiowa culture and reveals what a tribe is, why these particular Native Americans act the way they act, and what their lives mean in the flow of mankind's existence.

In the following example, taken from her second novel, which reveals a great deal about Medawar's style and method, a group of herders, thinking they have seen a witch in the form of a raven, build a fire to summon others to their aid. Owl Man has just been offended by the rude behavior of his companions but pays the offense no mind:

> Owl Man was not offended. He stood quietly beside me as he and I listened. Listening, I learned, as we all did, about the boys seeing a woman transform into a raven. Seeing that, the herders ran off to their homes. At first light, the fathers of the boys came back to check on the abandoned herds. Many voices spoke excitedly, and I quickly discovered that when one is robbed of sight, the other senses immediately hone themselves to a fine edge. The air was so crisp that it carried every voice. I easily recognized each speaker as if that person were speaking directly to me. But the most incredible thing was that visualizing the speaker helped me hear through what was being said. I was able to read the tone much more precisely than I would have been able to read an impression. (*Witch of the Palo Duro* 52)

Although these novels are primarily Native American crime fiction, they are also clearly intended to serve, at least tangentially, as a reminder of the white people's view of and mistreatment of the Native American, and their reaction to the lives they are forced to lead. Medawar states explicitly her purpose in an "Author's Note" appended to *Witch of the Palo Duro* and *Death at Rainy Mountain*. She writes that she has used real names for the majority of her characters, "and this work is based on the actual lives of these very men. I have done this intentionally. On too many occasions their names have been misused, their extraordinary lives distorted. I am only a storyteller. As such it is not my responsibility to right a plethora of wrongs. But during the course of telling a story, I can give my people back their heroes. I can restore to these heroes their names" *(Witch; Death)*.

Throughout both books she also tries to correct wrong impressions whites have about the Kiowa. At the beginning of *Death at Rainy Mountain* she says: "We Kiowa have never lived as the white man has portrayed us, in big groups, in a gigantic village sprawling across the prairie. It's a very romantic notion, but stupid" (2). She points out the impracticality of such grouping: various bands and subbands with individual chiefs who were fractious and easy to rile against one another; pollution of water supply; vulnerability of whole tribes to enemies. She describes the Kiowa persons and their religion:

> Compared to the Comanches, we Kiowa are a tall people. I suppose it's because we Kiowa were created differently from other men. Every nation has its own genesis, this is ours. Our beginning name was Kwu'da. It means pulling up out. Our religion, like our life structure, is complicated, but the basis is this. The creator, Saynday, called the Kiowa out of the hollow world by striking a stick against a huge hollow log. With each strike a Kiowa person emerged. We are forest people, literally born from a tree, which is why trees are sacred to us and why we were much taller and more complexioned than our friends the Comanche." (*Witch* 30)

Medawar's first novel in this two-book series, *Death at Rainy Mountain*, illustrates effectively the line she is to follow in both. The setting is the "verdant land just above the Red River" in Texas. It was in the summer seasons of 1866, after Little Bluff, who "had been responsible for keeping an independent, furiously stubborn people, lacking even the basic understanding of the term *compromise*, united as a single race" (1), died and all the Kiowa met at Rainy Mountain for his funeral.

In this fractious group Medawar introduces all kinds of people, male and female, their attitudes and actions, psychological drives and hangups. Her main character is Tay-bodal, an Indian name meaning, as Medawar makes clear without any belligerence, "Meat-Carrier" (the hindend portion of the buffalo, no less), translated into vernacular American as "horse's ass." He often manages to behave in a manner befitting the name. Deprived of his family in his early twenties, Tay-bodal has remained a loner, like his father. He followed his father as eagle catcher, and loved to play with plant and herbs. He has always wanted to stay apart from others, and this inclination has been assisted by a society at large who found his looks, his character, and his inclination to be a medical doctor somewhat off-putting.

The other characters are The Cheyenne Robber, Tay-bodal's friend and hero, who is accused of murdering Coyote Walking, his love and wife. Among numerous other characters who provide comedy is Tay-bodal's newly acquired wife, Crying Wind, a widow with a four-year-old son who decides that Tay-bodal is beautiful and worthy of becoming her husband. She is easily stirred to jealousy, flightiness, impetuosity, and lust. The combination drives her into comical situations and actions.

The plot of the novel revolves around succession in leadership, now that Little Bluff is dead. His death at a ripe old age unleashes several ambitious men who want to become his successor. The Cheyenne Robber is a logical choice but he is accused of murder. Tay-bodal gives himself five days to prove his friend The Robber innocent, but takes only three. By careful medical evidence, what we in white society would call forensic evidence, on the day of Bluff's funeral, Tay-bodal proves that The Robber could not have committed the murder. The scene and book close in Indian paradise for Tay-bodal and his bride, though, as we see from the next book, with Crying Wind a state of bliss is always subject to the storms of change.

We see the change in *Witch of the Palo Duro*. This book begins years after the earlier one had ended. Medawar had used *Mountain* to outline the Kiowa nation, a tribe of four hundred people in ten groups. In this second book she is interested in continuing the development of Kiowa culture and customs.

The Palo Duro is a deep canyon north of the Red River in Texas in which mists cloud all visibility, causing the credulous to believe witches live and work there. When The Cheyenne Robber mysteriously disappears many think that a witch has caught him. Tay-bodal, of course, knows better. The disappearance is linked to a complex domestic situation where one girl-woman is causing all kinds of trouble to The Robber. She is killed, and Tay-bodal must find the murderer to clear The Robber. He does, of course, with his usual medical and human insights. Medawar ends the novel with an outside interview with Tay-bodal, now grown old, which indicates that the old man has told the story from his distant past and which "seems" to end the series at two books.

Ravens are important characters in Kiowa legend as with all other Indian tribes. Raven plays an important part in his novel. At first accused of murdering a horse, it is proved innocent of any part in the slaughter. Instead the killer of the horse was a human being, a Shape shifter that had a purpose for the sacrifice: "Shape shifters need a powerful sacrifice before they can work the Dark Way power." Shape shifters, which can be male or female, in the light of day, must "return to their true identity. It is in the light of day when a shape shifter is vulnerable and can be destroyed" (53).

This second novel is more successful than *Death at Rainy Mountain.* It has more tradition to build on and the author's tone is surer as she spends more time developing the story than in creating the rather heavy atmosphere of its predecessor.

Medawar's third novel, *Murder at Medicine Lodge,* swings to a new conflict, this time between Indians and whites. In 1867 the Kiowa, Comanche, Arapaho, Apache, and Cheyenne rendezvoused at Medicine Lodge, Kansas, to meet with representatives of the U.S. government to sign peace treaties. Tay-bodal, along with his wife and son, goes with his tribe. There the tribal members immediately start bickering among themselves and with the U.S. Army officials. The bugler turns up missing and is found on the prairie murdered. The Army immediately suspects one of the Indians. Tay-bodal finally works through the skein of leading and misleading evidence to find the real killers.

Although she is just a little off the reservation of her usual subjects, Medawar makes this her finest piece of writing. She is hard on all the people, but at the same time very sympathetic and understanding of the curse of being human. She sees and describes her characters unforgettably. One of the soldiers, for example, Captain Mack, "a tall, dark, brooding man, had something of a scooped face. His brow and chin were so prominent that his profile put [Tay-bodal] in mind of a quarter moon wearing a droopy moustache and muttonchop sideburns" (154).

Medawar is at something of an impasse in the matter of language. Tay-bodal, who tells the stories in the first person, is a Kiowa who speaks only a word or two in English, therefore at times has great difficulty in understanding what is going on. The author emphasizes this linguistic fault line by at times having Tay-bodal and the other Indians try to speak or understand English words, always with laughable, sometimes nearly catastrophic, results. For example, they pronounce the proper name Harrison as "Hawkeye" and paper as "paa-pass." Yet as Tay-bodal tells the story, apparently in Kiowa, he is almost poetic, at one point describing an area as "pristine." When Tay-bodal is writing the story he does so clearly, cleanly, and poetically. When he moves to the tricky business of explaining how the various Indian languages are understandably mixed with English Medawar has a little trouble but succeeds.

In *Murder at Medicine Lodge*, when Medawar turned Tay-bodal into an elderly man, it seemed that she had reached the point where she would have to kill him off. But in fact she had apparently maneuvered herself and him into a new way of telling a story—a kind of time warp, Alice in the Looking Glass approach by distancing the storyteller from the event by a near-lifetime. She places a time-distance between the event and the disclosure of the guilty party, and by doing so washes away most of the passion and excitement from the detection and makes punishment of the criminal of less significance. In her method of achieving the return to the reality in her fourth novel, *The Ft. Larned Incident* achieves considerable success.

Tay-bodal gets up one morning tired and dispirited. He drags himself to the mirror and looks at his old, time-lined face and thinks of the past. As he gazes at himself his face slowly dematerializes and turns into the face of his youth. He undergoes a mysterious experience, the thought of which used to frighten him but now offers comfort. The mist of change of reality forms on the mirror and Tay-bodal's face as he gazes. "This mist was not like the kind that comes whenever cold air meets warm. The mist was more like smoke. It moved. It swirled. And in the center of this movement, a face formed" (3). The face is, of course, his own. The rejuvenation of youth rattles him with joy and expectation of the pleasure of reliving a part of his past: "And I was so very glad to see him. So glad that I was nearing crazy with happy, as my wife used to say. That young man's specter slowly dominated the glass. I knew that I, the old man that I am, still existed, but what I prayed, and mightily, was that the young man now gazing steadily back at me would stay for as long as possible"(3).

The portion of his former life that he remembers is less dramatic and crime-ridden than in her earlier stories. This is mostly a domestic romance, in which love, happiness, and Indian harmony are replaced by rancor and fighting between Tay-bodal and his wife, Crying Wind. For no real reason at all, Tay-bodal thinks his wife does not love him anymore and goes into exile, in the Indian fashion living apart from one's spouse and thus constituting divorce. Neighbor Indians become suspicious of Tay-bodal and Crying Wind and of their own spouses. They suspect and come to dislike their children because of imagined wrongs. Wives have illegitimate children. The extended Indian family is threatened.

The heroes of earlier books play diminished roles. Skywalker is still the wise man but is less important than he used to be. He plays only a peripheral role. The Cheyenne Robber, such a dominant figure in earlier stories, has almost no role at all. He is a seducer of all women, especially wives, and is stabbed and nearly killed. Crying Wind and Tay-bodal discover the error of their suspicions and are reunited in the retold story. But as the account shifts back to the real world—back out of the mirror of remembrance—she is dead and only a few of the old group still survive.

Tay-bodal gets them all together, and in a conventional Classical Detective denouement he clarifies the old mystery and points out the guilty. It turns out that loose sex and envy and impotence among the men had finally fired one woman to become the murderer of the man who was playing around with Crying Wind.

With this new approach to storytelling Medawar still makes her book interesting and informative. With her gentle prose she recounts daily Indian life in a style that almost colors it bleached-white, flaunting sex and seduction and the ways a community copes with these transgressions. Having developed her new working method of flashback storytelling, Medawar leaves Tay-bodal alive and though old, as garrulous as ever. All in all Medawar is one of the finer storytellers in Indian crime fiction, with a gentleness yet thoroughness all her own.

The story is a closed-community Indian affair and has nothing to do with Indian-white conflict or injustice. Intrusion of the white world comes only in the geography. But that and the accounts of Indian life instruct whites in what Indian life used to be and still is.

Peter Bowen

In a literature whose characters sometime look like a parade of freaks, each needs some distinguishing feature that will make him or her unforgettable. Peter Bowen's do. Gabriel Du Pré is a Métis Indian whose clothes consist of "High moccasins and Red River sash and hat, the doe skin pants and the loose shirt and leatherjacket, buffalo with the fleece in" (*Wolf, No Wolf* 19). His companion, a Métis lady named Madelaine, is always picturesque. In *Notches* (58) Bowen describes both Du Pré's and her appearance, Du Pré's first:

> Bright red shirt with black piping and fiddles over the pockets made of porcupine quills. The shirt was heavy silk. Du Pré picked it up. A red silk Métis sash was folded underneath. Fiddles on that, too, and DU PRÉ on the back in black beads. Very fine beads. Two circles on each side with coyotes howling at yellow moons on them. Du Pré felt something crinkle in the sash's pocket, on an end that hung down. He fished out a dollar bill.

She is even more exotic in appearance:

> Madelaine came out of the bathroom. She was wearing a heavy tur-
> quoise silk/satin shirt with yellow flowers embroidered on it in fine
> beads, a long yellow skirt, and yellow cowboy boots. Her rings were all
> turquoise and silver and coral.

Du Pré inspects cattle brands seared onto the rear ends of livestock.
He is often called upon to double as peace officer because the small law
force of Toussaint, Montana, is often overwhelmed. Du Pré, though
loud in trying to refuse to help law and order, once his moral indignation is raised is obsessed with routing out lawbreakers and cultural
degenerates. Madelaine generally acts as Du Pré's sounding board and
governor of his rage. But she is lusty and pragmatic, and her sense of
outrage once it has been released, as we will see in *Notches,* is virtually
wild and uncontrollable. These two are joined by an aged mystic named
Benetsee, who appears and disappears mysteriously and often unnoticed. He is criticized by Du Pré or Madelaine for being wherever he is
or is not. But they cannot get along without his help. He is, in every
sense, the spirit in their adventures.

These three and with several other strong characters who play important roles in Bowen's stories form the nucleus of people inhabiting
Bowen's books.

Both Madelaine and Gabriel are Métis, whom Du Pre describes in
these terms:

> We the voyageurs. Some French they come, Scot, Irish, all them Cath-
> olic, with the Black Robes, them Jesuits. Very tough priests, them Jes-
> uits. And they marry indians and here we are. Some of us, we live on the
> reservations, some of us don't, most of us are gone, part of what Amer-
> ica mostly is, you know. Indians call us white, whites call us Indians. So
> we are the peacemakers, catch all the shit from everybody. (*Wolf* 35)

Du Pré is uninhibited in what he has to say and the language he uses
with everyone. Madelaine is the rhetorical mirror image though because
Du Pré is forty-eight years old and apparently more than normally lust-
ful she devotes half her talk to teasing him sexually, talking about sex in
general in the most explicit language. He responds in kind. So generally
being around them is to be in the midst of heated rhetorical innuendo
where the main concern is sensual. But no matter how violently Du Pré
talks and how sexual their language, both are fine citizens — though Du
Pré would rather say "fine Métis," since he has little respect for the

white world because the people do not practice the Métis morality and because they believe in the now and present-day. Du Pré hates all aspects of the world that are contemporary.

With these characters in his society, Bowen creates literary *persona* who are compelling and quaint. His storytelling is discontinuous and disjointed and therefore requires close attention. Because the Métis are not quite in the mainstream of American society and rhetoric, their vernacular, as is illustrated in the quote above, like the genuine vernacular of the Louisiana Cajuns, is somewhat peculiar and different. Métis expressions sound different, with omission of prepositions and other connectives, but generally is understandable.

Bowen calls it Montana language. Personally and linguistically he is fiercely Montanan. As author he writes what he pleases, he says, and if readers don't appreciate the stories, that is really no concern of his, though it undoubtedly is to his publisher, now St. Martin's Press. He writes quickly, spending only ten working days on each novel. He says that when he is proofing his stories, he reads them as though for the first time. He complicates his communication with his style of narration other than speech patterns. When he is writing description or internal dialogue he follows through with the Métis style of thinking and talking. Sometimes when he is advancing his story, Bowen writes standard English. But with no sign to the reader he may switch to Métis vernacular and carry on in a kind of stream-of-Métis rhetoric that is a little misleading until the reader retraces his steps and shifts gears from one language to the other. His novels consist of hard-driving stories played out by quaint characters, and those stories, though they may appear less important than the sharply developed characters, who are not so much described as allowed to develop, not so much analyzed as allowed to unfold themselves, are to Bowen of the utmost importance.

Peter Bowen, like Jake Page studied elsewhere in this book, is a man with a varied background. As noted, he has been a carpenter, a barkeep, a cowboy, and a fishing-and-hunting guide. He has also dabbled for a short period in the creative writing program at the University of Montana. He has published three Yellowstone Kelly novels not discussed in this study. So he, like Page, brings knowledge and skills and experience from several genres outside the novel. Perhaps because of this wide experience they are fired by a fierce democratic point of view and a demonstrated irreverence for canons and conventions. He is proud of being a Montanan and stands straight and tall, so much an independent person that his mailing address is General Delivery.

Each Bowen novel is a book with a single purpose, a solo intent. Sometimes this purpose is clearly stated. At other times it dissolves into a general discussion about Métis culture. At times it disappears into Métis symbolism that is difficult to understand. But if the book is to be clearly comprehended the ending needs to be caught.

Coyote Wind is the vigorous first novel in the Du Pré series. It is set in small-town Montana, among the Métis. Bart Fascelli's brother, Gianni, was killed by Du Pré's father, Catfoot, because he ruined one of Catfoot's women. But this murder was long ago and has not been solved. As the book opens a skull with a bullet hole through it is found alongside the bodies of two people just killed in a plane crash. Du Pré becomes virtually obsessed with finding out whose is the third skull, since it obviously had not resulted from the plane crash, and who put the bullet hole through him. When he finds that the man was Bart's brother and the murderer was his, Du Pré's, father, Du Pré tells Bart, to whom the news is interesting but the murder justified. Bart, who is indolent and immensely wealthy from a source not revealed, becomes close friends with Du Pré and Madelaine, and the children of both from former marriages, and is very free with dispensing his wealth. He and Du Pré rant against the English who hated the Métis and chased them from their Canadian homeland.

Du Pré is an anti-hero and wants nothing to do with being a hero. He really wants to be left alone so that he can inspect livestock's rear ends and be with Madelaine. Bowen's novels are single-purposed. Although they are filled with the vitality of a whole culture, at the end Bowen wants to make his point, and generally he does, though sometimes more to his own satisfaction than that of the average reader. Bowen ends this first novel with Du Pré's resignation about the affairs of man: "My father a murderer and your brother needed killing and I am very tired of this" (154). He then turns away and starts whistling "Baptiste's Lament," an old Métis folksong, and Bowen turns his camera toward the sky and says simply, "Many stars above." It is a quiet resignation or perhaps desperation but Bowen seems to be saying that when all else fails one can return through music to the culture and the realization that with the mean people killed there is hope for the future.

In this first novel in the series Bowen sets the background for most of his characters. Du Pré knows all the Métis songs, is an excellent fiddler and plays often. He is a drunkard, but faithfully Catholic. Madelaine is here more vulgar and earthy and profane than she is in the later books.

In *Specimen Song,* his second novel, Bowen shows his disgust with white society and preference for the Métis's backwoods existence. Du Pré is attending a Smithsonian Folklife Festival in Washington, D.C., featured to play Métis songs. He has been invited by a Smithsonian director named Paul Chase, who is an egomaniac and nut (like most of the people in Washington). Du Pré meets and talks with Louisiana Cajuns and discovers that they are really soul mates. He gets out of Washington as fast as possible, but not before one of the Indians who has been helping out in the Festival is murdered. He is subsequently invited by Chase to go on an expedition that will retrace a portion of the old fur-trade route through Saskatchewan and Manitoba for the "voyageurs and trappers of the Company of Gentlemen of Hudson's Bay, or the Hudson's Bay Company, or the Here Before Christ" (15).

After first declining the invitation, Du Pré accepts the trip, which turns out to be long and cold. A murderer stalks the group. He might be from the Quebec power company, which wants to dam the Red River against the wishes of the Indians in order to generate electricity. The murderer turns out to be one of the Indians with the party. After a long search and finally running him down in upstate New York, Du Pré causes his death by hitting him with a rock from a slingshot and the Indian falls off a log and breaks his neck.

Bart develops from his indolence into a decent and lively individual who goes to Washington, meets and falls in love with Michelle, a big, busty detective on the D.C. police force who is just as earthy as Madelaine in language and outlook, though just a little more sophisticated. Maria, Du Pré's youngest daughter, is turned from a worthless hippy into a very determined young lady whose education at a prestigious college is going to be paid by Bart. She saves her father's life when he has his final showdown with Lucky, the Indian who stalked the canoe trip and who has now been run to the ground. The point is that Lucky kills because he likes to kill. Du Pré hates people who like to kill. When he has killed Lucky, Du Pré consoles himself: "What do I got to say? Du Pré thought. I kill that sack of puke and don't give a shit for the opinions of no one at all in the matter" (278). The ending is complete and well crafted.

Wolf, No Wolf is Bowen's strongest and most direct statement about a subject to date. This book is about the war between the environmentalists and the ranchers over how the west should be used. The environmentalists say it should be restored in natural life to the condition it was in when the Indians lived there. The ranchers claim that they have been living there and grazing government land for over a hundred years and it is therefore their right to dictate how the land should be used.

The book begins with two environmentalist teenagers coming in and cutting the ranchers' fences to let the cows out on the range and then shoot them. In turn the two are found shot dead. Then eight more environmentalists are found murdered up in the mountains.

Du Pré is sympathetic with the wishes of the ranchers. His people have been living around there since being chased into the Dakotas after the British excluded the people who spoke French from Canada. He knows that both sides think they have valid arguments for their point of view but he knows that somebody is going to get hurt.

Bart Fascelli, against his will, becomes sheriff, Du Pré remains his helper. The FBI sends in a local agent, named Corey Banning, a foul-mouthed big independent woman who has lived all her life in Montana. She knows the desires of the ranchers but also her obligation as an FBI agent. She speaks the language of both parties and seems to be getting along with both, possibly bringing peace to the warring factions. But she is blasted away in her car. To replace her another FBI Special Agent is sent in. He understands the situation but is determined to reestablish law and order.

Although Du Pré hates the actions of the environmentalists he is first of all a kind-hearted humanitarian. When a group of eight skiers goes skiing on Wolf Mountain he warns them that avalanches are about to destroy everything in their way . They go nevertheless. At the last moment Du Pré rushes out to try to save them, only to be caught in an avalanche with the only girl he can possibly save. Both are buried for hours under the packed snow, and the girl's body is lost. Du Pré manages to save himself.

It turns out that the environmentalists have been killed by two ranching brothers, arrogant and determined to maintain the way of life that their forefathers had lived. They will kill anybody trying to take from them what they think they rightfully own. When Du Pré and the FBI are closing in on the pair, one takes his own life, and the other comes to Du Pré, confesses the murders and threatens Du Pré in such a way that Du Pré has to shoot him.

Du Pré actually admires and respects the brothers not because of what they have done but because of their courage. They are brave, "like Indians," and there can be no greater praise or respect than that. Du Pré says the brothers have a lot of Indian blood in them.

The ending of the book reveals how Bowen has brought Du Pré to the point where he represents and speaks for the old West. Despite the killing of all the wolves that have been released so far, the environmentalists bring in another group by helicopter and release them in the mountains. Determined that these shall not live there but apparently not wanting them killed, Du Pré loads a group of heavy, fifty-pound wolf traps and heads to the mountains to trap the animals. Speaking for all the people in the West and also for himself as their control, Du Pré says: "You know, this is my land here. And I like them wolf all right. And when I am ready they can come back" (*Wolf* 213).

Notches, Bowen's next work, takes Du Pré into another world, more in touch with the everyday life of whites. Young women, mostly prostitutes, are turning up dead along the interstate highways, mostly skeletons eaten by coyotes and ravens into a nonidentifiable state when found. Du Pré is outraged at the murders and the inability of anyone to catch the perpetrators and put an end to the crimes. Then Madelaine's daughter runs away from home and is feared murdered. She is, however, brought back home and delivered safe to her mother's arms by a young cross-country truck driver named Rolly Simpson. After picking the young lady up on the highway, Rolly had gone out of his way to see that she got home safe and sound. He is impressively handsome, looking like the perfect candidate for truck driver of the year award.

As it turns out there are two serial killers working the highways, one on the East-West Hi-Line run and one on the North-South road. Through means not quite clear to the reader Du Pré, after disposing of the East-West killer, concludes correctly that the North-South killer is Rolly. Through a telephone call stating another purpose for the meeting of the two, Du Pré sets Rolly up to be killed. The two meet at a rest stop, and as Rolly steps down out of his eighteen wheeler thinking Du Pré wants a friendly conference, Du Pré pulls his pistol and threatens to shoot him. After a little talk, the magazine from Du Pré's pistol drops to the ground, Rolly jumps into his truck and drives away, but five miles later the truck explodes. Apparently in the action, somehow Du Pré had planted a time explosive in the truck that resulted in a collision and an explosion. Badly burned, Rolly is taken to the hospital and eventually recovers, though he had to have his arm amputated.

The book ends with an inexplicable twist. Du Pré visits Rolly in the hospital, and while there Madelaine paints Rolly's face and apparently inducts him into the Métis society. When he is released they have another festive meeting, apparently the best of friends now that Rolly has paid a certain price for all the murders he has committed. Du Pré says that he hates serial killers, who "ain't human." But such murders are apparently more acceptable if involving only prostitutes. After all Rolly did not murder Madelaine's daughter. It is a strange, horrible, and inconclusive ending, explicable only with some kind of conclusion that some things are more valuable than murder. Du Pre explains his behavior by saying that Madelaine's loved ones are safe. It is at best a narrow sense of societal justice and protection entirely personal for Bowen and perhaps a Montana sense of justice.

In the next book, *Thunder Horse*, Bowen changes to a theme almost ever-present in Native American fiction, archaeology and environmental degradation. A Japanese consortium has bought Le Doux Springs, an idyllic pond on land next to Bart's vast holdings. The consortium people say they want to develop the spring as a tourist trout stream. But because of the spring's location and because he does not trust the Japanese, Bart suspects that they want to develop some kind of outlandish tourist attraction and ruin the land.

In the preliminary digging for the Japanese, Bart exposes some archaeological ruins, a large fossil tooth, of Tyrannosaurus Rex. Two archaeologists are brought in to examine the tooth and the rest of the archaeological ruins. One is a good guy, the other bad. It turns out that the tooth has been stolen from the museum in Billings. One of the archaeologists, the nasty one, is murdered. To help in the research a ninety-three-year-old archaeologist is brought in as a consultant. Du Pré is caught by a group of Indians, blindfolded and taken to a secret cave of the Crow tribe, former allies of the Métis. There he meets an old man, learns of the dinosaur bones and is released. Knowing the full story of the T. Rex bones, Du Pré returns home, catches and kills two of the Indians who had formerly attacked him, but does not kill a third member of their group, a worthless man who has tried a dozen jobs and failed in all.

As *Notches* had ended somewhat off the point with some kind of off-center symbol, *Thunder Horse*'s conclusion is even more enigmatic but makes its point. Le Doux Springs, after having been temporarily diverted by an earthquake, returns to its clear, cold water and fills up deep and symbolic. Du Pré, Madelaine, and Burdette, an outsider character, strip down to their underwear and dive into it, alongside Benetsee, the Indian mystic, who is already there. The water is so cold they can stay in only a minute, but that is long enough for the swimmers to get the message and Bowen to transmit the point to us. This is the land and the spring of the Horned Star People, also called the Red Sailors, in other words water people. Now that the land has been saved from the outside exploiters, it is again the land of the Horned Star People. It has been preserved for them and they are at least symbolically reanimated. As the four people climb out of the cold water, Benetsee "pointed down where the water shimmered. A red skull looked up, the eye pits deep and black with time. The skull moved a little." Thus it acknowledges the good deed of the living Métis and the rejuvenated life of the tribe. Recognizing the rebirth of their ancestors, the swimmers celebrate joyously. "They laughed and laughed and then they made for shore" (243).

Long Son (grandson), is Bowen's style and approach carried to its extreme. As usual the story is placed near Toussaint, Montana, where Larry Messner, the son of one of the oldest ranching families, decides in the end to auction off his remaining cattle and household belongings and apparently leave the area for good. This closing of the book on this chapter in Montana ranching opens another in the past of the Messner clan that includes several unexplained deaths. When Larry Messner himself is murdered, Du Pré is labeled as the killer by the gang of obvious thugs who have lived around and off Messner. When the FBI joins in the investigation of Messner's murder, Du Pré agrees to help them, as much to save his own scalp as to ferret out the real murderer. Messner's intended exit from Toussaint and death are explained by his involvement in drug trafficking and the risks always involved.

This novel differs considerably from Bowen's other ones. Here the author is more concerned with developing atmosphere and character than in telling a story. Madelaine and Gabriel, for example, often sit around in the bar-cafe and talk, often with the owner and other customers. Bowen seems awed by the power of words. They flow from the mouths of the characters in a stream as unending as the Montana wind. But the gusts are shorter and choppier, Bowen using the comma to serve as prepositions, periods, and other elisions.

Take for example the compression in this sentence: "Good place to camp, had water and cover and wood, plums would have grown in the draw, good for making pemmican, and there were good places for riflemen to guard the paths" (238), or this enigmatic explanation by the mysterious Benetsee about one's strange behavior: "Get lost, the graveyard. . . . It is next the church, he don't see it, though" (243).

There is also a major change in the characters involved. The usual standbys Bart and Benetsee have their roles reduced to minimal involvement. A fascinating and powerful character named Ripper is brought in to serve as Du Pré's strong left hand. In an unusual development for Bowen, *Long Son* becomes a kind of children's story. Here more than before, Du Pré is overwhelmed by the fecundity of his own children and those of Madelaine—all from former marriages. There are children all around his feet, in his arms, and on the backs of all other adults. Du Pré takes much time off his adult masculine activities to play with the numerous children stirring around, to tell them folktales, and to sing folksongs to them. Another of the amusing new participants is an owl—perhaps we could call it a fleeting character—which in a collision has been knocked out and blinded in one eye. Du Pré and the kids nurse the owl back to health and since it cannot be self-supporting in the wild keep it around and feed it. Both kids and Du Pré are amused when the owl begins eating up the cat population and destroys a big bull snake.

Long Son ends not in a circular development that ties all things together but in an enigmatic line that leads into new territory. These darts into the wild blue yonder point out how easily novels dealing with mysticism, especially the mysticism of Native Americans, can lead to symbols that stretch the imagination of readers not themselves a part of the tradition the symbols inform. But the messages carried by those symbols are well worth the necessary unraveling of the language in which they are presented. Bowen's single-message novels are entertaining journeys with the statement at the end a kind of independent, solitary affirmation of the old ways of life of America's early citizens.

Ash Child, to the contrary, is a yet another kind of book, and is probably Bowen's most complicated and successful novel to date. It is his resolution of the protests, especially against environmentalists and other do-gooders, especially those in the eastern United States, that have gone on for years.

In this novel, Montana is ablaze, the fires set, although the firefighters do not know it, by drug traffickers who have come in from such places as Chicago and made Billings their western capital. Intentionally or unintentionally the fires they have set with their bombs threaten to burn Du Pré's little town of Toussaint and its favorite saloon-cafe and the society it represents. The havoc they have unleashed threatens to destroy the Western civilization as it pushes the citizens farther and farther toward the obscured sun: "The sky was white and hazy, and the sun yellow and vague" (11). The blazes climb ever higher up the mountains and down the valleys. In combating the holocaust it is a battle between age and experience, and aggressive and irresponsible profit-making and self-indulgent youth.

Finally the combatants are driven to the top of magic Wolf Mountain, the symbol of the gods and of the past. There they encounter the leader of the drug cult, who is performing her ritual to the cacophony of weird chants and dances. Having overcome the enchantress Du Pré and Madelaine are rescued by a helicopter and take the woman and the man she has killed down the mountain back to the saloon.

Readers of this book will find that Bowen has changed or modified his attitude in several ways. He is still very much against the drug-infested East and their pollution of his West. But the government in Washington is combating the evil with the FBI, DEA, and other agencies, and for once is doing the right thing.

But the East is still the origin of evil and the West the center of the good of the past and tradition. *Ash Child* is a combination of mystery wrapped by symbol and sealed in mythology and magic. The animal world is close: the porcupine is the Ash Child, which moves, though slowly, away from fires. The coyote, with its superior wisdom and intuition, is always just out of vision singing his songs, but always possessing superior wisdom: at the end of the book Madelaine puts a coyote tooth around Du Pré's neck as a symbol of protection. The magical wraith-man Benetsee, now at least three hundred years old, is an even more mysterious spiritual-earthly creature.

The book ends in an optimistic reversal of the gloom of the burning west. The fire has been put out and the East and West joined in one world: "The Great Plains rolled away to the east, the horizon purple in the sun. Harmony and safety all round" (209).

Readers of this book will find the symbols and language a little more difficult to interpret than usual. The humor, however, is Bowenesque and obvious. The novel begins with Du Pré in the hospital recovering from a ruptured appendix that he waited too long to report to the doctor. As he is recovering, his friend Booger Tom comes in and hands him the HOLY BIBLE, which gurgles when Du Pré holds it up to look inside. A Ph.D. in psychology comes out from Washington, calls herself "Phud" and says that all people with this degree don't like others with it because they are competition. J. Edgar Hoover, says the Ph.D. psychologist, "is our founding fascist" (45).

The novel ends on two high notes of superiority. After the fire is extinguished, everybody who had fought it—hundreds of professionals and amateurs—assemble at the Toussaint Saloon where they have a songfest and festival far superior to that at Woodstock years earlier and end it with the "Coyote Fire Song" in a return to the ways of the past. "The Music," said Madelaine, "it is pret' good."

Such is the story and the triumph and promise of Bowen's West.

J. F. Trainor

Indian life is sometimes portrayed in crime fiction in a dazzle of action that reveals a great deal of Indian culture as background and setting for the character of the hero. Sometimes the actions are larger than the culture in which the protagonist works. With J. F. Trainor both are developed and displayed in a way that is a positive commentary on the Indian culture as well as on the development of a truly unusual and extraordinary character, a female giant incorporating the characteristics of Don Quixote, the Lone Ranger, and the Spirit of the West, all in all a spoof of all the nonsense about the Frontier West that has inspired and directed American and world culture for 250 years. All this is personified in a mixedblood female who for her own purposes writes her version of the laws and straddles lawry and outlawry as she desires. She is a delightful and awesome figure.

Joseph F. Trainor, who sometimes teaches in the adult education program at Brown University, writes of a forceful, imaginative, inventive, larger-than-life heroine named Angela Biwaban, a feisty Anishinabe princess from Duluth, Minnesota. Anishinabe was the correct name of the Chippewa before whites changed the name into Chippewa. The Chippewa or Ojibwa are Indians of the Eastern woodlands and plains with an Algonquin language stock. Though Trainor does not give a complete background of the Ojibwa he does explain in considerable detail the background and nature of the people in the person of Angela Biwaban.

She is twenty-eight years old, unmarried, and stands five-feet-four-inches, though with her energy and wit she at times seems to stretch to at least seven feet. She is well equipped for the many roles she plays in her adventures. She describes herself in these words:

> Well, if you took Crystal Gayle and painted her copper-brown, trimmed that long, sleek hair a bit, stretched those well-shaped legs, added a quarter-inch of meat to the shoulders and fanny, and upgraded that class orthodonture into a truly dazzling four-hundred-watt smile, well, that's me, folks. Crystal and I even share the same contralto voice.

Trouble is, whenever I sing, I sound like a sick buffalo calf—which is why I'm here in Utah and not in Nashville. (*Dynamite Pass* 8)

In all books she is faced with adversities that only a clever person could survive. Her adversaries are powerful and deadly men who think nothing of snuffing out a life. In addition, she has what can only be called domestic troubles concerning herself and her extended family. She was convicted of embezzling $300,000 and sentenced to three years in the South Dakota Correctional Facility, where prison personnel and life in general were unpleasant. Released, she has been assigned a parole officer, Paul Holbrook, to whom she must report in person or by telephone once a month. With her active lifestyle she often forgets or is unable to force herself to make that report. Consequently her parole officer, with whom she may be in love and he with her, is always harassing and threatening her. These threats, however, are tame compared with the others she receives, not life-threatening, just freedom-cramping. She is called by her aunt, "the avenging debutante" (*High Country Murder* 3), and she does not suffer injustice and threats to herself lightly. But there are two sides to her.

Her grandfather Charles Blackbear reads Angela and her actions directly and accurately. "You don't fool anyone, young lady," he tells her. "You really enjoy this Lone Ranger business." To which she replies, with an impish smile, "Well, I am rather good at it." When the Chief compares her to Nero Wolfe, she is disdainful. "*Nero Wolfe*. . . . That old couch potato wouldn't have lasted five minutes up on Grizzly Peak," where she combated freezing weather and a cold-blooded killer (*High Country Murder* 388). In Native American crime and action fiction, the fat brownstone effete ratiocinative flower-grower does not fare well in comparison, as he would not in real life. Indian crime fiction needs more useful figures for comparison than those housed in conventional stories.

Angela's extended family of both Indians and whites touches on nearly everyone she meets. One or more she generally has to help in one way or another. Her helpers are, sometimes, Paul Holbrook, and her grandfather, Charles Blackbear, who assists her through sage counsel and cautions.

Target for Murder, Trainor's first novel, begins with a full background of who and what Angie is. She lets us know straight away that she, unlike some other Native Americans, is not to be called Indian, as Holbrook mistakenly does. "I am not an Indian. I am a Native American. Indians are people who wear turbans and live in places like Varanasi and

Calcutta. They're very nice people, I'm sure, but I'm not one of them."
When Holbrook corrects himself and calls her a Chippewa, again
Angie does a little teaching: "There is no such thing as a Chippewa.
That's a nonsense word invented by white people who were too lazy to
learn our language. Our name is Anishinabe, and it means people" (8).

On her doorstep one day appears her oldest friend, pregnant and
broke, having just been scammed out of a large tract of land by scam
artists who have forced her to swallow the loss and endure the resulting
poverty. Angie, outraged, resorts to highhanded and unusual strengths
to elude her parole officer and rebuff her friend's defrauders. The book
is high adventure among white crooks, where cheers go to the Native
American victor.

Dynamite Pass, Trainor's second book in the series, is the story of how
a white lumber company and developer try to scam the Utes out of part
of their land in northern Utah. Angie gets involved because she goes to
the site for a powwow and finds that her cousin, Bill Shavano, a Sha-
guache County forest ranger, has been found dead, his skull supposedly
crushed by a falling tree. Angie, however, learns that he had opposed a
fast land deal that would have allowed a lumber company to clear-cut
the Ute's forest, and that is why he was eliminated. In her usual thorough
way, Angie manages to stymie the deal and uncover the murderer.

The third novel in the series, *Whiskey Jack,* takes up one of the plots
constant in Native American crime fiction, environmental degradation.
Moira Grantz, an environmentalist on the West Coast, has been accused of being a Nazi and murdered. Angie, herself a fierce environmentalist, goes under cover to learn the identity of the murderers and is
almost killed in the attempt. The environmental degraders are shown
also to be sexually perverted, at least in the person of the murderer
who got a real sex thrill out of killing Moira. With the whole scheme
brought to light, the environmentalists win the case and preserve their
interests.

Number four, *Corona Blue,* has an unusual setting. Angie is operating a corn combine in a South Dakota cornfield when she plows into a
dead body in the row in front of her. She rushes off to summon the police and when she returns with them the body has disappeared and the
police will not believe that she had seen one, nor that her car windows
had been shot out by a gunman as she drove away to get them. Again,
there are people trying to force farmers off the land so that they can buy
the property for their own development. Angie, working with the farmers, thwarts the criminals and saves the land.

High Country Murder, number five, moves Angie into new, strange, and dangerous territory. Working as a secretary for the most prestigious law firm in South Dakota, she is taken by her boss, Sarah Sutton, to Denver for a conference. In Denver, Sutton starts acting strangely, giving Angie privileges and an equality she has not enjoyed in the past, and in turn arousing Angie's suspicions and apprehensions. Mysterious telephone calls and appointments have lead Angie to investigate, at the risk of her life, since she seems to be mistaken for Sutton or to need to be eliminated to clear the way for some criminal's purposes. Sutton, it develops, has a past that opens the way for murderers to begin horning in. In one of her more trying adventures Angie chases a killer from a Colorado ghost town across the Rockies until in a showdown between a killing man and a threatening nature, Angie manages to overcome the former and elude the latter.

In these five novels there is an unusual and strong message carried by the settings and the characters, Biwaban especially. She, as we have seen, is a clever and witty person who claims she will do anything to achieve her goal because despite the black legal mark against her she is deserving of greater achievements. Although resorting to every guise and manipulation to achieve her goals, Angie is really a straight arrow who skirts many obstructions to reach her desired end, which is always honorable. Her technique drives with and against the winds, dodging right and left until she reaches the heart of the problem and the solution.

In addition to admiring Angie, and the author's wit in creating her, the reader of these books learns a great deal about Anishinabe practices and culture. For example, Angie dances a prayer song: "As the others took up the prayer song, I gave my eight willow hoops a firm shake and toe-stepped into the circle's center. The step is called a *fancy,* and it's really not too hard—if you've been practicing since babyhood, that is. Bounce, bounce, sidewinding kick. Twirl to the right. Bounce, bounce, kick with the left. Twirl again" (*Pass* 9).

The novels are strengthened by Biwaban's clear and explicit tie-in with the Anishinabe tribe. Angie never lets us forget that bond. Her strength comes from her heritage. Trainor has Angie speak to someone in Anishinabe and explain the terms to the reader. Often Angie carries on a conversation in her language so that whites can't understand. Angie is also in one way or another always associating with her people or explaining why she is away from them. She is not only pro-Indian but also strongly pro-feminist. She is an amusing and appealing character.

These books are high-tension fast action that feature a Native American acting like a Native American generally against present-day whites and their law that makes her and other Native Americans vulnerable. Her actions are hardly credible because they occur on a kind of Indian Mount Olympus where only the fast and supercharged survive. But most crime fiction exists in a bubble of make-believe that requires a willing suspension of disbelief before it can be believed. If one can make that suspension here, this is Adventureland with a capital A. It is Indian mysticism grounded in very earthy characters and explained through the barrel of a gun that has a grin on its muzzle.

Aimée and David Thurlo

Aimée and David Thurlo know the craft of the novel, and they know especially well the Native Americans about whom they are now writing. As they say in a biographical note after *Second Shadow:* "Their knowledge of and pride in Native American and Hispanic peoples and their traditions are on full display" in their works. This novel is brimful of both knowledge and pride and brings full display of both to the forefront.

From the first page the novel begins to reveal the tension under which a Native American lives in a predominantly Anglo profession and community. Irene Pabikon, a beautiful Tewa Indian, is an accomplished professional architect. Although she has been urged by the elders in her pueblo to marry an Indian, settle down, and live according to the old ways, she knows that personal ambition drives her to become something more than just a member of her clan, a small cog in a small wheel. She wants to become a dignified professional member of the white community so she can fulfill her personal ambitions. Doing so, however, is difficult. She will be cast out of her Indian life yet will be despised and ignored by the white community of which she wants to become a part. She becomes an architect, thus becoming a member of a cutthroat profession where under-the-table dealings and sabotage are easy.

She is especially vulnerable in the assignment given her in the novel. She bids on and is awarded the job of restoring the Mendoza hacienda, the palace of the Mendoza family who in the past have ruthlessly exploited and abused the local Indians, particularly Irene's family. Although Irene knows she has the greatest potential for doing the restoration correctly, she fears that hostility from all people—Indians and whites—might threaten her success. She is right. Other architects try to slow her down and prevent her from completing the job on time. The construction firm that she must use, headed by a man named Cobb, tries in every way to undermine her efforts, and the Mendoza family with its two off-center members poses bodily and professional threats to her. That she succeeds despite all difficulties is testimony to the strong potential of the Tewa people.

Evidence of this strength is generally seen in the Tewa workers along with Spanish men and women that Cobb has hired for the construction. Pabikon suggests to Cobb that since there is always tension between the two races during work hours, Indians should work together and Spaniards in their own groups. Despite the clear logic of the proposal, Cobb, though he knows the potential for conflict and perhaps because of it, insists that the two races must work together and iron out their conflicts however they please. Conflict does result, several times in near physical violence. Finally, despite all troubles the task is finished.

The Thurlos people the book with strong characters. Pabikon, of course, is unrelenting in her determination to be a splendid architect. The two brothers and their sister who live in the Mendoza hacienda are inflexible, though one brother and the sister are slightly deranged. All feel their strong inherited aristocratic blood and demand respect. Cobb, the chief of construction, is strong, condescending, a male chauvinist who hates Irene both for her gender and for her authority over him.

The book is filled with Indian legends, folklore, and mythology. Throughout Indian culture, nighttime is alive with skinwalkers, witches, and allied evils. Pabikon feels threatened in the darkness, and her Indian associates always remind her of the danger. Whites use the Tewa mythology against them. Daytime is also filled with dangers. The owl is an especially sagacious agent in warning the Tewa of impending danger. One day, for example, one of the Tewa workers is told to dig a trench but requests that some of the Spanish workers dig the trench because he has heard an owl and does not want to go against the bird's warning. The white overseer says, "It's just an owl up there, not a vulture. If you don't like the damn bird, chuck a rock at it." But, "the Tewa man shook his head, and looked up at the rocky ledge about two hundred yards up the mountain, where the owl was perched on a pine branch. 'It wouldn't change anything. It's a bad omen. You can't ignore things like that,'" he says. The bad omen is ignored and the result is that the Tewa worker is scared to death with what ensues. When he screams out, and is castigated by his boss, Pabikon walks over to the trench and "her eyes locked on the skeletal hand resting in the worker's abandoned shovel" (102, 104). She knows what the hand signifies.

Discovery of the skeleton constitutes a kind of Gothic horror in the work. The construction zone is definitely a Gothic psychological hardhat zone. And there are more. The construction area is a hazardous workplace. The Spanish and Tewa workers are always only a foot away from accident. Near accidents follow Pabikon all the time. One day, for example, she is on the roof of the hacienda checking the quality of materials used in the reconstruction. As she starts to climb down she narrowly escapes a nasty fall when she discovers that the ladder has been intentionally taken down.

But threats to life and limb are more common and more dangerous at night. One night she is really spooked. She hears sounds in the hallway just outside her door. At first she just shivers in her bed, but when she gets enough courage to open the door she sees dreamlike shadows receding down the hallway. At other times she hears noises outside her window and when she looks out she sees only indistinct shadows which could be man, beast, or skinwalker. Although most of these spooky occurrences are eventually explained, their supernatural nature is not diminished for the Tewa.

Meanwhile the book develops like Daphne du Maurier's *Rebecca*. Raul Mendoza, part-owner and major domo of the hacienda, is a strong, silent, reserved man who was once married to a beautiful woman named Reina (Queen). She is now dead. His younger brother, Gene, sensitive and unmarried, was in love with Reina and does all he can to keep her memory alive. Their sister, Angela, is emotionally off balance as a result of a trauma in her youth. Raul broods as he walks about the hacienda appearing aloof and withdrawn. Soon, however, he starts following Irene around and finally admits that he is more interested in her than in the restoration. Irene at first fears her boss, then at the end of the book marries him.

Regardless of its deep saturation in Gothic horror, *Second Shadow* more than accomplishes its purpose as revealing Tewa mythology and culture and the role of the Indians, especially the females, who want to get away from the culturally incestuous life of the Tewa and join the larger community around them. Irene voices the conflict when confronted with the possibility of loving Raul: "I used to think my ways were just the ones of the white world; I went to school on the outside and I've learned how to adjust. But I'm finding that some of the beliefs I grew up with are very much a part of me. I'm not as progressive as I thought. I reach out for the things I know and hold on to them without even thinking, especially when I'm away from the pueblo. . . . Being

Tewa is a culture and a religion all rolled into one" (97). Although this scene might be somewhat overly melodramatic, it reaches to the heart and brain of the intent of the novel and as such should be considered a success.

Luckily for the novelistic growth of the Thurlos and the accomplishments of Native American crime fiction, however, the authors gave up Irene Pabikon as a protagonist and turned to a more important and useful character.

Blackening Song begins this new series that develops conflicts of lifestyle on the Navajo reservation and has as its protagonist a woman named Ella Clah, who left the reservation when she was eighteen in order to develop her own lifestyle in the broader society. She became an FBI agent in Los Angeles but was called home upon the murder of her father, a preacher in a liberalized church on the reservation.

The chief suspect is Clifford, Ella's brother and son of the slain preacher. He is a *hataali*, or traditional medicine man, and therefore opposed to his father's more liberal teachings. Although forbidden by FBI rules from investigating her father's murder, Ella goes to the reservation to comfort her mother, Rose. Because she is a Navajo Ella knows her people's customs and is therefore inevitably drawn into the investigation. At first assisted in her effort only by a childhood friend named Wilson Joe, she is eventually joined by brother Clifford who has been smoked out of hiding and now assists his sister and Wilson in trying to corner the perpetrator. He is finally identified, wounded in a shoot-out with Ella, and turned over to the authorities.

This is a remarkably powerful book, much stronger than *Second Shadow*. It is essentially about the same people, the Navajo of New Mexico, and about the same subject matter of Indians leaving the reservation in order to pursue their individual dreams and ambitions, but this book excels in its development of character, the verisimilitude and naturalism of plot, and the use of Indian customs.

Of all the characters, Ella Clah, naturally, is the strongest. Although a first-class FBI agent, Ella is a loner. When other agents celebrate the successful closing of a case, she spends the time alone, not joining in the festivities. The preference to be alone is a holdover from her youth, when she had been alone not by choice but by necessity.

> *Alone.* That word suddenly had many meanings to her. As a girl, the feeling she had attempted to describe with that word had really been the desire to find someone who could understand her needs and fears. Denied that, she'd eventually tried to become another person entirely,

hoping to ease the chill inside her. But she'd never quite fit in anywhere." (290)

Successful in her role as an FBI agent, she had never settled down,
instead she moved frequently from one post to another. Now she was in
Los Angeles, still alone. Her husband was killed in the war. She had
found her identity being her husband's wife. When he was killed she
had to find her identity on her own. The FBI had taught her to be herself. "The Bureau taught me to stand on my own, and gave me confidence I never had before. I realized I was capable of accomplishing
anything I set my mind to. I made a place for myself, and I made a difference there" (150). Her being an FBI agent runs counter to feelings
about that agency found in most writers of Native American crime novels. Jake Page, for example, lists the FBI among the half-dozen most
hated things in life, Stabenow makes fun of it, and Peter Bowen associates it with all the things he despises.

But Ella is neither a typical FBI agent nor a typical law enforcer. The
stereotype of the hated FBI is personified in the person they call FB-
Eyes, whose name is really Blalock. Sent to the reservation as the resident law enforcement officer FB-Eyes is both a threatening figure —
threatening because of the power he represents — and comical — comical
because of the absurdity of his attitude and pose. He is haughty, condescending, humorless, and insecure; consequently, he demands compliance
with his orders no matter how ill-advised they are. He has been "in this
wretched backwater for two years — in other words, forever" (36), and he
knows how to handle every situation having to do with law and order.

The other characters, though minor, are clearly and carefully etched.
Rose, Ella's mother, is an understanding woman who although she did
not always agree with her husband, always supported him in his mini-
sterial work. Clifford, the *hataali* who wants to maintain the old way of
living, is imaginative and resourceful. Working with his sister Ella, he
makes a formidable opponent to the murderer of their father. Wilson
Joe, the youth lover of Ella, is in many ways her mirror image psychologically. As a young person he was always an outsider, the oddball who
wanted to join but was always relegated to remaining just outside the
circle. He loved Ella but never got to show it. Here in this book, he is
both imaginative and helpful.

Because the characters are strongly drawn and the plot riveting in
many ways, the book is valuable for what it does toward revealing Navajo

life and ways. It supplements the accounts given by Tony Hillerman and others. The skinwalker, or witch, for example, is omnipresent and detailed on several occasions. One example will suffice as illustration. Ella and Wilson are parked on the side of the road investigating a strange artifact before them. They approach a hollowed-out circle surrounded by several rocks. Wilson comments nervously, "I don't like this." Ella, however, continues to probe. "She crouched down on the far side of the circle, trying to make out a pattern in the ashes that had been strewn there. 'It almost looks like a dry painting, but's made from ashes, not sand. Here's something that looks like a bird. And what's this?' She pointed to a human-looking figure with two faces."

Wilson reminds her that these are "skinwalking rituals." The two faces depict the intended victim of their slaying. Ella chills at the reminder.

"Ella was at a loss to explain how, but without any warning, the feel of the place suddenly changed, and she felt cold all over. She stood, suddenly uneasy, as if some sixth sense worked overtime to alert her to danger" (130). She wants to get back to the truck.

They move quickly back to the truck and drive off. In a minute Wilson stops the vehicle to see if the tires are all right. But Ella feels a threatening presence: "Ella took her pistol out of the glove compartment, fastened the holster to her belt, then stepped out of the truck. Her hair stood on end, as if she were about to be struck by lightning. She'd felt this way before, usually before a case went sour."

Just as Wilson starts to get back into the truck, Ella spots an elderly man coming down the arroyo. Neither of the two recognize him. His face is hidden in a blanket but he has a threatening demeanor. The unknown man approaches to within twenty feet, points a bony finger at them and then prophesies, "'You can't escape what surrounds you,' he warned, his voice hollow, as if he were speaking from a cave. 'Death wraps itself around you even now.' He began a bizarre, incomprehensible chant, which grew progressively louder as he repeated each stanza" (132).

The demented man does not frighten Ella because she knows that, after all, he is human. But Wilson steps in front of Ella and scatters pollen into the air, a Navajo cleanser and protector against witches. The man suddenly throws the deformed head of a recently killed goat at them, the goat's head without eyes, meanwhile continuing his chant. While still chanting the "fanatical mystic reached inside the blanket and pulled out a desiccated, skeletal human hand." Terrified, Wilson points his rifle toward the sky and fires two shots. To the amazement of both, the cloaked man collapses to the ground. Ella is in for a shock when she rushes up to examine the apparently dead man. "Ella stopped three feet away from the bundle of blanket and cloth that lay crumpled on the sand. Scarcely breathing, she studied the shape. Something was very wrong with it, she realized, heart pounding. There was no body—nothing lay beneath the blanket except ground. Before Wilson could stop her, she tossed the blanket aside and stared in mute shock at the expanse of grayish sand beneath. No prints or marks marred the smooth surface" (131). To Wilson's insistence that the spook was a *chindi*, Ella insists that it was a man, not a powerful skinwalker, and she realizes that the whole scene had been caused by a trickster or illusionist. When Wilson will not allow Ella to put the blanket in his truck, she vows to come back later and retrieve it. When she does, it is gone, as well as all signs that anything had happened at this spot. Navajo skinwalker ways are terrifying mythology, and the Thurlos are excellent at depicting them.

Although far less intrusive than in *Second Shadow*, the ending of this book smells too much of the romance. In the earlier book the heroine falls in love with the owner of the hacienda, they are going to get married and live happily ever after. In *Blackening Song* romance artificially creeps in at the end. FB-Eyes, who really is a pompous ass that only a mother and perhaps the office in Washington could love, has decided that he likes the reservation and has asked to be assigned there permanently; he has turned into a pussycat that all will love. Perhaps more strangely, Ella, who left the reservation in order to develop her own personality and career and has been successful in her FBI character, has decided that she wants to give up her FBI future and remain on the reservation, among her people where she can find self-fulfillment. She hopes to become a member of the tribal police, perhaps the chief of police in the town. She is needed by the Navajo, and has accepted the culture and rituals and the duty of supporting prayer rituals. The Indian gods approved of her decision.

The development of the Ella character and this story is interestingly explained by the authors in an afternote to the book. They wrote that once while driving back to the Rez for David's high school reunion they noticed that on the thirty-yard line of the football field lay the body of a dead horse, and no children looked at it or approached the body. "Avoidance of the dead and anything connected to it was simply too ingrained." Immediately they realized "how old beliefs and modern education could exist side by side." To portray life on the Rez realistically, they realized, Ella Clah "would have to have her feet planted firmly in two very different worlds." In the series, the Thurlos hope to "write an entertaining story, not to suggest answers to any of the problems facing the tribe." They want to present their readers "with a glimpse into this special world" (interview). That they have done. The book is dedicated to Tony Hillerman who "gave them a hand" when they needed it. The book has succeeded in providing an entertaining story about much of the reality of life on the Indian reservation, and in so doing the authors have provided pictures of what needs to be done to improve the situation and some insight into how the problems can be helped. Without meaning to aim the beam of a flashlight directly on that world, they have provided some guidance.

In *Death Walker,* the second Ella Clah story, which continues the homicidal adventures on the Navajo reservation near Albuquerque, the Thurlos have found the right mix and the correct combination of character development to produce a powerful novel.

The story picks up a few months after the end of *Blackening Song.* Peterson Yazzie, Clah's demented cousin who was sheriff but who was also a murderous religious fanatic, is in a mental institution. His evil powers are so strong that he is able to almost hypnotize the personnel of the institute. He is determined to get revenge on Ella, who broke his power on the reservation, and her brother Clifford and mother Rose for their role in frustrating his earlier plans. While Yazzie is still locked up a series of serial murders begins. It soon becomes clear that the people being murdered are those knowledgeable in and teaching the history and traditions of the Dineh—the Navajo. Ella and her family are in constant danger. Her job is to cut the line of strength flowing from Yazzie, to break the chain of murders and to find the perpetrators.

This book is by far the stronger of the two starring Ella Clah. The Thurlos have found the right venue for Ella and have developed the proper character in her. She is strong and self-confident. She has been sufficiently accepted by the tribe to accomplish her goals as newly appointed special investigator on the Navajo reservation; she almost feels at home. Although she works comfortably with men, she now has been given an assistant, a female cousin named Justine Goodluck, who becomes her close confidant and assistant and saves her life. Her next closest assistant is Carolyn Roanhorse, the medical examiner on the reservation. Dwayne Blalock, the FBI agent nicknamed FB-Eyes because he has one blue eye and one brown, is now in the FBI office in Albuquerque and is only marginally associated with Ella and her doings.

Wilson Joe, with whom Ella was getting almost romantically chummy at the end of the earlier book, is now back to teaching school full time and not making love.

Most important for the success of the series, Ella has matured into a credible police officer and respectable figure for all readers. She has made it clear to Wilson Joe and all others that she is not interested in the potential romance suggested at the end of *Blackening Song*. Her mother is always intimating that police work is dangerous and Ella should settle down and get married, and mother has precisely the person in mind for the coupling. But Ella's future is clearly indicated at the end of this book. When the murders have been solved and Peterson Yazzie has been finally dealt with terminally, mother Rose decides it is time to steer Ella toward the romance road she so definitely needs. Rose arranges a dinner to which only Ella and Wilson Joe will be invited. But Ella, knowing her mother's intention, asks Carolyn and Justine to come also. Rose can hardly be rude enough to uninvite them, so the dinner party is held, quite successfully from Ella's point of view, and quite unsatisfactorily from Rose's. But Rose is not to be deterred. The last few lines point up the developed character and determination of Ella. Rose tells Ella that now that everything is over she can rest. "Maybe you should call Wilson. Spending a quiet evening together would do you both worlds of good." But Ella has her own future: "'Rest? Quiet evening' Ella chuckled and shook her head. 'No way. I've finished the fieldwork, true, and the Packrat is locked up and under guard. But now I've got to face the real scourge of every cop's life'

"'I don't understand. What can be worse than what you've already confronted?'

"'Paperwork,' Ella answered. Giving her mother a quick hug, she headed for the exit" (338). Apparently no page is to remain unturned in Ella's determination to be a professional.

The book is powerful. It reveals the tension in the life of the Navajo as they exist with skinwalkers and *hataaji* and with the Anglos. The book is excellently paced. The atmosphere is constantly tense and charged. Sometimes the action is almost frantic. The outcome is satisfactory.

Bad Medicine, the third novel in the Clah series, demonstrates growing control of characters and story development by the authors, and there is considerable advancement in the series and their characters as it would be in everyday life. There is consequently more than the usual amount of Indian culture presented, with the fears, prejudices, and biases in the reservation community that one would find in the society outside it.

In this story, Ella sees the daughter of U.S. senator Yellowhair running off the road in an obviously drugged condition. She is killed. Her father, refusing to believe that his wonderful daughter could possibly have been mixed up with drugs, thunders all kinds of threats on Ella and the police department, but especially on Carolyn Roanhorse, the physician and autopsist because she discovered drugs in the dead daughter's tissue. In a parallel story conflicts between Indians and whites flare up at a silver mine owned by the Navajo. These conflicts are fueled by two secret organizations, the White Brotherhood and the Navajo Fierce Ones.

The novel, perhaps the strongest yet in the series, is especially notable for the amount of Indian lore brought into it. Still working in two worlds, neither yet fully mature, Ella is developing the skills she learned as a member of the FBI, and those learned from brother Clifford in shamanic medicine.

Ella is growing in her professional skills yet she cannot separate herself fully from tribal culture. Rose, her mother, is still a fountain of wisdom and a mountain of strength. In moments of uncertainty and frustration, Ella goes to Rose. But she is reaching a crossroads where she has to make a decision about her future, and she does so. For example, Wilson Joe, the local schoolteacher whom Ella was somewhat in love with in the first novel but less so in the second, wants to get married. Ella has decided against him and probably against a second marriage at any time. Her first marriage had led to unhappiness. Now Wilson pulls her aside and tells Ella that he is going to marry a fellow schoolteacher. He invitingly gives Ella a chance to say that they should marry instead. She does not. Rose tells her she should, that she had better get married soon and avoid a life of professional loneliness. Ella says she will accept the professionalism. The decision strengthens her for her readers and also keeps her available for future love affairs, though obviously the authors have thrown in the element of Wilson Joe's withdrawing his availability for other reasons. It is interesting to speculate on those possibilities.

Dr. Carolyn Roanhorse is given a more central role in this book. In the past she has served as physician and forensic examiner and friend of Ella. Now she is the center of one of the plots. Senator Yellowhair's daughter has to be autopsied because Ella was sure she was murdered. The Senator, however, is so unchangeably opposed to the desecration of the body in the autopsy process that one begins to think he was in on the murder. He is determined to destroy Roanhorse because of her involvement in the autopsy. Roanhorse gets sick and Ella begins to wonder if a witch caused the illness.

Whereas earlier books had ended in rather precise turns made by Ella, away from the reservation and its mystism, *Bad Medicine* concludes in a happy mix of Navaho mysticism and police realism. Realizing that neither the Brotherhood nor the Fierce Ones have been lastingly defeated, Carolyn asks, "Do cops ever win a complete victory?" Ella, looking at her brother Clifford, replies: "Evil always exists. It's part of the balance, and only by accepting that, can we walk in beauty" (340). Navajo well-wishing and inconclusive. But the major accomplishments of this novel vis-à-vis Ella and the Navajo, or the Thurlos and the Navajo, are numerous.

In the development of Ella this book shows that she can stand alone as a professional without being sustained by a man, her strong mother, or the tribe. On a larger scale it demonstrates that Navajos can exist in both worlds—Indian and Anglo—and succeed in both. It takes character, integrity, and strong will, and Ella especially, and other Navajos in general, have this integrity and strong will and can succeed. The next book in the series, *Enemy Way*, continues with this cast of characters that includes Clah, Rose, Clifford, and Wilson Joe.

In *Shooting Chant*, the authors take a slightly different tact. Although they are not interested in writing novels that urge Anglos to pay back Native Americans for injustices of the past, they write a strong advocacy novel not on a tribal or national issue but on one of broader range—equality and independence for women.

In this new work Ella Clah, still a special investigator for the Navajo Nation, is caught between two tensions that are tearing the reservation society apart. On one side the Traditionalists believe in gradualism and persuasion in achieving their rights and justice. The Modernists, on the other side, led by the firebrand Fierce Ones, are threatening chaos and are causing disruption through sabotage, vandalism, and murder. Their object is the LabKote factory, located on the reservation, that produces sterile vessels for medical labs but does not employ what the Fierce Ones think is a fair number of Navajo. Of course no number would be sufficient. So Ella is caught between the confines of Indian versus Indian and of Indian versus Anglo. The militants believe that harmony cannot be restored through Anglo law, and Ella is convinced that it must be restored through that very avenue.

But she is also caught in the elemental battle of nature versus independent desires. She is pregnant. The child's father wants to marry Ella but she will have nothing to do with the idea: the two people, though maturing independently while separate cannot develop fully when coupled to each other. Ella's mother, Rose, has managed and flowered after her husband's death. She points out the hazards of single parenting, yet she also supports her daughter's decision to establish a female line of heredity. The child will not be marked in bastardy because on the reservation sex is not linked to morals but "was just a part of Nature." To the Navajo "Nature moved in harmony with its surroundings and what was part of nature was not to be condemned" (60). So the female child will have a stronger and wider opportunity to carry on her mother's wishes than she would have off the reservation.

And she can further her mother's quest better here than in the wider world. Ella, when asked why she remains on the reservation when she has to fight battles between rival Indian groups and between Indians and Anglos, answers that she tries to plumb the depth of Navajo life as she reads it. In the depressions of poverty, despair, and frustration on the reservation she sees more than culture. It is something spiritual. "It's what we call *hozhq'*. It means all that's good, orderly and harmonious . . . that makes us one with the land and gives us an identity that's more than the name Navajo" (107).

Throughout the book the main point is stated and restated. She has no medical confirmation, but Ella knows the fetus is female, as does her mother. Their sixth sense tells them this fact. Both refer to the fetus as "she," and both depend on the girl baby to continue and expand the matriarchy feebly taking shape.

At the end of the book, after the conflicts and tensions have been released, we have a fast-forward to after the baby—a girl, naturally—has been born. Ella named her *Deezbaa,* which means "She goes off to War," with her first name Dawn because "the baby will have a happy voice and will be an Everlasting and Peaceful baby" (348).

In this book the Thurlos have burst forth from the terrestrial and territorial conflicts between natives and invading tribes and based their hope on a more fundamental freedom and justice, that between the sexes. Their proponents are two strong, independent, and capable women, with a third in the cradle of infinite hope and opportunity. But in getting to this hopeful conclusion, the authors' reach almost exceeds their grasp. The novel becomes sentimental at the end. But when one is fondling a baby, how is hope to be separated from sentiment?

In their next book, *Red Mesa,* the Thurlos saddled themselves with new pitfalls and expanded opportunities they could not cover. *Red Mesa* does not stand up to the promise of its latest immediate predecessor. It is an extended domestic quarrel that has no reason for being and holds little interest for the reader.

Ella Clah and her cousin Justine, who works in the office next to

Ella's, have an irritable working relationship. Ella is devoting more and more time to her daughter Dawn, and Justine, after a broken love affair, is seeking a new one. The general atmosphere of the tribal office is tense, as are matters throughout the Rez. Ordinarily Indians on the Rez do not feud and when they do it is not among members of the same tribe. But now all people's tempers are brittle and easily broken.

Ella and Justine hold a secret meeting, an unidentifiable corpse is left behind—which is thought to be Justine's—and Ella is suspected of murder. She should be taken off the case because of the kinship with the supposed corpse, yet Ella continues to investigate. In the end, Justine is found by Ella trussed up, beaten, and in bad physical condition but alive. Then the tension is released and suspicion returns to sisterly and family respect and love.

The writing is certainly professional, but the plot on which it is strung will not sustain a powerful story. The reader—unless specializing in family squabbles—will find that the motivations for disagreements do not sustain family hostility. And the novel is disappointingly weak.

The authors' hoped-for strength is not recovered in their next novel, *Changing Woman*. The story continues with the tradition of the "changed" Ella in the preceding work, and the Thurlos turn back to conventional detective fiction, this time on the reservation. A family and extended family affair, *Changing Woman* includes the whole police force. Justine, Ella's officemate and assistant, has lost her trigger finger and since she can't use a pistol effectively may be let go from the force. This upsets Ella, who is determined to fill in and cover for Justine and keep her on the force. But the police force is threatened with being understaffed. As a result the whole unit supports one another against the threat of a gang of hoodlums committing arson in an effort to intimidate the tribe into allowing a gambling casino to be built on the reservation. Everyone knows the disruption the casino would bring, but the only person strong enough to stand up in public and speak out is Ella's mother, Rose. In this novel time has passed, as I intimated. Justine has suffered a mutilated shooting finger, Ella's ex-husband is less of a nuisance, the whole Indian police force is more closely knitted. Unfortunately, Ella has not benefited from the passage of time. She is, as the title of the book suggests, a Changed Woman. As the Thurlos say at the end of the book:

> Changing Woman, who was at the center of Navajo beliefs, stood for creative feminine power—life restoring itself in an endless array of new cycles. [Ella had] found that life brought a different kind of peace to

those her age—one that would give her the confidence and courage to walk a new life path for herself and for her tribe. (369)

This consolation may be more satisfying to the authors and main characters than it is to the readers of crime fiction who want more tension and conflict and heroics. We must wait and see where the authors take Ella Clah next.

The journey they do take next, in *Tracking Bear*, is back toward their earlier works featuring Ella Clah, though they do not abandon the new situation in which Ella, Rose, and Justine are close to one another and to the larger family of the local police force.

Here they in fact pit the Indians, their way of life, and the police force against the whites. In the conflict between the two races, the whites are trying to Americanize the Native Americans and they in turn are endeavoring to Indianize the whites. The whites are trying to exploit the reservation properties by mining the uranium-rich ore and establishing an atomic power plant to generate electricity to supply the needs of surrounding states. Most of the Indians—except those who will directly benefit—think this just another effort of the powerful whites to exploit Indian lands. Representatives from both sides of the conflict—whites and Indians on both—suffer from violence and threats. Although one Indian policeman is killed, the native police force wins out in this conflict between the two races. It is they who are in control of the situation, they do the policing, they find the guilty parties. The two opposite forces reach an agreement about the atomic generator but it is through the efforts of the Indians.

Tracking Bear is essentially a crime story about whites in conflict with Indian traditions and holdings. As such it tells a good story well. But its emphasis is more on good story than Indian life, tradition, and essence. Ella Clah never manages to get outside her skin and become the heroine she has been in earlier works. Little Dawn is now a three year old, and Ella is increasingly concerned with being a good mother. Consequently this is a mother-daughter-family-tribal novel that would have benefited from more heroics.

Jake Page

Jake Page is an author distinctly out of the conventional crime fiction loop. Page's hero, T. Moore "Mo" Bowdre joins Jack Wilder of Robert Westbrook's series in being an unusually powerful character in crime fiction, certainly in Native American mystery, because of physical appearance. The two remind the reader of many of the characteristics of eighteenth-century English lexicographer and social philosopher Dr. Samuel Johnson (as fictionalized by Lillian De La Torre), of American social critics Ambrose Bierce, H. L. Mencken, and Mark Twain, and of country music star Willie Nelson. All, except Nelson, were acerbic and bilious commentators on the human condition Throughout the Page novels Mo is called the "redneck Nero Wolfe," but the effete New York flower expert hardly stands a comparison with the New Mexico investigator, and the reference is apropos in body size only.

In crime fiction, investigators, like other heroes and mythological creatures, sometimes possess physical attributes that speak of their character and ability. Edgar Allan Poe's French detective Auguste Dupin, for example, behaves somewhat batlike, isolating himself in the back library of a crumbing Gothic mansion at Faubourg Saint-Germain during the daylight hours, and venturing out into society only after dark. Sherlock Holmes has eccentricities that both amuse and annoy his companion Watson but endear him to us. Nero Wolfe, a kind of downsized version of what Mo perhaps most closely resembles, carries his one-seventh of a ton of weight around his Manhattan brownstone, eating voraciously and spending exactly two hours a day in his rooftop garden caring for and loving his ten thousand plants.

In the 1930s and 40s American pulp fiction, straining always to create unforgettable characters who would appeal to a buying public, stretched the limits of credibility with the physical characteristics of their investigators. Writer Paul Ernst, for example, created a character named Seekay who wore a mask because he had no face behind it.

In the story named "Madam Murder and the Corpse Brigade," Seekay is like Sherlock Holmes in his ability to read external aspects of life. He surmises, for instance, that the client who has come to ask his assistance in trying to save her brother does not live in Chicago, where Seekay works. In answer to her astonished query of how he knows she does not live in Chicago, Seekay answers: "There is more to tell me you're from out of town. There is a sharp crease down the side of your spring coat. You have been seated in the same position for a long time — probably, several hours. In a bus or train. A bus almost certainly — in a train you would have taken off your coat" (in Hoppenstand and Browne, *The Defective Detective* 10).

More akin to the Mo tradition is Seekay's acute sense of smell. When Marian, the woman needing help, walks into the room to see

Seekay for the first time, he says. "Tell me what happened to you at the hospital." In answer to her query, "How did you know I had been to a hospital?" Seekay replies: "I have a nose, and the smell of a hospital persists in your clothes" (in *The Defective Detective* 10).

The tradition that Page follows by having Connie fall in love with Mo, probably because he is blind, is nurtured in this Seekay story. Marian is attracted to Seekay, and at the end of the tale wants to work for him and thus be with him. The dialogue of this move runs thus:

> "You are intelligent, Miss Ford."
>
> Marian drew a deep breath. "I'm glad you think so. Because I . . ." The words came in a rush. "I'd like to work for you. You need someone."
>
> For a long time Seekay stared at her. Then his eyes smiled if his lips could not.
>
> "Shake," he said, extending his hand. (In *The Defective Detective* 24)

The dialogue is, of course, only prelude to greater intimacies, here only implied.

Closer to Mo's blindness is the character Peter Quest, in "The Brain Murder," by John Kobler. Quest is going blind because of glaucoma, and "like an electric bulb which burns brightest before final extinction, so Peter Quest's doomed vision possessed abnormal keenness," and his "deft, artisan's fingers are good at breaking locks" (in *The Defective Detective* 26). Like Page's Mo, Quest is abnormally sensitive to atmospheres both climatic and cultural, he senses a quickening of pulses around him, a sudden unhealthy alertness that disturbs him. Conventionally, of course, the woman in the story falls in love with him.

Various other writers use the blindness motif on which to develop their characters. In the Middle Ages, charlatans, quacks, and people with no eyesight were more insightful than were people with normal vision, at least that was the folklore and tradition. Present-day authors of crime fiction set in the Middle Ages and earlier use this tradition. For example, one historical crime fiction series has a scholar–wise man aided by his bad sight:

> Jehozadok's [the sage] partial blindness did not prevent him from being unusually aware of everything that went on around him. Indeed, his affliction probably aided his knowledge of activity across the scholarly city, for many people made a point of dropping in on the old man to ensure that his poor sight did not cut him off from the world. Each one brought a tidbit of news like busy starlings feeding their young, flitting between the outside world and the security of the nest.

Without leaving the Scola, Jehozadok gathered more information than any of his able-bodied feeders. (Ian Marson, *Falconer and the Face of God* 52)

In a series about eighteenth-century London, Bruce Alexander writes of the real Judge Sir John Fielding of the Bow Street Runners who is blind but is a superb investigator when aided by a thirteen-year-old boy whom he rescued from a life of degradation and crime. Generally all stories about the Middle Ages are so filled with details that readers have nicknamed them ODTAA (One Damned Thing After Another). Mystery fiction about the same period could easily be called ODCAA (One Damned Crime After Another). Such is *Remedy for Treason,* by Caroline Roe, the first in a series about a physician in Spain, during the fourteenth century, a member of the Jewish ghetto, who is blind and uses a young ten-year-old Moorish lad for his eyes. He is a blind medical doctor but not a surgeon, as Page's Mo Bowdre wanted to be.

Another series of crime fiction approximating Page's hero is the successful pair of investigators created by the contemporary author R. D. Zimmerman. In the series including the titles *Death Trance: A Novel of Hypnotic Detection* (1992), and *Red Trance . . . Mystery of Hypnotic Detection* (1994), Maddy Phillips is a blind paraplegic forensic psychologist specializing in forensic hypnosis. Her brother, Alex, is her eyes and contact with visual reality. After he has witnessed a crime or crime scene, he is hypnotized by his sister and recreates the crime or enough of it for her to intuit a solution. The parallel for Mo's accomplishments is close, though he calls on "his eyes," Connie, very rarely, usually having intuited the reality before she is needed. But she is vital to his life. Mo once says, Connie's "absence makes me blind" (*Strings* 236). Also writing today, Michael Collins (Dennis Lynds) and George C. Chesbro have their deformed detectives. Collins's hard-boiled holdover from the earlier tradition is Dan Fortune, a private eye with only one arm, and Chesbro's man of many talents including former experience as a circus headliner and black belt karate expert, is a dwarf. In the tradition of dwarfism, Chesbro goes back to least to Homer and fits into a rich tradition of people apparently exceptional because they are small.

Page's use of folklore and folk motifs in developing Mo's character gives him unusual strength. Himself a square peg in a round hole, Mo is the son of a man who was widely known for being eccentric and fiscally "tight." He never threw anything away because he argued that one can never tell when something might be needed. He even had a box of cord ends labeled "strings too short to use." He ran a hardware store under the same philosophy, which meant that although one could not buy anything that was new in his store, he could sometimes find replacement parts. Mo thinks his father is somewhat strange because he is rather embarrassed to be the nephew of Charlie Bowdre, an outlaw who had died ignominiously in the Lincoln County wars of the 1880s. In every book Mo has to explain away his inheritance from this lesser figure of the famous war, and Mo is not ashamed. In fact he rather glories in being a redneck from a wide and deep family of rednecks.

Further aspects of Mo's character and development mature in folklore and folk motifs. One such belief is that people who lose one sense compensate for its loss by super-development of the others. Mo is not at all reluctant to admit his blindness. In fact he glories in his ability to overcome it. In one book he admits he is "blind as a bat on a foggy night" (*Strings* 68), and in another he glories that he is "blind as a mole on a bad day" (*Lethal* 240). Since he cannot see, Mo must be able to use his other senses to a keen degree. His hearing is superb. He can be talking to people at one table and unconsciously hear and register what is being said at an adjacent table; this added information often serves him well in his ferreting out solutions to crimes. He is especially gifted in being able to identify birds by their calls when nobody else can even hear them. In desert quietness he hears a car motor two miles away when all is silence to his companions (*Canyon* 219).

Mo reads Connie's moods and reactions like a thermometer. He can "even tell her mood from her body temperature sensed across the room" (*Strings* 66). He senses her every change in mood by the sounds she makes. He once tells her that when she is smiling, "[your] voice is different when you pull your lips back that far to the sides" (6). His olfactory sense is perfect. In one story he is clued in on a lawyer's guilt by smelling his cologne—it is too expensive. In another he goes into a person's office and smells opium, which leads to the man's being arrested.

He is also gifted with perfect pitch and can hear whistling wind and tell when it is off-key. One day, for example, when he is visiting a woman for whom he sculpted the figure of an Indian, he hears the wind whistling through the statue and reprimands the woman for having placed it, against Mo's advice, in a spot where the flow of wind would make the statue whistle half a note off-key.

Page's other characters—major and minor—stand out as effective creations. In his five novels to date four stand out as "major." Samantha

Burgess, paparazzi reporter, is a person who grows in professionalism through the first two books. At first she is a naive freelance investigator and observer. In *The Deadly Canyon* she has grown into a bona fide reporter.

Mo is giant-sized, profoundly dignified in the true sense of the word, absolutely independent of all human needs except the association with his lady friend Connie, and without regard of his impact on society. He is a regular mountain of a man and a mountain man. To accompany him on his various escapades Page creates a Barnum museum of off-center characters, always bigger than life, always surprising and entertaining. The only other authors of Native American crime fiction to even approach him are Robert Westbrook and Peter Bowen and his barnyard of people who live around Gabriel Du Pré, the inspector of cattle brands. Like Mo Bowdre and Bowen's Du Pré, Westbrook's Howie Moon and Jack Wilder stand out firm and in bold face type. The two are comic figures almost unique in crime fiction, certainly in Native American crime fiction.

In the world of literature we may not be what we read but what we read certainly contains a great deal of what we wish we were. We therefore project into what we read our fantasies and hopes. We especially like to dive deep into humor because laughter makes us all five feet tall, or sometimes seven feet tall, and leavens the bread of life. Mo Bowdre is a special pepper in Native American crime fiction.

To achieve his purposes in stretching Hopi culture to its fullest dimensions in and against Mo Bowdre, Page has made him the ultimate Ur-Redneck, the father of them all, a mythical hero with all the trappings and traits necessary for his unusual behavior and accomplishments. He is, in other words, the blue-collar American, the person who has always dreamed of and peopled the West by moving out to it. He is the culmination of the dream of the New World, of the Citie on the Hill of early Puritan dreams and mythology, though with him, as maybe with us all, the Citie is really an outhouse.

Like most heroes' origins that are shrouded in mystery of religion, Page does not quite know how Mo was born. His wife, photographer Susanne Anderson, and he were doing a piece on Billy the Kid. One night they drank a lot of wine at dinner and the next morning Mo "sort of existed," Page recalled in his interview with me. Obviously the Muse was dining with the couple that night for Mo's first birth. His second was more conventional.

Mo stands six-feet-two-inches tall, with white hair, white mustache, and beard. For dramatic effect he likes to wear a black Stetson that is too small for his oversized head, and dark glasses. He is overweight with a stomach that cascades over his belt. His ego is also overdeveloped. His arms are like hams, his hands immense though sensitive. He is not a man to go unnoticed.

He advertises his presence and character with a loud and grating laugh that only friends can tolerate. Page variously describes it as similar to the squeal of a pig with laryngitis, a greased string stretched between two tin cans, and other parallels that make the reader's flesh crawl. In the automotive world it could be compared to the unpleasant sound of a Volvo's horn. Mo can be seen and heard for half a mile. This noisy exterior, which is at times hard to tolerate, shields the personality of a sensitive man who is determined to succeed and be useful to society, to make his few years on earth somehow beneficial to mankind. He pretends to be too cynical to try to do anything to correct it but peoples' misbehavior pains him nevertheless, and behind his mask of acting he is determined to right wrongs and relieve some of the curse of Mark Twain's "damned human race." Mo is always thinking of man's inhumanity or the "world's inhumanity to people" (*Strings* 18).

Page's choice of his protagonist as the prototypical redneck serves two purposes. Primarily the redneck is the ultimate voice of democratic America, the blue-collar worker who is after all only one color away from all other Americans. Mo represents the most democratic level of American society and therefore the largest number, the most abused, and the most potentially rebellious of worthy citizens. The elite in Page's novels are the scoundrels, or the scoundrels are the elite, especially those that abuse the Hopi. Page does not explicitly say it, but he demonstrates that the common people are more likely to attempt to atone for the national sins against the Indians than the elite who are more disposed to continue to exploit them. Not all the common people are good guys or women, Page has to demonstrate in order to write a credible story. But Mo as representative of them demonstrates the innate goodwill in common people.

Mo has the advantage of being able to move between the two societies, the common and the elite. In the words of one of the characters in the novel *The Deadly Canyon*, Mo "was a country boy who got himself educated, could slip in and out of it, from redneck to—what do they say, urbane—and back to redneck" (71). Mo explains his mobility by voicing one of the means of the redneck in achieving his goals in life: "Just 'cause you're a country boy doesn't mean you got to draw up the wagons of ignorance around you" (2). Page is personally comfortable with all levels of American society.

Although Mo may flirt with the elite he knows the dangers. He explains to his girlfriend Connie: "You know, you mess around too much with the mind of a man from the dominant culture, you get your ass in trouble" (*Canyon* 73).

Mo was blinded in a mine explosion, and this seeming handicap gives him certain freedoms in actions that would be denied to a sighted person. Connie, his girlfriend, though at times sad that Mo cannot see the beauty of nature around him that he so deeply loves, realizes that if he could see, Mo would "just be a normal slob, like other men (*Strings* 66). So she accepts him warts and all, or in this case blindness and all, and glories in the resulting superiority it brings. In fact, Connie loves Mo "because he sees so well" (*Gods* 99).

Does the extraordinary Mo stand examination in the novels as human being and redneck sculptor? Is he credible? Generally Mo is successful as an appealing, or at least interesting, character as attested to by Page's readers and critics, and as a blind person once told Page. Page states in his interview with me: "For the most part, I'm satisfied with his believability (who would believe an amateur detective these days anyway?) but as a blind man he seems to work. It turns out, I discovered after the first book, that there is a blind sculptor (from a Rio Grande pueblo) out there who is well thought of. I've heard from him and his wife who said that Mo worked just fine, and noted some other coincidental similarities. This made me very happy."

So Page knows the type of character he is portraying as his hero, as well as the other people who walk along the lines of his novels. He should. He is widely experienced. He has been a ranch-hand, hard-rock miner, editor at *Natural History* and *Smithsonian,* and a book publisher. He has authored hundreds of magazine articles and newspaper columns and has accompanied his wife in her many assignments as professional photographer. In all his books Page uses and reflects his wide-ranging experience and acute observations.

The direction and flow of Page's novels are consistent. In *The Stolen Gods* he sets the parameters and internal development he is to pursue in the next four novels, though he will change dramatically in his fifth work. His setting is very much Hopi. The motivation is exposing the continued injustices done to Native Americans, in this work with the theft and presumed sale of the Hopi's most respected and treasured deities, gods in whom reside the very essence of their being. Without these gods, the Indians are a ship of religious ritual without power or compass.

The scene of action is the Meyers Gallery, run by Walter Meyers, a shady and despised art dealer whose philosophy and modus operandi is that everything is for sale. No matter how intrinsically beautiful and valuable an art object is, its real value is the price it will bring—and the profit resulting from the transaction. Meyers is brutally murdered in his gallery in Santa Fe, in an efficient action that leaves behind few clues. His will gives his collection to a KKK kind of group in the South unless his widow, Marianna del Massimo, can raise 10 percent of its value immediately. If she does, this down payment will go to the Southern group. Meyers has so many enemies, however, that though the clues are scarce the murder opens out to virtually the whole world. Narrowing it down is the problem.

The finger of guilt seems to point to a Hopi Indian, clan brother of Connie, Mo's roommate and love, half-Hopi counter to Mo, the one person who makes him and his life complete. The FBI is called in to the investigation since the murder seems to connect with four Hopi gods stolen some time earlier. The gods are carved wooden figures, attractive only to the Hopi and to those who understand the value of such holy figures. The mystery deepens as the FBI discovers that Meyers had been talking regularly to someone in Singapore, apparently about some hush-hush art deal. Another suspect character the FBI has been shadowing is Willie Blaine, who is dedicated to working his way out of poverty and off degradation row at any cost. Mo with his extraordinary sense of smell traces the murderer through the use of a particular herb. The many loose ends are tied together, with Mo the intellect, and his acute senses, behind the solution.

The Deadly Canyon, the second novel in the series, revolves around a more mundane group of characters. Mo and Connie have arrived at a research center in the boot heel of New Mexico. Mo advertises that he has been commissioned to sculpt an appropriate figure for the center but in reality he is there to sniff out illegal smuggling activities that have been going on, maybe among the group of scientists who are always bickering, gossiping, and lying about their research. In addition to other kinky kinds of activity, every one of the researchers has some sexual involvement with graduate students on a yearly or summer basis. People, including the lovers of the research scientists, start getting killed. Others, with their worry compressed into irrepressible restrictions, begin acting in bizarre ways. Mo ferrets out the motivation and objectives of the murderers and leads a posse for apprehension of the guilty ones. The research center has to go out of business, a victim of the evil that guided it to its success.

The third novel in the series, *The Knotted Strings,* is a triple theme story woven together in an episode near Santa Fe. Because of the complexity of two themes and near triviality of the third, the story is less artistically powerful than its predecessors.

A movie company has come to town to film a factual episode from Indian history, when the Native Americans were victorious over the Spanish invaders of their part of the world a hundred years earlier. Some Indians resent having the movie people there and are determined to disrupt the filming.

The Indian authority who granted permission for the movie suddenly dies and the movie star who was slated to play the leading role is murdered. Since everyone in town is either a movie star or a hero worshipper, or hates the whole business, no clear pattern for suspicion develops. Mo is especially sensitive to the nuances in behavior and motivation of all people present. That motivation turns on a quaint often overlooked aspect of the agreement between the U.S. government and the Indian tribes, and knowledge of the possibilities of that law has driven some unlikely characters to sow disruption and commit murders.

The novel is difficult to sustain and difficult to work through. The Hopi claims about their holy lands and rights must be respected but Mo's development as a sleuth must be maintained. The making of the movie is certainly the least important aspect, except as motivation, and in developing it, Page may have let his dislike show through too prominently. Anyway, the novel, though competent, suffers by comparison with the others before and after it.

A Certain Malice is by far Page's most ambitious and accomplished fiction to date. Complex and convoluted, it is a quantum leap forward. The story develops on an extended symbol within a symbol of ritualized and real personal rebirth from ignorance and self-centered concern into universal understanding and empathy. *A Certain Malice* in the profundity and reach of its searching for ultimate truth is one of the most penetrating novels of its kind. In subject matter and method of treatment it reminds us of the finest efforts of Herman Melville. One other author of mythology-crime fiction, Arthur Upfield, approached at times this artistic accomplishment. In *The New Shoe* (1968), in a mixture of Melvillean and Dickensian prose, Upfield toyed with the finality and the absurdity of death. He has one of his characters, Mr. Penwarden, who builds coffins, invite Bony, the protagonist, to lie down in a coffin so that they can get his measurements for the time when he will need one. Mr. Penwarden, a Dickensian character, then philosophizes, "We all want a corrector . . . sir, and there's nothin' like the sight of a coffin to melt away pride and vanity" (54). But in *A Certain Malice* Page probes more deeply. It is a modern variant of Sophocles' *Oedipus,* this time with a woman trying to slay her father. It pulsates with the deepest truths that crime fiction, or any other writings, all too infrequently investigate. It is the *Moby-Dick* of crime fiction, diving into the very bowels of existence.

Melville's deep echoes chronicle Ahab as the collective ego of the human race fighting for humanity against the evil forces of a malignant God out to destroy mankind. Ahab will do anything to drive the harpoon of justice into the vital organs of his oppressor. Page's Annie is outraged womankind, revenge for women's felt injustices of the past. She is victim rampaging against victor. She is created fighting against her Creator. She is lost body searching for her soul. Melville's drama plumbs the very being of human existence, with biblical sonority; it is lightning voiced in thunder. Page's cry against man's assumptions and mistreatment of his creations is woman's steel insistence on recognition and equality. Though of different timbre, both books address the human condition and plea for betterment.

A Certain Malice is actually two loosely tied stories that are developed concurrently and come together in the end, bound in a Gordian knot by an encircling lifeline. It is only nominally about Native Americans except as they are everyday Americans. Instead it is about blind lack of human understanding and empathy. Melville's *Moby-Dick* is the adventure of an obsessed person determined to find and destroy Nature's supposed killer of people, the white whale, and through it God Himself. It is a search-and-destroy epic, a kind of spiritual crime story, with Ahab the investigator trying to locate the guilty party and bring it and him to justice at the bar of human independence and hubris. Ishmael is the personification of mankind who survives Ahab's monomania and returns to join society. Mo, Page's Ishmael, searches for the truth of his commitment to humanity. He realizes that he owes humanity something. The question is what and how much. The quest is the answer to those questions. Mo is pitted against his Moby-Dick in the person of the demented Annie, his putative daughter. *A Certain Malice* lacks the biblical sonority, wild adventure, and epic sweep of

Moby-Dick, but approximates it in seriousness of subject and ascendancy into myth.

Because the book develops in the mythological, Page goes further than in the past in suggesting the significance of Mo's heroic birth, and in fact uses it as the heartbeat to drive the development of the story. At the beginning of the work, Mo suggests he was born by parthenogenesis, immaculate conception. He is about to utter the unutterable, his divinity, but Page has the self-revelation interrupted by the appearance of the starkest reality, the police sergeant Ramirez.

The implications of this announcement do not end with Mo's interrupted confession. He tells more of his past in this book than in any other. He admits that as a young man in Denver he sold sperm to help himself financially. In such a practice he now feels that he was distributing anonymous fatherhood, with all kinds of implications. If all men sold or gave away sperm for general use they could look upon themselves as at least theoretically fathers of any and all the children on earth. Therefore every man "should look upon all children as potentially his and should treat them as such" (112). In developing this story Page has two approaches.

Of the two stories the first is about two young people—a woman from India, three months pregnant, and her white boyfriend—and one other woman on whose ranch the first two murders took place, being killed in a particularly grotesque ritualistic way by a religious zealot from India who cannot abide the idea of his daughter marrying an "infidel" outsider from his religious faith. So they are murdered. Here we have the timeworn Romeo and Juliet theme again. The other, far more important, story is about the development of Mo the private investigator as he is mistreated by a woman afflicted with borderline personality disorder, and how through being tormented by her Mo is reborn into a different kind of person and achieves a new empathy for people afflicted with such diseases and, far more important, for people in general, who may suffer some of these symptoms though in much milder form, or surely some kind of adversity.

In this story, as in all accounts of mythological-religious development of heroes, the growing figure is despised and hounded by people or an individual.

The first story has a minimal development of Page's interest in Hopi life and crime. But the role of Connie, Mo's partner and representative of the Hopi tribe, is reduced to a distant participation and limited to a few telephone calls after page eighty and reappears at the end thematically to cinch Mo's tie-in with the Hopi and humanity. She is the alpha and omega, the beginning and the end, of the book.

The second story leaves Hopi life altogether and concentrates instead on the development of Mo's character, from a person who is incomplete to one who understands and has become whole. In the mine explosion that blinded Mo, he "lost something else," something other than his eyesight. "What is it he has lost?" the author asks. "There's nobody to tell him of this other thing he has lost. In that same instant, he knows he'll have to keep coming back to this place of tunnels, where maybe one day he'll remember" (4). Finding that which he has lost will develop Mo's character in universal love and empathy, and in so doing make him into Everyperson.

The novel begins in a ritualized setting that Page has named "Meditation," in an underground chamber that the Hopi call a kiva. The fire in the center of the floor emits light and smoke that "dematerializes in the cold night air the way a prayer disappears into the world of the spirits." In with the Hopis sits Mo as the mysterious atmosphere of this spiritual occasion intensifies. Mo realizes the power of the darkness, with the "rhythm of human pulses, free the people in the kiva from the constraints of time, allowing their minds to journey."

In this meditation Mo is taken back to an earlier profound event in his life, when as a mining engineer, taking molybdenum from the earth, he was blinded by an explosion in the mine in which he was working. Like all of us under similar circumstances he did not understand at that time why it was he who had been blinded. But he knew he would have to create a new world for himself because the old had been destroyed. In his agony he brooded on the loss of a spiritual meaning. He is thus unconsciously open for an adventure that will possibly allow him to gain some insight into the cause and meaning of his being blinded.

Page delves into the second theme–the search for truth and empathy—indirectly and painstakingly. The ranch on which the three corpses—one of them the wife of the owner of the ranch—had been discovered in the early part of the novel was owned by a family with a son, named Conrad, who had slipped into unusual and wayward behavior. The parents want him to be rehabilitated and think that he might be if Mo will take him on as an assistant and keep him around and act as a model and guide. So Conrad is taken to Mo's household and becomes Mo's social responsibility, his "child" to be brought up right.

The second strand of the novel's rope of life encircles a twenty-one-year-old woman named Annie, who turns up unannounced and begins stalking Mo. A hypochondriac, Mo one night cannot sleep so he walks in his yard and sits on a bench to think. He slips into a meditation that in effect is a continuation of the one begun in the kiva with the Hopis at the beginning of the book. His train of thought leads him to remembering the mythological "hunchbacked flute player that was a favored icon in these parts from Anasazi times right up to the gallery-mediated present. Kokopelli was politely described as a fertility figure, and the actual fertilizing of pueblo ladies was surely something the old flute player thought about" (111). Impregnating pueblo ladies was necessary, Mo reasons, because they needed to repopulate the world against the ravages of disease, drought, raiding party, etc. Mo realizes that this functional use of sex was important, but he reasons there must be more to it than mere utility.

He also realizes that he had in his youth used semen only functionally when he sold it in Denver or distributed it in casual love affairs. The conventionally religious would look upon this as a kind of onanism and therefore sinful. Mo wondered how his semen had been used, how many women through this nondirected and impersonal ejaculation he had made pregnant, and how many people he saw around him were really his children. And what was the nasty potential from this unidentified siring. Suppose, for example, two of his children met, fell in love, married, and had their incestuous offspring. "The implications of his anonymous but widespread sowing of wild oats suggested that he should look upon all children as potentially his and treat them as such" (112). His mind then turns to his young companion, Conrad, and he wonders if he could be in fact Conrad's biological father. Here Mo is beginning to be reborn into universal love for humankind. He becomes immersed in a symbolic sex act, as "He heard a rustling of leaves and felt a breeze on his cheek that came and went like a lover's sigh." He hears something, "less a sound than a rhythm, a regularity," and he figuratively fathers a real child, as Mo asks in the darkness who the person is making the sound and is told, "I'm your daughter" (113).

This announcement, bringing Mo back from theory to reality, tests his unusual philosophy to its limit. Here a twenty-one-year-old claims to be Mo's daughter, unknown and hitherto unsuspected, the result of some youthful sperm carelessly distributed when Mo was a mining engineer around Leadville, Colorado. This self-proclaimed living result of earlier sperm distribution sorely and almost tragically tests Mo's theory of universal and anonymous fatherhood. But as in tragedy and death we sometimes achieve life and wisdom, Mo survives his crisis, passes again through his experiences of being blinded in the cave in Leadville, in effect is reborn, and has the scales of ignorance fall from his eyes and sees the wisdom of universal love.

Annie's insistence that Mo is her father, and his intense doubt, continue to drive Mo into further and deeper investigation of her charges. Finally, he decides to return to Colorado, see his former lover—Annie's mother—and get to the truth. Mo, Annie, and Conrad make the trip by automobile. As they get closer to the place where Annie's mother is supposed to be living, it becomes clearer that she is no longer there and that Annie has been exercising a giant and powerful con game on Mo. But he is determined to see the act through.

They stop the car to investigate and Annie lures Mo into a cabin. She realizes that she must control him if she is to master the situation. To do so she smashes the back of his head with her gun and he falls to the ground unconscious. As is symbolically appropriate, Mo drops in a "near-fetal" position. Annie sees Mo "as a gigantic baby, curled up in sleep" (250). To make his point Page turns again to Steinbeck's *The Grapes of Wrath* as he had elsewhere in his use of the folk joke about the fornicating squirrels and the man's expressed desire to be like them only to be told that all he had to do was find a cooperative female squirrel. In a symbolic return to raw nature, Annie then pulls off her shirt and curls it into a ball under her head. She stands before Mo with bare breasts. She reaches over him, her naked breasts touching his shoulder as she "pressed her head against his, and wept. She didn't want to hurt him" (253). She wanted to mother and protect him.

Her gesture constitutes the very basic drive of the human community, or at least what men think is the foundation of nurturing in such a community. John Steinbeck illustrates this drive graphically in the concluding paragraph of *The Grapes of Wrath* (1939), an epic about humanity's need to help one another if the race is to survive. Rose of Sharon has just delivered a stillborn baby and her breasts are swollen with milk. When Pa and Ma lead their family into a barn to escape the rising rain water, they see a very hungry young boy and his father lying in one corner, afraid that they will be chased out into the rain. The boy tells Ma that his father, in the unselfish generosity of the ideal parent, has starved himself almost to death while giving all available food to his son. Now his starvation is so far developed that he cannot hold down any food. The boy says the man must have milk or he will die. Ma is Steinbeck's symbol of perseverance and the drive to endure. She and Rose of Sharon know intuitively what must be done. Ma's eyes "passed

Rose of Sharon's eyes, and then came back to them. And the two women looked deep into each other. The girl's breath came short and gasping." "Yes," she said, meaning that she would feed the man at her breast (472).

In all human cultures the female breasts have erotic significance. Yet in some societies breastfeeding is looked down upon by females as a kind of male-dominance and by males as perhaps prolonging sexual continence and disfigurement of the breast. As Malcolm Potts and Roger Short say in their book *Ever since Adam and Eve: The Evolution of Human Sexuality,* perhaps because we are embarrassed by our fixation with female breasts, we use every kind of derogatory term possible for them except *udders* (157). Still in our fantasies, at least, adult men think of them as possible sources of life-giving milk. Nicholas Regnier (ca. 1620–40) in his painting *La Charite Romaine* pictured the famous Dr. John Caius, the founder of the Cambridge college Caius school of medicine, as being suckled at the female breast, as he was supposed to have been done in life, though in the painting he looks robust and not on his deathbed.

In the secular epiphany of his novel, the pressing of the grapes of wrath into the wine of love and empathy, Steinbeck describes the supreme offering of the female to the male and to mankind: "Rose of Sharon . . . bared her breast. 'You got to,' she said. She squirmed closer and pulled his head close. 'There!' she said. 'There.' Her hand moved behind his head and supported it. Her fingers moved gently in his hair. She looked up and across the barn, and her lips came together and smiled mysteriously" (473). She has nurtured mankind. And after the man is fed she will release him to his own purposes and pursuits. Symbolically she has animated the core in which life perseveres.

In Page's work and immediate purpose, Annie must control Mo. He has not yet been reborn, which is necessary. In her need to direct him she then ties his hands behind his back and secures them to a rusty pipe beneath a sink, under which Annie sees a black widow spider. Annie knows that female black widows don't harm anyone unless attacked; she sees herself as the black widow spider and knows that she wouldn't harm anyone unless threatened by all the injustices of the world. The only trouble is, of course, that she imagines those injustices, whether they actually exist, are attacking her. She looks upon herself and her female role as mother of people as being threatened. The ensuing scene is a close symbolic parallel to the birth process and develops graphically Page's mythological-Christian message.

Mo with his hands tied to the pipe under the sink is the fetus bound to the mother's womb by the umbilical cord. Ready for birth, Mo saws through the cord and thus releases himself for birth, though ordinarily in the birthing process the umbilical cord is cut after the baby has emerged from the mother's body. Here, however, Mo, having cut himself from the connection with the womb, emerges and stumbles down the black shaft of the cave, that is the birth canal. He remembers the contours of the mineshaft-birth canal because he has been through this lane at least twice before, when he was born physically and when he was in the actual cave and was blinded by an explosion.

Like an angry goddess, or mythological mother, who is afraid to have her son born, Annie rushes after Mo, determined to control and guide him so he cannot harm her, his mother, as males ordinarily do in mythology.

The ensuing scene in the cave with Annie trying to find him so she can kill him approaches an intensity seldom achieved outside mythological literature, as the following few lines told largely in sexual terms illustrate:

"I'm coming, you bastard, you fucking bastard. I'm coming I'll *kill* you. I'll hurt you. I'll *hurt* you." [Annie] was shrieking, her voice trailing off into a high-pitched howl in the drift. She was coming closer.

"You're sick!" Mo shouted. "You're sick, sick!"

"Damn you, damn you!" The gun fired again, the awful noise swallowing the air. Three shots? Five? The ricocheting of the blasts, how many? It had to be empty. They kept echoing, further and further off, lower-pitched, now closer, merging into a growl.

He lunged forward.

The world was falling, the rumble now a roar. A stream of dirt and pebbles and then rocks hit his shoulders, his head. There was a scream, Annie screaming, and another, a searing scream of wood breaking, and Annie again: "Auugh, no!" (273)

The final scene in an exit from the cave contains the essence and summation of the whole book. It needs to be examined closely:

The shaft. She was at the shaft. He dove forward, arms out in front, wrists cinched tight, felt her falling into him, snatched, clutched her, hit the ground—no, her, fell on her legs . . . grabbed at her shirt and pulled, yanking her torso up, out of the shaft, and crawled away from it, scrambled, hauling her over the rock. It was pounding on his back, his shoulders. Another. Shit. Shit. The mountain falling in. The noise. Christ, the noise was awful, all this rock, this rock. (273)

It becomes immediately apparent that Mo's earlier joke about parthenogenesis (birth from an unfertilized ovum, seed—immaculate conception) is now made serious. Mo is being reborn but not alone and not in the usual way. Annie, who has gone mad, falls back into the source of life, Mo's regenerative possibilities ("felt her falling into him") and is reborn, as Eve had been born from Adam (not from the rib cage but from a more natural part of the body). But not of Mo alone, for he "fell on her legs," the physical extension of her recreative anatomy. So it is indeed a strange birth, both male and female giving birth to the new—cured—female.

But Mo has undergone a rebirth also. As he approached the saving of Annie, Mo's "world was falling, the rumble now a roar. A stream of dirt and pebbles and then rocks hit his shoulders, his head" (273). So his birth canal was tight, dangerous, and noisy. For this double birth, nature, as is universal in folklore and mythology, takes notice and acknowledges the grand event, this time with what is in effect an earthquake and Mo recognizes that God is a part of this whole event: "The mountain falling in. The noise, Christ, the noise was awful, all this rock, this rock" (273). With this paroxysm of nature, the mixing of Christ in with the acknowledgment, and the rebirth of the two people into better persons, the thesis and message of the novel comes through loud and clear: small groups and cults should not exclude other kinds of people; one should not use violence in trying to possess what might be rightfully one's own; and people should be understanding and empathic to the needs of others.

This novel is Mo's return to the "place of tunnels," and his working his way through them to at least his own personal "salvation," in the realization that he owes something to mankind in general and in that realization is his personal triumph.

In this remembrance Mo turns full circle. Thrown by Annie, the young woman who claims to be his illegitimate daughter, into the same cave in which he lost his eyesight twenty-one years earlier, he is faced by the mad female and asked, symbolically, the same question two times, Why did he "betray" her. The first betrayal was Mo's not being near Annie when she needed him in the past. Second, now that she needs him again and has found him, he is denying her a second time. On the third—implied—response, however, Mo no longer denies her. He tells her what she needs to know, that she is in fact mad.

So unlike the biblical Judas who denied Christ three times, Mo does not turn from Annie thrice. In the agonizing re-enactment of his earlier experience when he lost his eyesight, he grapples with Annie, who is trying to shoot him, has boulders falling on the two of them, protects her from sure death, and though blind, manages to stagger from the cave, this time with a newly awakened inner vision, saving both himself and Annie. Although still physically blind, Mo has been reborn with a sight that he could never have known before. He has come through the biblical eye of the needle and now enjoys a knowledge and freedom he could never have enjoyed earlier.

Through the symbolism of the events in the cave, Page suggests his true meaning in the novel, and rounds out the prediction given in the introductory "Meditation." The eventuation begins, as nature would dictate, with Mo physically situated to be born. He has been struck on the back of his head by Annie and has fallen in a near-fetal position. Mo escapes, runs down the tunnel, reverses his direction, manages to get through a narrow aisle in the cascading rocks, saves Annie, and they both emerge.

The Christian—or universal—symbolism builds up after Mo and Annie get out of the cave. In their absence from his sight, Conrad has called for help. When that help arrives, both are taken to the hospital. It is Friday, the day, of course, when Christ was buried—Good Friday. When he recovers consciousness—from his burial—Mo is told by the doctor that the man who murdered Conrad's mother—and the two young lovers—has been caught, Mo murmurs, "Jesus," again tying the whole series of events into the supernatural.

Mo wants to go home "tomorrow," but is told by the doctor he cannot for some days. After having been told that Annie will be all right, Mo explains that, "She was looking for her father." "Oh, God," the doctor replies, again directly pointing toward religious interpretation of the episode (276). The whole book has been laced with oaths and references to God, as in the ordinary vernacular of people, but this time the oaths take on a deeper meaning, like references to and genuine supplications to the all powerful. A little later the doctor tells Mo, "You saved her life, you know." Mo replies with a deeper sincerity than he usually has been able to summon: "Yeah? That's good. I owed her *something*" (277). So Jesus-God saved her life.

The something for which he is indebted to Annie is his realization that he owes both her and all mankind empathy. In the beginning Page has said that "something else has been lost" and that Mo will have to return again and again to recover it. He needs to feed that realization of this debt every so often.

From the crisis and experience Mo emerges a man with widened and sensitized new realizations. He entered the cave blind but emerged with a new vision. He lost a female daughter but gained a son, Conrad. Conrad had been "given" to Mo by his father and stepmother, who owned the farm on which the two young murder victims had been found. Conrad's stepmother had become the third victim and his father had been paralyzed at the site of the original murders when he found his wife. A young irresponsible and worthless young male at the time of the murders Conrad through his experience with Annie and Mo has taken on a new persona and worthwhile character. Mo too has developed into a new person. Annie has been medically treated and returned to some degree of sanity. But she could not become Mo's real daughter, despite the fact that Connie had said that she would love to have Mo with a daughter. But it is not to be. He must settle for a son. Why Mo could not have a daughter perhaps ties in with the conventional father-son mythological symbol. Maybe Mo has become a god, with a little g.

Annie survives her borderline personality disorder. Most important for the novelist Page, though Mo has emerged a wiser man he has not lost his affection for the "Indian woman," Connie. Having returned from the funeral of her uncle, she has come to the hospital to see him, and he, the new man, wants to see her. So his connection to the Hopi, the Indian nations, has been re-established. To rise above this accomplishment will take a great stretch of imagination and will.

Robert Westbrook

Robert Westbrook is one of the more ordinary writers of Indian crime fiction on one level and one of the more accomplished on the other. He stands ankle deep in everyday life but is at his strongest when he looks up into and through mythology and develops his stories through the upsurge of *homo sapiens* spiritual aspirations.

Ghost Dancer begins in a Mt. Olympus atmosphere. Howie Moon Deer, the Indian hero, and Jack Wilder, Howie's boss, in a much needed assignment, have been hired to meet a customer halfway up a ski slope and are riding up the ski lift in a dazzling display of sun and snow. "They cleared the first tower and suddenly found themselves high above the white ground and climbing fast into the frozen sky" (18). Changing ski lifts Howie and Jack sit alongside a woman and a young girl, obviously the woman's daughter. The woman dazzles Howie with her beauty and supernatural appearance. Howie immediately names her the

"Lady in White," a "snow maiden," and though rebuffed at first from any effort to get to know her better, he later learns that her name is Alison, and she is a physician who performs abortions in Albuquerque. The daughter's name, significantly, is Angela.

Howie and Jack's appointment is with a sexually dissolute ex-senator who is to meet them in a rest house on the slope of his ski resort at a spot sacred to the Indians. Before he meets them he seduces one of his ski patrol members. After he leaves, the woman calls someone on the telephone and says that the senator is on his way. He is shot with an arrow and falls into a ravine on the sacred spot. Jack and Howie find him and begin to investigate his murder.

The senator has lived two lives, one respectable and conservative, the other predatory and selfish. He married and fathered one daughter, and seduced a half-Indian who worked for him and fathered a daughter with her. The respectable daughter is Alison, Howie's "Lady in White," who practices medicine in Albuquerque, performs abortions, and cannot work in her hometown because she is harassed by the very militant group Christians for a Moral America—the CMA.

The daughter of the Indian mother, Josie, has through the years hidden her hatred for her father because of how he mistreated her mother and is determined to get revenge, as well as hasten the inheritance of a considerable fortune from her father.

She has tried to get her father to sell the sacred ledge halfway up the ski slope to a gambling group who want to put in a casino there. Her father has stoutly resisted the idea. It is Josie who shoots her father and her guilt is determined. Although a kind of "supernaturalness" about "The Lady in White" is established and she has pointed out a vision toward higher aspects of life, she must disappear to make room for Westbrook's heroine in his next novel. So Westbrook sends her to Ghana to practice medicine unselfishly. She promises to keep in touch but it is clear that she will not, and Howie does not expect her to. Westbrook ends the novel with a lonesome cry of abandonment from Howie: "*One day I'll find my own tribe!* he vowed as he turned over the ignition. He knew they were out there somewhere: a whole damn tribe of bookish, misfit Indians. But meanwhile he felt so suddenly lonely he could hardly see the road through his tears as he drove away" (308).

Westbrook's second novel, *Warrior Circle*, is not as successful as the first, though it tries in thrusts to reach up toward the sky as *Ghost Dancer* had. It begins with a mythological-earthliness motif by having an introductory and leading character who stutters. Then later the group of wicked fake-Indians who are trying to rob the city try to reach their epiphany on the surrounding mountain peak but the book fails to reach the mythological triumph such efforts initiate through the development of the remainder of the story.

Outside San Geronimo a group of businessmen meet weekly in what they call their Warrior Circle, in which they play at being Indians. Their purposes are twofold. They give themselves fancy Indian names and go through the mental and physical gymnastics they think Indians used to perform to achieve ultimate peace. But they got their Indian lore from the Internet and other non-Indian sources and therefore were performing in a pseudo-authentic world.

But the main purpose of the Warrior Circle is to take over the land worth a quarter-million dollars they had already stolen from the city at five acres for $5.00 and convert it into a shopping mall that would ruin the rest of the city. One night in their Indian playacting, one of the men is shot in the back of the head by a masked figure with "eyes bare human" that Westbrook calls "Death." The murder is hushed up, but word about it gets out and a search is begun for the murderer.

As the Warrior Circle is investigated about the murder, the members become vicious. The sheriff especially becomes uncontrollably mean and intends to murder Howie, as he and Jack Wilder begin their investigation. Although they work on the solution, Howie and Jack do not solve the murder, instead the investigation is cleared by an outside source, a local reporter, who likewise had been the subject of an investigation over her supposed murder.

The novel begins after the reporter, Aria, and Howie have just had sex and she jumps out of bed, dresses, leaps into her car and drives away. Thinking that she will return, Howie drifts off to sleep until hours later he is awakened by the sound of Puccini's *Turandot* coming from her car. A search is conducted in the neighborhood, but neither Aria nor her body can be found.

Subsequently and illogically as the search continues for the murderer of the Warrior Circle man, Aria comes back to San Geronimo and tells Howie that she had run away to Hawaii in order to be alone and think through her future. She was not ready to be tied down and had to live independently.

She is not directly guilty of the murder though she has been investigating the Warrior Circle for years because of what they had done to her father in New York City. She had sowed the seeds of suspicion and hatred that had caused the discord among the members of the Circle that caused them to start killing themselves. She had begun this internal strife because her father had been irreparably harmed by this group. He had run a successful small pharmaceutical business until members of the Circle had ruthlessly destroyed it. Now Aria was out to expose them. She is determined to prevent the rape of San Geronimo. She is still not ready to settle down with Howie, so he leaves town. As it turns out the leader of the Warrior Circle who had been murdered at the beginning of the book had been killed by his wife because she did not like what he was doing to their lifestyle.

Howie is not really interested in the solution to the Warrior Circle murder because of the time that would be needed for the law to take its course, so without any explanation he goes to Colorado, leaving justice about the Warrior Circle in the hands of whites, which could take years but not of his life. His feelings about whites are summed up in Westbrook's pronouncement: "These people were interesting, sometimes funny; often tragic. But when push came to shove, they were not his people. They were not his tribe" (262).

After a short period spent in Colorado he returns to San Geronimo and almost magically meets a woman named Claire Knightsbridge who has left her home in Iowa because she discovered that her professor husband was sleeping with his female graduate students. Although offended by her husband's behavior she immediately has sex with Howie, then returns to Iowa and her husband but writes to Howie saying, "You made it possible for me to go back to Jim and the kids and face reality again" (228). Thus apparently is the power of uninhibited sex.

But she returns. As he walks the streets he hears someone playing Bach's Prelude from Suite No. 1 and knows it is Claire returned to his town and him. Howie talks to Jonathan, Claire's young son, and expresses one side of his philosophy of life: "Home is a very wonderful thing. But sometimes home isn't what you've left behind in the past — it's what's lying ahead of you in the future, waiting to be found." Howie's future moves are around his passions which are reawakened by Claire who makes him feel "suddenly alive again" (226).

Despite Claire's physical stimulation, or perhaps reflected in it, Howie in this novel is a very naive and romantic man. He wants a "princess-type" lover but realizes he can't have one. He is not misled by the notions of the whites that Indians of the old days were noble savages.

Although Westbrook generally does not openly criticize whites, in this book he pulls all stops and allows his cynicism of the whole human race to boil through:

A hundred years ago, the white men were making jewelry from the genitals of Howie's murdered ancestors, soldiers from the Seventh Cavalry had been known to cut vaginas from Sioux women and turn them into handbags. But palefolk were sentimental creatures: they got very misty-eyed about all the things they destroyed; pristine forests, rivers, buffalo, and the native people who once inhabited this continent. It was like Hitler in his old age, had he won the war, saying to his grandchildren, "Oh those Jews! Weren't they a lovely people!" (35)

Westbrook sees all people, the predator and the prey, especially the former, as pretty much the same at all times: "Underneath the latest haircut—ponytail or crewcut—it was remarkable how nothing much changed from one stoned age to the next" (195). His wider attitude on man's folly is voiced in the final paragraph of the book in commenting on Howie's attitude about life: "Foolish, certainly. Still looking for love, at the mercy of lust, full of wild and unfounded hope. But what the hell. He had placed his bet on the great Indian roulette wheel in the sky, and it would be interesting to see how it played out."

Although it expresses in no uncertain terms Westbrook's attitude toward certain aspects of American society, this book is at best only moderately successful. It is too complicated. It seems to have been cobbled together without a successful plot, or with overly complicated plots with characters who do not stand out, and with Howie not towering head and shoulders above the others. It is an Indian pseudo-romance filled with considerable violence.

The third novel, *Red Moon*, is a return to Westbrook's strongest style and is in fact a powerful story that reaches some of the spiritual heights that *Ghost Dancer* had achieved. The story begins with a mystical and "supernatural" figure who calls himself the Rainbow Man. He shuffles into San Geronimo pushing a grocery cart in which he carries all his earthly belongings. He has pushed the cart over rugged land all the way from California and is obviously on a "divine mission." He is befriended by Claire Knightsbridge, director of the San Geronimo Art Institute, who gives him a $5.00 donation when she is returning to work from a comfortable lunch. He mistakes her for an angel who had "shown him some mercy."

The Rainbow Man begins to stalk her, not intending any harm but because he considers her the most beautiful and angelic figure he has ever seen. He walks around her house and sees her naked taking a shower and sketches her three times, always with wings and looking angelic.

The Art Association is supported by an old lady, Barbara Vandenberg, rich with a husband twenty years her junior, dissolute and robbing his wife. Bab's son, Robin, by a first marriage, is sylphlike, "elfin," "like Peter Pan," and a playboy.

Robin hires Jack and Howie to investigate his father-in-law and see if he is stealing money from his wife, then he unhires them telling them that he had been wrong in hiring them. Naturally, this curious behavior arouses the suspicions of the two detectives and they refuse to quit.

San Geronimo is filled with artists, talented and phony. One of the major true artists is an Indian named Gilmer True Day, who uses an Indian girl named Anna as his model. She is also mistress of Sherman, Bab's husband.

Thirty years earlier someone had stolen from the Vandenberg collection at the Art Institute Georgia O'Keeffe's painting *Red Moon,* and one of the thieves was the Rainbow Man who has now returned to San Geronimo to restore it. Before he can do so he is murdered, as it turns out by Sherman and Anna. The importance of the attempted return of this major art treasure by the Rainbow Man he murdered is underlined by the fact that it is done in a Wagnerian thunderstorm that shakes mountains and men.

Although he has been murdered to prevent the return of the art treasure, the Rainbow Man has outsmarted his murderers. In the last hours of his life he gives to his angelic Claire Knightsbridge four gifts, three of which are immediately visible, the fourth of which is a mystery. As it turns out, the Rainbow Man had long ago sent the picture to his sister and asked her at a certain time to send it back to the Art Institute. She takes this time to return it as her brother had requested. So the circle is complete.

Westbrook always closes the door on one novel while opening that on the next. Here he has Claire Knightsbridge, the director of the Art Institute, Howie's love and lover, clear out to make room for the next. Claire is an accomplished cellist and has received word from a friend in Chicago that the friend is establishing a string quartet and wants Claire to play in it. Claire is torn between her attraction to Howie and his passion for her and for her future on her own path. She chooses the latter, declaring that she will always love her "noble savage," as she calls him as she boards the train for Chicago. She must play her own song in life.

Albeit a little melodramatic *Red Moon* is a heroic and accomplished novel. Claire's exit on the train is sentimental, but earlier Westbrook had imparted a little homely counsel that ought to stick with us, at least with the impressionable. When the Rainbow Man's sister sends back *Red Moon* it contains a note that reads, "Just look what you can do." That is always one of the messages of heroic fiction.

In his fourth novel, *Ancient Enemy,* Westbrook returns to the mundane world around us but his subject is more important than it was in *Warrior Circle* and his success much greater.

This story is situated in Chaco Canyon, historical home of the Anasazi in northern New Mexico, and is concerned with the question of whether those historic Indians were cannibals, the "Ancient Enemy" of scholars interested in them.

A stiff-necked British archaeologist, who passes himself off as an honored scientist on leave when he really has been fired, is digging in the ruin. He is interested in proving that the Anasazi not been cannibals. The Indians are determined to block his disturbing the ancestral resting place of these people. One night as he is secretly digging, one of the Indians, who is his hidden cohort, comes to the ruins to kill him. A head is later found thrown into a dumpster behind a local cafe. To try to prove that the decapitated head is that of the British archaeologist, though it is not, a shark's tooth is placed in the ear, where he usually wore one. This story does not reflect very well on the Indians. Beautiful Donna Theresa, who for her purposes married the British archaeologist, is sister to the Indians who murdered him, with her approval.

When the archaeologist's head is discovered in the dumpster Howie and Jack get involved in the case. Howie has been hired to check out the rumor that the restaurant is serving cat instead of chicken. This second investigation provides a leitmotif that echoes in crude humor and sexual innuendoes, not always to the improvement of the novel.

But Westbrook opens up and develops new avenues. Donna Theresa, the mysterious Indian sister of the guilty ones, enriches the novel with her heroic tragic flaw of stuttering. She therefore steers the novel between the two levees of heroic and anti-heroic. Jack Wilder is both heroic and anti-heroic. Howie also moves between the heroic and anti-heroic.

Jack's wife, who is ordinarily a fixture in the background, listening to and advising her husband but not taking part in much action, is unusually strong in *Ancient Enemy.* She is librarian in the San Geronimo public library and is diligent in making sure that books are not kept out overdue—surely a trivial matter in a murder investigation. In her search, however, she discovers that the British archaeologist checked out a book a year before and had not returned it. She sets out to his residence to recover the book, only to discover him at home with a closet filled with human bones. In effect, it is she who solves the mystery.

Although Westbrook is dealing with the important subject of archaeology and the cultural habits of the Anasazi he is content not to project his own conclusions. The British scientist has discovered a twig coprolite (fossilized excrement) that can be used in a DNA test to prove that the Anasazi were or were not cannibals, but Westbrook has Howie flush it down the toilet. "It felt right somehow to put things in their proper places," he concludes (302). It is interesting that Westbrook had a lucky roll of the dice or some kind of prescience for through use of DNA in the feces archaeologists are proving that the Anasazi were in fact cannibals. Westbrook does not make the point that the flush of the toilet is thorough.

In this novel, Westbrook has demonstrated that he can write of everyday life and artifacts and do it skillfully. He is more powerful when dealing with mythological heroic figures and least effective when writing romances and everyday crime and passion. But then everybody demonstrates greater strength when shouldering heavier burdens, and Westbrook has broad shoulders in novelizing mankind's stretch upward toward the stars.

CHAPTER THREE

Protagonists, Associates, and Development

To make their stories lively and to demonstrate their individual creative talents each author has developed protagonists with different, distinguishable, and sometimes unique characteristics. Frequently these characteristics are the latest adaptations of age-old conventional traits; sometimes they are essentially alterations of merely outsize characteristics. Often they are physical, sometimes rhetorical, but always they are, as they should be, author-based and as far as possible unique to that writer. The protagonists are idealized or dream-driven versions of the author, what he or she thinks is the style best suited to the society created and written about and to the expectations of the readers. The protagonists are always the high-reach mark of the author and of the author's accomplishments. In other kinds of fiction the story can survive with weak characters; in crime fiction the tale thrives best with a strong and accomplished protagonist. In crime fiction the authors are known, judged by, remembered by, recognized by, live or die by their operatives, detectives, protagonists.

Of all the heroes working today in Native American crime fiction the most powerful and amusing are Robert Westbrook's and especially Jake Page's T. Moore "Mo" Bowdre. So complex and important is

Bowdre's development in the Page canon we should outline in some extent the means and extent of that growth.

Leading Characters

Jake Page

Mo's birth and development are characteristic of the folk and mythical hero. Mo's unusual, almost unprecedented, heroic quality is doubly presented with two, not one, mysterious births, one by the author in creating him and the other by the author's creation of him in the novels.

Mo "mysteriously" appeared to the author as recounted earlier, after a wine-filled dinner during a time he was working on a Billy the Kid project. Page then has to have Mo explain his birth in the novels. In the first novel, to a reporter who asks Mo about his background, he fills in the details about his birth with the statement, "Hah-hah-yes I was born. Born a pig in the horse stable." The parallel though a rather barnyard reference may be uncomfortably close to "babe in a manger," but at least the language tells us the level of the heroic Mo that Page thinks he represents and in which he will try to develop him. This conceit is to grow more fully in successive novels, as it should be, and come to full bloom in *A Certain Malice.*

The same Muse that birthed Mo in the horse stable and ties him into a long tradition must have directed Page to develop him as blind. Sightless heroes go back at least as far as (blind) Homer. As Homer may have been a more sensitive teller of folktales because he was blind and could center his attention on aspects of life that transcend the usual, as many commentators think, Mo felt that his handicap gave him an advantage in reading his surroundings: "The sense of touch is a better guide to the three dimensional world than any of the other senses, including vision," he says (*Gods* 3).

He advertises his presence and character with a loud and grating laugh that only friends can tolerate. This noisy characteristic parallels the outstanding trait of all mythological heroes. All are marked with some sign or outstanding personal trait.

Page, of course, had the option of creating his leading character with any personality he chose. He decided to make him a "pompous redneck" in every external aspect of that word, with an appearance that is bound to make him stand out in any gathering, with a laugh that is "a staccato series of noises that lay somewhere between human laughter and the bark of a large dog" (*Canyon* 2). Although he would not seem to be the type physically, he is sexually always ready to perform. He is, in other words, the raucous outsized personification of the stereotypical universal "redneck."

Robert Westbrook

Contemporary Indian crime fiction has another strong character in this tradition in Westbrook's Jack Wilder, working with the naive-sophisticated Indian Howard Moon Deer. Like Mo, Wilder has suffered an accident that has rendered him blind. Like Mo, Jack has developed his other senses to an acute degree. Like Mo also, Wilder has the help of his wife, who plays a major or minor role as needed, his strong arm Howie, and his other senses. Wilder is like Mo also in being at most mysterious and at least mythological. Westbrook is inclined to develop Wilder's immediate past and his having been blinded by an aborted dope raid in San Francisco and the fact that his Sioux Indian assistant Howie is both "over-educated" and naive and vulnerable. In this axis, in other words, Westbrook has the democratic impulses and experience.

Howie is rather indifferent to the human race. Wilder, on the other hand, speaking for Westbrook, or Westbrook speaking for himself in the presence of Wilder, expresses a sardonic Jonathan Swiftean, Thomas Hobbesian contempt for the human race, which he feels cannot be saved and is not worth the effort. Such an attitude, and Westbrook's development of it, introduces a new strain of vinegar into Indian crime fiction, which might change the chemical balance altogether, driving it more toward typical old-fashioned hard-boiled fiction with a western setting.

Westbrook introduces something extreme into his fiction—pornography, or pseudo-pornography.

Ghost Dancer, his first book in the Howard Moon Deer series, begins with the sex act desecrating a sacred Indian spot on a mountain slope and later touches on the fact that some weird people have their genitals pierced with small gold rings, which makes the sex act all the more fascinating and stimulating. *Warrior Circle,* the second, begins with a tussle in the bed, what Howie thinks is "postcoital heaven," and then abandonment by the female partner. Later he meets Claire who has left her adulterous husband in Iowa but is ready for sex. They have barely met when Howie suggests that they have a drink, and Claire enthusiastically agrees, saying she "is in the mood for something stiff" (225). Her desire extends beyond the drink. They go to Howie's cabin and Claire undresses and plays her cello. Howie had never before seen a naked woman playing a cello and is excited beyond resistance. Then, as Westbrook tells it, they change to a different song. In *Red Moon,* Barbara Vandenberg, who ought to be too old for sex, marries the much younger Sherman Stone and maintains him no matter how much he abuses her because his penis is ten inches long. Howie jokes with her in an exchange that probably comes straight from the world of jazz:

> "I always supposed that for women it wasn't the meat as much as the motion," [Howie] managed.
> "It's the meat," she assured him curtly. (243)

When Claire leaves to return to Chicago, she tells Howie that she will return in good time but she refers to masturbation as the usual sexual outlet for men. She expects him to remain true to her but not to stay away from other women. "I certainly don't expect you to survive forever with just the old hand," she tells him (283).

In *Ghost Dancer* and *Ancient Enemy* Westbrook uses cunnilingus extensively. In the latter, while Howie is trussed up in braces that render the use of his hips inoperative, Claire suggests that they play a game of Scrabble and the winner get "a blow job," then she cheats by using an esoteric medical term and slides over Howie's face for him to perform the cunnilingus. She—and he—will do anything for sex. *Ghost Dancer* has as a second take on cunnilingus. A rich old lady with a fondness for felines has hired Jack and Howie to find her missing cats. She suspects they are being served at a local restaurant disguised as chicken and Howie is to investigate. Wilder, though he has accepted the job because he needs the money, makes a joke out of, a theme that echoes through the book from beginning to end:

> "They're eating pussy at the Shanghai Café," was how his boss, Jack Wilder, had put it, chuckling at his own joke. Jack had a truly awful sense of humor. "Your assignment, Howie—should you accept it—is to catch them in the act of putting Puss in the pot!" (1)

An unusual theme of development in Westbrook's novels is his use of classical music. In *Red Moon* when Howie has sex with Claire Knightsbridge, it is in a tipi where he is living and after the conclusion he feels that "a bear, a blonde and a tipi—as far as Howie was concerned, this was a fine way for any postmodern Indian to get in touch with his roots" (74), especially since Schubert's string quartet *Death and the Maiden,* was playing on the CD. Howie and Claire were deeply affected in another way with music. The Rainbow Man's sketches of Claire depicted her in an "upward surge," which in effect pictured her real desire to fly. "These were wings that desperately *wanted* to fly. Not fly in the exact same way that Claire flew, metaphorically speaking, when she played a few special pieces of music, particularly Beethoven" (75).

In *Red Moon,* after Claire has decided to go back to Chicago and play in the classical string quartet, Howie says to her as she gets on the train, "This is the first. I've never lost a woman to Beethoven before." Although Claire assures him that she will be back, we know that Westbrook is clearing the stage for the female of the next book and doing it on the wings of song he so much admires.

Supporting Characters

Jake Page

Page's other characters—both major and minor—stand out as effective creations. In his five novels to date four characters are "major." Samantha Burgess, paparazzi reporter, is a person who grows professionally through the first two books. At first she is a naive freelance investigator and observer. In *The Deadly Canyon* she has grown into a bona fide reporter for the *Nevada Intelligencer* who is mistress of all occasions and sucker to nobody. As such, because of her wit and charm, she becomes a favored reporter of the Santa Fe police department and acts as outside eyes for the events transpiring in the novel. She is a distant third in the hierarchy of characters who loom larger in some books, smaller in others.

The FBI gets sympathetic treatment in the person of Larry Collins, a loose-cannon agent who was exiled to the Southwest because the Hopi reported to Washington that four of their most important gods had been stolen. Collins had not wanted to report to the godforsaken desert of New Mexico but once there he had fallen in love with the country and the locals. Acting unexpectedly for an FBI man, Collins, always revealing his crooked teeth in his smile, is in sync with the locals and is generally liked by all—except the men back in Washington. Page calls Collins "eccentric but a bit thickheaded" (*Canyon* 100). In *The Lethal Partner,* because he has been ordered to report to Florida for duty and he loves the Southwest too much to leave it, Collins resigns from the FBI. He jokes that he will set up a dance studio in Santa Fe though he cannot make two moves in logical sequence. Collins is a useful second-rung character.

Another triumph in personality—perhaps second or third in importance in the novels—is Sergeant Anthony (Tony) Ramirez of the Santa Fe police department. He is half-Latino and half-Anglo. In developing Ramirez, Page is furthering his atonement for people who have been mistreated by the dominant white society. Ramirez is clever, has a quiet sense of humor when not kept straight-laced by his duty, and feels caught between the Anglos and the Indians in the Southwest.

Page's strongest supporting character materializes in his latest novel, *A Certain Malice*. Annie, as we have seen, is insane with borderline personality disorder. She drives and controls the second half of the novel and provides the stimulus for Page's developing this novel into a profundity he has not even approached in his earlier works. In her role she has to symbolize the earth mother, with whom Mo Bowdre undergoes a second birth and growth into a mythological dimension.

Except for Mo, however, the strongest character in Page's novels is Connie Barnes, Mo's heart and companion, his eyes, his everything. She is half-white and half-Hopi. Because Mo was conceived from the first as being an overgrown redneck with a colossal ego and overactive *cojones* and was going to work in Hopi land, Page knew he would need a Hopi girlfriend. "Since she was going to have to be a lot more worldly than a lot of Hopi women are," Page says in his interview, he "made her half-Hopi with a runaway white father. So if she did something wholly uncharacteristic, the Hopis would say it was because of her deadbeat father." And she is constantly doing something uncharacteristic of Hopi women. Although she never complains about doing the domestic work of a Hopi female and at times is treated condescendingly by Mo, Connie is far more than a "squaw." When Mo was in a desperate funk about the explosion that had blinded him, Connie coaxed him back to life and happiness. She is his enthusiastic sex partner. She listens to his whining, his dreams, his corny jokes, and his exquisite cognitive solutions to the problems of crime that he cannot see but can understand. She is his mirror image and complement.

All of Page's characters are as near flesh and blood credible human beings as fictional characters can be. They are a mixture of all kinds of sexual preferences and practices. They are a herd on the rut, always only one act away from sexual foreplay or one move short of played out. All are to one degree or another off-center and humorous.

Many of Page's more effective characters are the lesser ones. One of the more humorous is the throwaway character Señor Gutierrez in *The Deadly Canyon*, who, Collins thinks, "operated in a different time zone. Like maybe a century or two off" (54). He has been working at his outpost on the American-Mexican border for forty-five years, seven days a week, fifty-two weeks a year. He was supposed to retire three years earlier but cannot because he is caught in a catch-22: In order to retire he must go to Mexico City and fill out the necessary papers. But he cannot go to Mexico City because he has to remain on duty on the border. A replacement was sent but he was killed in an automobile accident on his way to report for duty. Señor Gutierrez is convinced that he will die at his post and his death will not be discovered for years. "One day I will put my head down on this desk and die"—he laughed conspiratorially—"and my government won't notice for months, maybe years" (55).

A larger and more fascinating character is Sheriff Jack Knott, a living stereotype of the fat, luxury-loving, lecherous incompetent. He is xenophobic and afraid of losing his job because of his incompetence. When he is needed for official duties he is always out whoring around with one of his mistresses. His misconduct is an open secret but few dare suggest that perhaps he should pay more attention to his official rather than to than his sexual obligations. The deputy sheriff suggests that life for all would be easier if the sheriff would straighten up and work right. When deputy Jimmy Snyder makes this suggestion, Knott paralyzes him with the wrath of authority and power:

> The Sheriff looked up at his deputy, his lower eyelids drooping. He stared at the younger man with pale hazel eyes, then turned his head and spat over the ledge. Breathing heavily, he said, "You know, Depitty Snyder . . . I could assign your ass to wearing a rabbit suit and make you Mr. Police Bunny . . . and send you around to all the damn schools in Hidalgo County so you could explain . . . to the little children all the nice things the sheriff's department does for them. I could do that right now, this very damn minute. . . . So you think about that." (*Canyon* 16)

The good sheriff gradually decides on more extreme punishment for his deputy. On another occasion when Snyder reminds Knott that the case they have been assigned has been taken over by the Feds and he should stay out, Knott blisters him with threats:

> "Depitty, I've decided that a rabbit suit ain't good enough for you. Now you get your butt over there to that research place and figure out a way to find out what I want to know or I'm going to hang you by the *cojones* from the courthouse flagpole and tell people that you got caught sending money to the Sierra Club, you hear me?" (*Canyon* 67)

The development of Page's novels so far, vis-à-vis both his theme of atonement to the Indians for white injustices and artistically, is interesting. The drumbeat of the deserts of Indians has not diminished, except in *A Certain Malice,* where it has been amplified to include all of humanity, but the craft of the novels and the development of the characters have grown steadily. There is almost a straight line of modification visible. Mo was begun as a hard-nosed big-assed redneck, loud and very visible, though sensitive and amusing. He is a late-developed frontier type beholden to no one.

Page recognized that he had a tiger by the tail. He needed a female to match or at least keep up with Mo. Connie Barnes, tall and beautiful, clever and long-suffering, stood in Mo's shadow, and since Page wanted to atone to the Hopi for their mistreatment he needed Connie in the spotlight more. She has increasingly come out of Mo's shadow. Achieving near equality with Mo though has not been easy. When she began to develop equal status with Mo, in *The Lethal Partner,* Mo was reduced in stature and respect to a whiner. So Mo has come to rely more on Connie, but in her supporting role, not as co-equal. Page says that he wants to make Connie the main character but realizes that it will be difficult to squelch Mo. In fact, however, he has already begun the toning down. The fear is that when he reduces Mo from the blusterous egomaniacal giant he is going to make him not a less strong supporting character but a weak, whining, minor character with none of his former charm and strength. So it is going to be unsafe to let the tiger go.

For the moment, in *A Certain Malice* Page has solved the problem by getting Connie out of the picture and replacing her with another very strong character, Annie, and facing Mo with a problem far greater than that in which he works ordinarily.

Tony Hillerman

Hillerman's Leaphorn and Chee, two who have developed and grown through the years, continue to dramatize the author's desire to write novels that both chronicle Navajo customs and sell well. Their personalities are well known and are revealed to us sufficiently in the preceding pages concerning their activities in Hillerman's novels.

Jean Hager

Jean Hager's Mitchell Bushyhead and Molly Bearpaw work well, each in his or her own story, and Hager has no plans to unite them in an adventure. Probably both would suffer, as Hillerman's Leaphorn and Chee do, at least to some of us readers. They can't grow when paired as half-heroes in one enterprise.

Louis Owens

Louis Owens has yet to settle on the protagonist with whom he wants to spend time. Cole McCurtain certainly has his strengths and provides a historical depth to Owens's work. He makes it rich in Indian and human tradition and profound in a potential that works in anthropological culture needs. But his role, or at least the novels in which he dominates, is probably outdone for the general reader in the third and fourth books of Owens' series. In the third book, the protagonist is a *developing* character who is defeated by superior forces and compelled to transform earthly existence into the mystical beyond. In *Nightland,* Owens, holding himself to the real world of daily existence, reaches high and creates action and heroic characters sufficiently strong to provide an interesting story befitting the dual Indian-white world they inhabit.

James D. Doss

James D. Doss operates in a shady world halfway between reality and dreamland, including the Upperworld, the Middleworld, and the Lowerworld. He builds on characters who can operate in all levels at the same time. His dwarf Utes from the other world are fascinating, as are his shamans who can talk with them and grow on their wisdom. Daisy Perika is one of our favorites, as she is of the author. Charlie Moon is undoubtedly going to take on increasingly important roles, to the satisfaction of the readers. And he is going to develop characteristics that have been only hinted at so far.

White Shell Woman, his latest in this series, is a divergence in subject treatment and a decided switch in tone from the earlier books. Doss is a scientist at Los Alamos whose greatest pleasure is to retreat to his hideaway where he can write. In the past he has pretty much managed to leave his professional life behind him and enter into the imaginative world of his creations. This time he does not manage to leave all his knowledge behind, and he is more given to indulge himself in humor. As for example one time in speaking of the heavy burden of owning the vast Columbine ranch his character Moon confesses that "I'm so poor I can't even afford to pay attention" (61). In the hospital Moon asks his doctor how Amanda Silk, who had fallen dead beside him in the Indian ruins, died. The physician explains, "Catecholamines." Moon has him explain:

> "Ah, yes. Catecholamines." Dr. Simpson's bespectacled eyes took on
> a dreamy look. "Dr. Silk must have suffered an incredibly stressful

experience. This results in a multitude of physiological responses. The whole point is to make the fight-or-flight mechanism kick in. The one of particular interest in Dr. Silk's case involves the hypothalamus. That organ signals the adrenal glands to start squirting catecholamines into the bloodstream—which increases the ability of the blood to coagulate. All of which helps prevent excessive bleeding." The medical examiner enjoyed the sweet sound of his own voice far more than the ethereal song of violin or harp. "This response is very handy if you are running from a hungry grizzly who is right behind you biting big chunks outta your ass." Simpson paused to chuckle. "Further questioning reveals, however, that Silk had coronary arteries an Olympic athlete would be proud of." (228)

Doss continues his speculation about theories and investigations in the scientific world that ordinarily do not make their way into crime fiction. At one point he muses, "I wonder whether space goes on and on forever" and finally returns to smack you on the back of the head. Moon speculates the same question in wondering about the universality of White Shell Woman and her gliding toward the vast emptiness beyond the reservation. Parris, Moon's friend, ruminates: "I wonder whether space just goes on and on forever and ever, or is it curved and twisted so that if a fella would eyeball it out there far enough, he'd see the back of his head. These are urgent questions about multidimensional string theory—quantum gravity—parallel universes. Not to mention this conundrum of entangled photons" (291). That is heavy stuff for crime fiction and reveals one direction, of many, into which crime fiction is currently developing.

It also may be leading Doss away from concern about the way whites are treating Native Americans and whether they owe some kind of recompense. In this book there is no hint of Indian animosity toward whites. Nearly all the actors—and all the culprits—are Indian or part Indian, and the whites play only minor roles. As the police chief says about the whites and the Indians: "The *matukach* [whites] are right. We are a taciturn people" (240).

Just as the early Doss seems more concerned with the feeling of remorse over the treatment of Indians by whites than the later author the same attitude seems to pervade Dana Stabenow's early works.

Dana Stabenow

One of the more satisfactory creations in this Native American world is Dana Stabenow's Kate Shugak. Not since Al Capp's Mammy Yokum have we seen such diminutive strength as Kate possesses, such wit and such delight. In her creation, Stabenow called upon people she has known, characters she has observed on the Alaskan frontier, and a fertile imagination fueled by the author's desire to see that women get their dues among the Aleut, in Alaska, and elsewhere. Since she lives in a dynamic society, Kate will undoubtedly continue to grow.

Thomas Perry

Thomas Perry, after searching around with several male characters who drove action novels, has developed a series on a powerful woman who can keep pace with any man and probably outdistance him. There are many adventures yet for her to have, many people for her to move out of danger. In doing this Jane Whitefield is going to continue to grow and develop in revealing aspects of Seneca territory and culture.

Margaret Coel

With Margaret Coel the story is more important than the characters, though clearly she must have Father John O'Malley and Vicky Holden to serve as guides to and through the adventures. They continue to grow in interest to the reader for their own personal lives but will be overshadowed by the cultures and conflicts about which they write.

Peter Bowen

Peter Bowen has created in Gabriel Du Pré and Madelaine two characters that are equal to every challenge and almost impossible to outdo. The society in which they live and play is different from others we read about. The Métis are not a common group for fiction, even about Indians. Nor are such people as Du Pré and Madelaine individuals to be found every day in literature. They have personalities created by someone who recognizes the picturesque, the powerful, and the unique. They live in a different world, speak a different language, adventure in a different society that is strange and exotic. They grow in strength and resilience and accomplishment with every story. One can only hope that more will be coming soon. They demonstrate not only the potential outreach of crime fiction but also the rich potential for adventure and character development in these new areas of culture.

J. F. Trainor

The same must be said for J. F. Trainor's powerful creation Angie Biwaban, the feisty Anishinabe princess from Duluth, Minnesota, who must at the same time serve two gods, the one of law and order and the other of herself, and finds the assignment difficult in both cases. But though she is somewhat larger than credence she is fascinating and a fine subject to read about. Trainor has Biwaban serving two or three purposes concurrently. She is a feminist heroine, determined to make females noticeably important. She is a spoof of the old Legend of the West. She is the Lone Rangeress. She is Mrs. Quixote touting at the windmills of the American West. She manages all roles in an amusing and informative style. She is probably what every active woman in our society wants to be and what many men fear they will become. Trainor must continually notch his six-gun of achievement on the accomplishments of Princess Anishanabe.

Aimée and David Thurlo

Aimée and David Thurlo have in the person of Ella Clah a splendid character who can dramatize the Navajo people as they see themselves and in so doing give us a fine story. She is a worthy heroine, an interesting person well equipped to carry a message, even when the authors are more interested in the story in which she acts than the message she reveals.

The interesting thing about all these characters is that they manage to be different from the usual cast in a genre that is generally filled with unusual sorts of people. Starring in an unfamiliar kind of crime fiction, at least to the degree that it concerns unusual peoples with different cultures, the protagonists must necessarily have qualities other than those in our more dominant society enacting scenes of violence and crime in settings we are more familiar with. The protagonists in Native American crime fiction are powerful and attractive. The authors are being joined by other writers of the same society and an increasing number of non-Indian authors, and are attracting readers, demonstrating not only the power of the subject but also the accomplishments of the authors.

Native American crime fiction is a powerful new literary subgenre that strengthens the entire genre of crime fiction and introduces new and unconventional literary areas and possibilities. Americans love the Western tradition and cling to it although according to historians it actually "died" in 1893 with the official closing of the frontier. The developing Native American crime fiction is in a position to keep that tradition alive not with false stereotypes of the past but with new and more accurate depictions of Indian-white relations and people who are not perhaps as picturesque as those of the past, especially in movies, but who take on a new and more rewarding profile because they are real.

They also perhaps serve an unexpected powerful role in demonstrating the closeness of the Indian-white races, or the lack of differences. This tendency has been growing through the years and through the fiction of our major Indian crime fiction authors. Tony Hillerman, for example, restricts his heroes to the reservation, where they are law and order but cannot exercise their power off the reservation, though they work in harmony with off-reservation authority. Jake Page cements the closeness of the two peoples by having Mo married to a half-Hopi.

Westbrook goes even further and has his "overeducated" Sioux Indian treated almost precisely like all other people in the novels. Once or twice Jack Wilder makes some reference to Howie's Indianness, but he seems to be the only one who notices it. The white women certainly do not, as they are jumping into his bed at their volition, not his. If sex is the key to the door of integration, Westbrook through Howie is forcing that door open permanently.

CHAPTER FOUR

Literary Achievements

Crime fiction though perhaps a subgenre of literature as a whole and though it has its own restrictions in which it should work nevertheless is increasingly developing into a writing with literary accomplishments. It is becoming more literature with crime in it than narrow crime fiction in the traditional sense of the word. It is a literature that many people can write, sometimes with a modicum of skill, and some with skill unsurpassed by most authors in more conventional kinds of literature. The authors studied in this book all seem to write effectively, though some are more "literary" in the usual sense of the word than are others.

Jake Page

Jake Page writes with one of the more noticeable and distinctive prose styles. We can perhaps best begin our survey with him.

Page has threads running through his fiction other than great anger at whites for their mistreatment of Indians in general and Hopis in particular. We have seen how Mo Bowdre is unusually sensitive to sound. He is especially attuned to music. His father had been caught up in his infatuation with old 78 RPM records and the music on them. Mo is even more deeply involved with music. In fact he and Connie believe that it saved his life.

Mo's musical preference mixes the mythological with "redneck choices." After the mine explosion that blinded him, Mo sank into a long and dangerous funk. No longer able to see the beautiful things of the world that he so sensuously enjoyed, he had to have "redneck" music to bring his soul back to life. In reviving his soul, Mo went back to the tradition inherited from his father, whose tastes in music ran to the so-called popular (*Strings* 42).

Page is almost lyrical in his description of Mo's salvation:

> . . . for a long time the world had not sung, but instead croaked, and T. Moore Bowdre heard no music. But from some small twangy place in his soul, he began to play for himself, on an increasingly insistent banjo of anger, a bluegrass cantankerousness. Slowly laughter returned to the diminished world, a world that lay outside him, but with enough left inside in memory and imagination and sheer greed for living. He made a quiet treaty with fate and quit feeling sorry for himself. He took up sculpture in a kind of defiance. (*Canyon* 274)

His popular music is more than spirit of life. It is also armor of love. When Mo and Connie are once threatened by a sniper who has Mo directly in his gunsights, Connie throws her arms around Mo to protect him, and he thinks of an old Fats Waller song from the 78 RPM days. Mo does not understand the power of the song or why he remembers it at this critical time. But when another member of the party whispers to Mo that he is safe, Mo returns again to Waller, and again explodes into the saving power of the popular song. "Jesus," he says, and, "Then another sound impinged on Mo's brain, sending Fats Waller off into the blackness" (*Canyon* 228).

But popular music means more to Mo than inspiration and shield. In another novel— *The Knotted Strings*—Connie has been given a non-speaking part in a movie. Connie asks Mo if he is jealous that she has been given the role and he has none, that she has momentarily taken the spotlight off him. Mo denies that he is envious but he obviously is. To prove his superiority to jealousy at least to himself he starts humming the dark and dismal popular blues song, "St. James Infirmary Blues."

Blues songs are by definition lamentations of injustice, of sadness. Almost always they are man-blues, the story of how men are treated unfairly and made sad by women. Page's development demonstrates how annoyed and self-pitying Mo belittles her good fortune. Then as he turns green with envy, he has to explain his behavior.

Mo denies being sick, says he is just restless and bored. The truth of the matter, however, is that he is jealous, a feeling that should be beneath

him but apparently is not. He knew the burden of the song he was singing, the revelation of jealousy it contains.

The essence of blues music is self-pity. Ostensibly the subject can
be the death of a loved woman, but the message is really the suffering
of the surviving man, or, more important, the injustice of the woman
dying and leaving the man in his lonely suffering. Usually the death is
the woman's fault, and in death she will never find a man superior to the
one she left. Mo Bowdre knows the burden and manifests it in his singing this song when he is feeling weakened by Connie's assumption for
the moment of the leading role in their relationship. Demonstration of
this interpretation can be given in almost any of the many versions of
this popular song.

In developing his characters and stories, Page resorts to other folk
practices and songs. *The Deadly Canyon* is partially built on a folklike
rhyme, "Poor Ol' Tuck he gone to ground"; first a "voice was little more
than a singsong whine rising from the gloom back around the dogleg of
the old mine shaft" (95). The rhythms and tones of this song can be
heard long after the lines have been cancelled.

In *A Certain Malice* Page makes two references to Disney's *Snow
White*, and in so doing digs deeply and revealingly into his own mind
and purpose in the book. Mo has been told that he is the father of
Annie and he is trying to decide if he is morally obligated to claim her
as his own. He asks himself what he owes her. As the message in that
question rattles through his head, his mind unconsciously shifts to the
reference in Disney's movie and Mo begins to answer himself (140, 159,
167). The mind may be turning to oatmeal but the unconscious association of his vocalized question with the Disney movie is revealing, for it
is the blue-collar workers of the movie, not Snow White and her elite
associates, to whom Mo's mind turns. The dwarfs who sing the song in
the movie are the redneck workers.

Perhaps even more important is the very backbone on which the
novel is developed. The first murder of the novel was of the two star-
crossed lovers, one white and the other a native of India, like Romeo
and Juliet. When Mo realizes who the victims are he immediately starts
thinking of the song "Maria," in Leonard Bernstein's operetta *West Side
Story*, which ran for 772 performances in New York and which featured
the song "Maria." In Bernstein's parallel to Shakespeare's story the opposing families are two gangs of whites and Puerto Ricans in New York.
The beauty of the song "Maria" is not about the girl in the story but
about the loveliness of her name: "The most beautiful sound I ever

heard. All the beautiful sounds of the world in a single word." But Page thinks of the conflict and murders in the unfair refusal of the conflicting gangs to accept the love affair, which he likens to that before him.

Music, nearly always faintly heard in the background of this novel, again comes to audibility when Annie first makes her appearance and Page brings up the song title "Old Devil Moon" perhaps as a belief of where Annie came from. Indeed the devil is unleashed and changes the nature of the novel and the people involved.

Throughout his novels, Page sticks close to the popular idiom. He writes in what he thinks is the equivalent of redneck prose—except when Page slips into a lyrical mode—which is sex-heavy, loud, blustery, grainy, earthy, in keeping with our stereotypical concept of redneck life and language. Familiar with and comfortable using this vernacular, Page writes easily and convincingly of his characters and their living culture.

His stories are filled with striking figures of speech that cause the reader to pause and reflect or chuckle over the image evoked. In *The Deadly Canyon*, for example, Eddy, the snake milker, runs into a rock "as implacable as a born-again Catholic. Like a nun with a ruler" (38). An unnamed canyon is "almost virgin" (49). In the desert old-fashioned gas pumps are "upstanding-burgher gas pumps" (49). Our ancestors "knuckle-walked their asses out of the forest, stood upright like timid little bears and said hey" (50). Men "wear their anger like tattoos" (*Lethal* 40). People are "lying around like a scarecrow without brains" (*Canyon* 110).

Much of the language points toward or reflects some sexual reference or innuendo. Mo is a redneck stud, always leering, and suggesting. He and Connie are frequently depicted going to or getting out of bed. These scenes indicate the domestic side of their lives and their close physical attraction. This physical attraction reveals them undressed, thinking of sex, talking about physical attributes, or having sex. Connie is just as eager as Mo for sex, always sighing and panting.

All the women are sexually vibrant and are described graphically. Breasts are always called "tits," and the women always use their breasts as political or professional weapons. Often they are preparing for sex, having it, or just finished. Mo never has enough and Sheriff Knott is so obsessed with sex that he cannot report to work on time. But Mo never treats Connie as a sex object or without love and respect, though she is always ready for action, appreciates it, and can tell a dirty joke with the foulest mouthed man. Connie is always a lady with respect and dignity.

At times the conversations and innuendos slant toward explicit sex. In *Canyon*, for example, Mo overhears a joke from an adjacent table in the restaurant about a "heroic" director and his love affair with his automobile. Mo repeats that the joke is, "The longer the sports car, the shorter the guy's" (62). Connie says that the Hopi have a saying about that also.

Sometimes the images are strikingly bizarre. In *Canyon*, for example, a graduate student has been working at the Institute and sleeping with the director, named Fitzhugh. When he casts her aside for his regular bedmate who is returning for the fall to work for him, the student, instead of threatening to bring suit against him, merely acts. Page's description, sounding comparable to any by William Faulkner, is vivid and amusing, as the student comes into his office and makes her displeasure quite evident:

> Fitzhugh stared as she unbuttoned her shorts, standing in red-and-white Reeboks on his desk, on his papers. She can't want . . . Fitzhugh thought, and he watched dumbly as she pushed her pants down and squatted on the desk before him, and he watched in stupefaction as the yellow stream made a puddle on his desk, on his papers. He stared as the warm liquid spilled into his lap. He stared as the woman pulled up her shorts and hopped backward off the desk. (*Canyon* 52)

Page is amusing in another episode involving students and staff. To the graduate students at the Research Center one of the researchers has the reputation of being uncontrollably promiscuous, accepting virtually any and every male. One day she and a male student watch as two squirrels are seemingly copulating. "No, it's a mock copulation," the woman says. The graduate student responds, "I wish I was doing that," expecting the woman to immediately invite him to begin on her. Instead she acted somewhat differently: "Ingrid lowered her binoculars and took the graduate student's measure, as if seeing him for the first time. His face turned red. She put a hand on his arm and smiled. 'That's fine with me, Tommy.' He smiled back. 'All you got to do is find yourself a female squirrel'" (*Canyon* 164).

Throughout his books Page's humor bubbles and blisters in various other ways. His figures of speech are hard, heroic, and extravagant. Once Mo goes to bed with his hat on. When Connie reminds him of it, he says, "Well, at least I took off my boots" (*Canyon* 98). When FBI special agent Larry Collins is in the hospital suffering with loss of memory, which he suffered in an automobile accident on his way back from Mexico, he gets up out of bed against the doctor's orders, dresses, and tells the nurse that he is fully recovered, though he has his trousers on backwards. In one of his many sexual allusions, Sheriff Knott, a veteran in lechery, knows that, "Matters of the loin can go sour" (*Canyon* 101). On another occasion Knott reminds his deputy that he has "sprung a leak in [his] braincase" (*Canyon* 101).

The books Page crafts are pieced together in short vignettes placed in a crossword puzzle. At times, especially at the beginning, they are short sketches pointing only generally in the same direction. Page confesses that when he starts a novel he has no idea where it is going. All pieces, however, wind up at a destination that has become clear as the parts of the mosaic fit neatly into the pattern and progress toward a climax. The prose is always clear, interesting, and convincing.

Jean Hager

Being a professional writer, author of many books, Jean Hager brings to her two series of novels about Mitchell Bushyhead and Molly Bearpaw a skill that evidences itself from the beginning. Sometimes she begins with a description that pictures the land and the people she is going to write about, as in this beginning paragraph from *Ravenmocker:*

> August heat held northeastern Oklahoma in an iron grip. It hung over the fourteen counties that had been carved, whole or in part, from the Cherokee Nation in 1907. West of the Grand River, dying yellow grass carpeted mile upon mile of gently rolling hills and prairie country. East of the river in the vast wooded areas of the Ozark plateau, hickory trees, native walnuts, elms, and blackjack oaks were already dropping rain-starved leaves. And south of Tahlequah, at the entrance to the tribal office complex, three flags—of the United States of America, the state of Oklahoma, and the Cherokee Nation of Oklahoma—hung limp and unmoving.

At other times she begins her story immediately, as in the first paragraph of *Masked Dancers:* "The sky was an ominous pewter color by the time Police Chief Mitch Bushyhead reached the station. He found Helen Hendricks, the dispatcher, looking anxiously out the window. 'Morning, Chief.'" Throughout her works she writes with the same direct, clear, and communicative prose.

This language is always earthy, precise, and sharply descriptive. Her figures of speech breathe new vitality into the subject. In *Seven Black Stones*, for example, Zeb Smoke is "older than dirt" (3), and shows his age. "His tough brown flesh had shrunk back against the bone, as if readying itself to start the decomposition process, revealing the shape of the skeleton beneath." Zeb is about as likely to warm up to Conrad's desire for a tape interview as "pigs to sprout wings" (7). In *The Redbird's Cry*, "An icicle of fear slid through" Daye Hummingbird at the thought of spending another night with her husband (6). In the same novel one of the characters, suffering from arthritis, was awake all night, "as wide-eyed as a tree full of young owls" (163). In *The Grandfather Medicine* a man's tongue is as "thick as a rump roast" (100).

Humor is not a requisite of crime fiction but it always leavens the mix of violence against ordinary life. Hager's is characteristic of both Cherokee humor, which is delicate in subtle understatement, and regular Anglo. The sexual statements and innuendoes, like her other kinds of humor, are clear and vivid. She does not lean toward the teasing pornographic in descriptions of sex, but she does not shy away from explicitness.

In describing one woman's behavior, for example, Hager says that she "came around the desk and leaned back against it, bracing herself with her hands behind her. The pose, which Mitch suspected was calculated, clearly exposed the outlines of her nipples beneath the yellow sweater. She wore no bra." She "could have posed for the center fold in one of the girlie magazines" (*Night Walker* 73). In another instance in the same book, another woman criticizes a female as one who "likes to see other people get their tit in a wringer" (83).

But Hager's men talk more explicitly about sex. In her first novel, she voices the male chauvinistic clichés that are commonly voiced when men are together talking about their virility and conquests. Mitch's assistants Duck and Roo agree that two old eccentric ladies who are always calling the police for imaginary intruders need "a good lay." Duck says that Roo should do it, he's "the big stud" (65).

In *Seven Black Stones*, a book deep in redneck characters, Hager uses more appropriate redneck language than usual despite the fact that in general she says she is not interested in or concerned with writing about that kind of people. Her language necessarily catches the tone of their references, especially sexual. She philosophizes, "A horny man is a determined man" (33). When Ed kisses Susan, "that brought the old soldier back to attention." But Ed's trying to talk Susan into sex, "made him go limp again." When Susan relents and asks, "What am I going to do with you?" Ed internally soliloquizes: "Shut up and let me get on with emptying my barrel, while it's loaded" (33).

In *The Grandfather Medicine* Hager is especially graphic. Her characters philosophize that, "Man has only so much joy juice in him. You use it all up in your twenties, you're gonna be one depressed dude the rest of your life." Again, "How long you gonna plow that field before you buy it?" And again, "He's got a catch in his getalong, or should I say his get-it-on?" (101).

All in all Hager's prose is well informed, at times beautifully poetic, and at other times direct and vernacular, as one would expect from an accomplished writer of effective crime fiction.

Louis Owens

Louis Owens is a mixedblood intellectual who is complex and very much aware of his background and desires and possibilities. His first hopes were to work and live in the physical outdoors world, to backpack and fish. He slipped into academia somewhat through the back door with a Ph.D. and began writing fiction, as many academics do.

Interestingly, when he began to write, he says in our interview, he turned to crime stories "never in fact having read one before." But he "wanted to write books that my brothers and sisters would read, that is novels with plots as opposed to precious symbolist poetry page after page. The challenge for me was to try to write fiction that could be page-turning, plot-structured, and still encompass all the complexities—both technical and intellectual—that I wanted to explore. So I ended up writing books that have layers." His goal, also, is to write books that "explode clichés and stereotypes." "No Indian braves in eagle-feather headdresses, no drumming shamans, no swooning Indian damsels. I really hate that stuff. Even worse is the dysfunctional school of Native American literature, the new Vanishing American garbage in which Indians are self-destructive drunks and darkly comic and nothing more."

Owens's object in his fiction is to write of paying back the Indian nations in quite a different way. He wants to atone by dignifying his characters and the Indian nations so fully that paying back is unnecessary and even impossible. Among equals there can be no paying back since there is nothing owed.

Owens gives more to and expects more back from his readers. He wants to extend his "readers' consciousness and challenge them by urging them to see beyond ordinary limitations." So he writes books that have layers and references. Like Tennyson's Ulysses, who drew into himself a part of all his experiences, Owens is a part of all that he has read and lived. Like T. S. Eliot he feels free to use those experiences and literary experiences as building blocks for higher experience, or conduits into richer experiences.

But he stretches this extension in a way that dignifies the reader. No author worth reading writes "down" to his reader. Some, however, provide more of a helping hand up and out. In the early pages of *The Sharpest Sight,* for example, when Cole McCurtain, the protagonist, is searching for the reassurance of knowing who or what he is, or even *if* he is, Owens enriches the statement of Cole's discovery of his existence and strength with a blending of two well-known literary and philosophical references. Cole says: "I shall fear no evil, for I am." In so doing he pumps religious reassurance through his and the reader's veins by recalling this partial quote from the Twenty-third Psalm, which reads, "Lo though I walk through the valley of the shadow of death, I will fear no evil. . . . " To that religious reassurance, Owens attaches the philosophical confidence provided by the Latin translation of the famous phrase provided by French philosopher Rene Descartes: "*Cogito, ergo,* I think, therefore I am." Owens, because he is what he is, will fear no evil and no one.

Owens's books are contrasts in spiritualism and the mystical as opposed to hard reality and pragmatism. In the former style, take an early scene from *The Sharpest Sight,* which pictures very well the two worlds in which the author feels comfortable. Mundo Morales is out in a blinding rainstorm that is to him probably filled with witches:

> And then, sliding slowly from beneath the bridge, was a face. The long black hair washed away from the forehead, and the eyes were open and fixed. He saw the dark eyes and broad nose and the mouth drawn back over white teeth and the body like one of the drowned logs swinging slowly so that now the feet aimed north. A hand rose in the choppy water as in casual farewell. And then only the river flowed on. (*Sharpest Sight* 6)

Owens's fourth work, *Nightland,* the novel that he was forced by the publisher to modify into a vernacular and simplicity that he did not like, is not really much different in its beginning from his other books, though the symbolism is more graphic and realistic. It is also extremely effective. The book begins with this picture:

> It looked like a black buzzard creased against the western horizon and angling toward him. But then the body twisted and he saw that it was a man, the black form of a man floating from the heavens with outstretched arms. The great arch of New Mexico sky, piled high in all directions with blue-gray thunderheads, held the dark shape, cupping it

so that to Billy Keene's eyes the man hung almost suspended between sky and earth. Then an object separated from the body and drifted like a leaf off toward the wooded ridge, and Billy saw the dead spire of the juniper at the same instant the body struck and was impaled, the silvered shaft through belly and back so that the man flailed for a moment and then hung limply, black-suited fish bait against the heavy sky. A snake's tongue forked deeped into the mountains, fire leaping from sky to earth and back again. (13)

Even if not forced to write more directly for the commercial publisher, Owens could hardly have created a more graphic picture and put a more supernatural stamp on a crucifixion, though it actually takes on the shape of fish bait slipped on the hook to catch the human fish. Throughout this book, and in fact everywhere in Owens's work, there is professional accomplishment that does manage to have both the Indian mysticism and white insistence on what we term reality merge into statements of not only the two worlds of the two peoples but also the points at which they meet and converge.

In his latest book, however, Owens has taken up a new direction and goal. *Deep River* is complex and complicated with two flows of the water in opposite directions. The top current is uphill, toward isolation and cultural loneliness. But Owens thinks, hopes that the underneath undying current reverses itself and flows out to sea, to community and home. He wants to be reassured that one can go home again. He apparently wants to write the elusive Golden Fleece of all American writers, "The Great American Novel," universalizing the Native American into the Noble American. He may or may not have been wise in choosing Hemingway as his model.

In this novel the sentiment may be Hemingway's, the language direct, frank, and vernacular. But Owens has not yet achieved Hemingway's simplicity and skeletal directness. Perhaps he shouldn't be seeking it. He has his own strengths.

James D. Doss

Of the writers of Native American fiction none is more deeply immersed in mysticism, Indian mythology, and folklore than James D. Doss. A white without any Indian blood, he manages to breathe in with his daily air the very essence of Indian culture and belief in a reality beyond the tangible and make it understandable. In this understanding sometimes the white reader has a little trouble stepping with one foot into Indian mysticism while holding the other in white reality, but a pause and a little contemplation usually accomplish the trick.

Perhaps his most telling example comes from Doss's *The Shaman's Game*, all of which is hip-deep in Indian mysticism and mythology. This passage shows how Doss can move in that world with no qualms or hesitation. In this passage, Charlie Moon, the deputy sheriff, has wondered if it is indeed possible that the dead Old Popeye Woman had come from her grave and caused the death of Delly Sands as the Indians are saying. So he went to the graveside to investigate. "Now Charlie Moon was not a man easily diverted from the path of common sense," Doss writes. But there was just one set of prints, leading *away* from the grave:

> The policeman moved closer to the prints in the sand, and kneeled. And felt a chill ripple along his spine. There had been some wind since even these footprints were made. The edges were softened . . . blurred. . . . They were small prints. Of bare feet. And one foot was terribly misshapen . . . there was a barely visible mark in the sand behind it. The lame foot had been dragged. (367)

As he stands there, Charlie hears approaching steps, obviously those of a woman and clearly someone who is dragging one foot. He is scared to death, but Charlie feels that common sense and police duty tell him that he must face the walker and discover the facts. Several lines, in the author's italics, tell Doss's own attitude toward Indian mysticism:

> *A soft pad-padding . . . bare feet treading*
> *encoded footsteps . . . one short . . . one long*
> *a hollow rapping . . . a tap-tapping*
> *someone who had awakened . . . and departed*
> *was returning . . . to sleep once more?*
> To know . . . to know. All he need do was tarry here. . . .
> But his flesh crawled as if he had worms under his skin.
> Maybe a man could know too much. . . .
> Charlie Moon turned his back upon it all. Upon the one who approached . . . upon the oval basin of dry, shifting sands . . . the pitted walls of empty tomb. He set his face toward the mouth of the canyon.
> The Ute took his first step . . . of his long walk home. (367)

In both the Indian and the white world, Doss is a neat, clear writer, with interesting and graphic figures of speech. For example, Aunt Daisy is out in the mountain evening, where it is "Cold as frog spit" (*Shaman Laughs*, 270). In the same book one is told that he should never outrun his shadow.

In his two latest novels Doss takes on other stylistic and plot mannerisms. In *Grandmother Spider* he carries them perhaps to an extreme. The fantasy of the plot is too long and too unreal for its frame, and though it is peopled by all kinds of bad guys, the plot strains the credulity and patience of the reader, who before the end begins to beg, "Come on now!"

But the reader sticks to his reading because Doss is obviously having so much fun. Released into the world of fantasy he lets himself go and shake with laughter. His characters all stand a little oversized, larger than their lives. Daisy Perika is a little meaner than usual. Several other elderly ladies stand outside their rugged outlines. Charlie Moon reaches higher than in the earlier novels and is somewhat clumsier and more naive, wearing a suit of near indifference and irresponsibility. We don't know we can count on him.

This novel, especially, is held together with strong bands of irony, exaggeration, and humor. For example, the sister of one of the murdered characters returns unexpectedly from a trip to Europe. She explains her sudden appearance, saying, "I've just returned from Europe. Flew all night after I got my brother's telephone call" (173). Her brother, brooding on her disheveled appearance, "imagined his sister crossing the Atlantic on a broom." One elderly man who calls himself Pinky Packer explains his means of travel: "This here's an African zebra that can speak sixteen languages. . . . I painted over the white stripes with road tar" (197). Pinky puts a knife between his opponent's legs and begins to raise the sharp edge against the man's genitals, causing him to stand higher and higher on his tiptoes. The knife-wielder explains his weapon to his victim:

> "This ain't some pissant foldin' knife, sonny—this here is a genuine Arkansas toothpick, fired in a Pine Bluff forge. Blade's a good fourteen inches long . . . and sharp as a Birmingham barber's best straight razor." He lifted the heavy blade a half inch. (198)

Doss pays no mind to whether he is painting the Indian as a noble savage or just one of the boys. He refers to them as ignorant heathens, redskins, and other vernacular words and phrases.

Doss writes a neat book, closely encased in theme. Page one opens on a fantasy legend and dream world of the traditional Ute. It ends in another fantasyland, this time of the policeman Charlie Moon and his dream that he can give up his police work and laze his way through life. In between Doss may have reached his limit on the setting of crime fiction. Such stories must be anchored to some kind of reality. It can flourish in dreamland but not altogether in fantasyland. It needs some mean streets to walk on, not exclusively on yellow brick roads.

So far, however, Doss manages the very difficult. He walks close to the dividing line between the real and the spiritual world, something like the equator separating the two halves of the world, and succeeds in using language that covers both worlds or allows reasonably quick exit from one and entrance into the other. Sometimes the transition is just a little dizzying to the reader but if one can, as Louis Owens suggests, let oneself go and believe concurrently in the two ways of looking at the world, then the transition is not impossible.

Dana Stabenow

Dana Stabenow has a sharp, experienced eye on the actions of human beings, especially the various kinds of Americans living in Alaska, and she has the computer fingers to describe them and their way of life. As we have seen, her characters are forcefully brought to life through hard-hitting and graphic prose. Some other examples will demonstrate just how close to the bone her prose cuts.

Her leading character, Kate Shugak, is a small-bodied explosive force with a physical characteristic that makes her immediately notice-able. A livid scar that runs from ear to ear has made her voice a "low husk of sound ranging anywhere from rough to rasping . . . from harsh to horrifying" (*Dead in the Water* 33).

Stabenow is a close female observer of man when sexually stimu-lated. When Jack, for instance, is aroused, Stabenow says, "If he had had a tail it would have been wagging hard enough to power an electric generator" (*Blood Will Tell* 102). She calls sexy girls "trophy blondes" (118). When Kate Shugak is forced to wear nice clothes to attend a din-ner of the elite, she is handed a bra that "didn't look as if they would hold up a sneeze, let alone Kate's breasts" (105). On another occasion when evaluating the mentality of some employees, she observes that the company "didn't hire its employees off the back of a turnip truck" (103). Once she observes that bears have "an I.Q. a good ten points above that of the average pipeliner" (*A Cold-Blooded Business* 80), and once Kate's mental superiority is asserted by Jack Morgan when he tells her, "Kate, you're smarter than the average bear" (*A Cold Day for Murder* 82).

Stabenow writes to entertain, yet entertainment is never pure amusement. It always consciously or unconsciously—covertly or openly—carries a message and lesson. Stabenow's readers see beneath the surface to one depth or another, peel back the veneer and really *see* the action and hear the language in their subtleties and implications.

Peter Bowen

Peter Bowen uses a uniquely picturesque language and style since he is writing of the Métis, a mixture of Crow-Choctaw-French, and, as he says, Montana language. But Bowen is also a master at turning the picturesque into the amusing and delightful. It is often not the figures of speech that are memorable but the nonpoetic locutions about the everyday that are striking and memorable.

For example, in expressing the practice of making love the language can be so terse and uneventful it is poetic. In *Coyote Wind* it is as undecorated and direct as a computer-generated weather report. Madelaine curses Du Pré for not having time for her sexual needs. Bowen reports the response to that demand: "They went to bed, hot flesh, need, lay spent" (21). At other times, the language is more expressive. In *Notches*, for example, Du Pré says "I say . . . old bastard, you go fuck a lame three-legged coyote, got clap" (121). In *Coyote Wind*, to return to that book for another example, the law tells Du Pré that he must give up his gun because he is shooting too much at the wrong objects. Du Pré makes an ironic confession about how dangerous he is:

> Du Pré let the hammer down, spun the cylinder, two rounds gone, three left.
> "See," said Du Pré pointing, "here, this first one is where I shot myself because I was behaving in a threatening manner, the second is where I killed Higgins's kid because he was behaving in a threatening manner." (139)

Bowen recognizes that generally speaking the more unusual the messenger is in fiction, as in life, the more attention is paid to the message. No one can fail to pay attention to his messengers and probably the word he is bringing. Bowen seems to be speaking through the masks of Du Pré and Madelaine. He has a very personal and firm attitude.

Aimée and David Thurlo

The Thurlos are dedicated to telling fine and interesting stories about the Navajo and doing so while having the Indians live in their vernacular everyday existence, with dignity. The result is that the Thurlos have found in their presentation of Ella Clah a vehicle worthy of their efforts and of the Navajo they are successfully presenting. They are able to depict the civilization they want to write about and to develop a powerful character who develops realistically the more powerful elements of that culture. They are prepared to go beyond the bounds of conventional crime fiction. So far they have been successful.

Margaret Coel

Margaret Coel also successfully presents her chosen tribe, the Arapaho. Approaching these Indians from a slightly different angle, Coel succeeds in presenting their conflicts with the dominant outside white society and their resolution. Her approach borders on the mystical and unusual and therefore she can present the Arapaho as she believes she should. Her style is also innovative and experimental. In her most recent books she has developed an approach leaning toward Native American science fiction crime fiction. So far she has managed to carry off the new approach with aplomb.

Mardi Oakley Medawar

Mardi Oakley Medawar, through a tangential and slanting approach, is perhaps the gentlest presenter of Indian culture, in her case that of the Kiowa. It is an unusual approach but successful. Her angle of vision and her achievement is successful; her creation of Tay-bodal is a minor triumph. *The Ft. Larned Incident* demonstrates the wide range into which she can open, with its various possible conflicts among the Indian tribes and with their constant battles with the whites.

Thomas Perry

Thomas Perry's Jane Whitefield pushes the envelope of tribal life. He has her work as an outside agent who uses her Indian blood and connections to maintain a service that is dedicated to changing the lifestyle and environment of individuals who need new starts. Perry never says so, but in a way he is pointing out to the Indians that there are new lifestyles available to them. They can build on the past, and use it as necessary, while concurrently moving out and into the broader American culture. He seems to be essentially an author of action novels and finds it difficult to restrain himself from rapid-fire action, sometimes to the cost of rich development of his characters.

J. F. Trainor

Of the authors now writing on Indian culture no two exceed Jake Page and J. F. Trainor. Page has, of course, molded a giant larger than life. Trainor is not far behind in the proportions of his heroine, Angie Biwaban. He has dedicated her to being offbeat, out-of-character, satiric, and determined to bring both reality and comedy to the tradition of Native Americans in the West. Although she claims Indian blood, in fact she belongs more accurately in a tradition of nationless people who wander about making the world seem *ridiculous*.

Robert Westbrook

All these authors to one degree or another push the edges of the envelope in one direction or another—in subject matter, such as the treatment of Indians and Indian culture by whites—or in their style of development. In his own way Westbrook mixes the old-fashioned hard-boiled philosophy and writing style with a new attitude toward the Native American and white culture, mixed or separated. He is a Mark Twainian philosopher who loves individuals but cares little for the human race.

To him the Anasazi may have been cannibalistic but he does not much care. White soldiers in Custer's Seventh Cavalry may have abused female Indian genitals—which he condemns—but that is little different from what he expected.

He is dedicated to telling good stories effectively and realizes that in order to do so he needs to raise them above the ordinary plane of existence. So he tells his heroic stories in the vernacular and they are ordinarily effective.

They have him pointed toward an achievement that may force him to lift the everyday back into the heroic and in so doing reinstitute old-fashioned fiction on a new subject—in effect urban-Indian crime fiction.

Tony Hillerman

The steady author of Indian crime fiction through the years has been Tony Hillerman, long the dean of such fiction and recognized as a major writer and authority on American literature in general. Hillerman in most ways is a "naturalistic" and natural writer. When he sets off on one of his stories he says he has no idea how he is going to get to his goal and indeed does not know what that goal is except that it is dedicated to demonstrating how unjustly Indians have been used and abused in American society. He has experimented in several ways, using an older protagonist in one series and a young one in another. Not known for his brilliant flashy style of writing he is recognized worldwide as perhaps the authority in the field of Indian crime fiction.

Altogether these authors present their subjects realistically and faith-fully The vernacular is peculiar to the people about whom the books are written and is aimed to a readership that is particularly interested in that group of people and their culture. As is necessary for a proper reve-lation of the culture of the people who are the subject, the language must be tailored to fit the different and peculiar world about which it is used. With these authors that goal is reached.

CHAPTER FIVE

Realities and Implications

A detailed analysis of Native American crime fiction reveals a great deal about the current state of the art in the genre and demonstrates an upcoming and developing direction.

The increasing number of authors of crime fiction that involves Indians or Native Americans, whichever one wants to call them, is expanding for at least two reasons. Those authors with Indian blood who want to write about their people do so for obvious reasons: they know the subject and they think that the subject needs to be written about or at least that writing about it will be instructive and entertaining. Those who do not have any Indian blood but want to write about the Native Americans do so because of geographical or cultural contact. In the past many authors of fiction about the West, like Zane Grey, Max Brand, and dozens of others, included Indians if not for thematic justifications then necessarily because of physical and geographical proximity. Often their main source of information was maps or literature or the breath of mythology. Nowadays, most authors on Indian culture, Indian or otherwise, live or have lived in or around Indian communities and are interested in them *because* of their cultures, or at least because those cultures can provide useful material for fiction.

These cultures provide the exotic flavor of newness, a field necessary to authors and readers of crime fiction. On this new field they are not only allowed to work in a new cultural geography, that of new and different people, but also are allowed to develop new protagonists and heroes/heroines with new characteristics and new dimensions. These new protagonists retain the general generic qualities of the crime-fighting protector of society, but also can be more closely tied in with the age-old mythological heroes. They can, therefore, be more closely associated with and tied to the people, as the mythological heroes were, and can allow for the development of heroes with radically different qualities. Jake Page's Mo Bowdre and Peter Bowen's Gabriel Du Pré are two excellent examples of the new type of hero that can be developed in Native American crime fiction.

The result is something like that created by Elvis Presley when he shocked the world with the introduction of his rock 'n' roll music. Much like the effect of rock 'n' roll music, which has changed popular music forever, the introduction of protagonists of different dimensions and cultural attitudes is likely to influence the direction taken by mainline crime fiction heroes in the future. Bowdre and Du Pré are close to the people, of the people, and for the people. Their potential is not likely to be overlooked. Nor is that of the other new and original main characters who people Native American crime fiction. They, too, move us into cultures that are largely alien to us, reveal dimensions of cultures and people who are at least somewhat strange, and thus provide us with new references of mankind's attitude toward and treatment of infractions against the body of society. Because these heroes move from the hard world of reality into the soft spiritual existence around them, we the readers are likely to attain new realizations of these unfamiliar worlds and the attitudes of the people who inhabit them.

Exotic people and atmosphere enhance another desirable ingredient in the fiction about most minorities, a sense of fair play and remuneration for past injustices. A sizeable percentage of authors who write about Native Americans declare that they are interested not in "paying back" for past injustices, a major drive for such authors as Jake Page and Jean Hager, but only in telling interesting stories interestingly. .

In the field of Native American crime fiction there is no agreement as to what the earlier Americans call themselves or want to be called. Louis Owens, himself a mixedblood of Choctaw-Cherokee-Irish descent, insists on calling himself and people like himself either mixedbloods or Native Americans with the feeling that not to do so is insulting. But Peter Bowen, who writes of Métis Gabriel Du Pré, a mixedblood of Choctaw-Cherokee-French blood, is a fierce advocate of calling Native Americans by the traditional name of Indian; he says that of all the Indians he knows not a one would want to be called by any other name. So the Native-American-Indian societies are becoming sufficiently self-confident to be, like black Americans in society today, concerned with what they are called and insisting on the term they think most appropriate.

The various authors are mixed in their treatment of the cultures they represent. Some, like Jake Page, and to a lesser degree Tony Hillerman, Jean Hager, and James Doss, are definitely concerned with "paying back" the Native Americans for the injustices they have suffered through the centuries. Others like Dana Stabenow, Peter Bowen, J. F. Trainor, and the Thurlos are primarily interested in writing excellent fiction, though both Trainor and Bowen in their powerful stories create anti-heroes who stand upright and tall. In fact, however, all the authors and works studied in this book are making notable contributions to the genre of crime fiction and to literature in general.

In achieving their goals, these several authors are somewhat mixed in their treatment of the cultures they represent. Some, like Jake Page, tend to stay outside the psychological and religious depths of his subjects, and like Jean Hager to count on the reworking of legends and mythology to provide depth. Others, like Louis Owens and James Doss, are especially perceptive and thorough in the degree of participation in and belief in mysticism, the supernatural, and dreams, and the creatures who represent those layers of existence.

Indian cultures incorporate the mystical and otherworldly in the daily lives and activities of the people, far more so than do Anglo cultures. In white societies, European or American, the supernatural world has always been accorded existence but has been held at arm's length as a wish-fulfillment or a visible threat. The beneficent forces have generally been the philosophical-religious citizens who believe in the Citie on a Hill concept, so omnipresent in colonial America, a heaven to be reached after death. P. C. Doherty, historian author of English crime fiction set in the Middle Ages, for example, makes a clear distinction between the good folk—Us—and the forces of evil—Them. In *Ghostly Murders*, for instance, he takes up Chaucer's pilgrims on their journey from London to Canterbury, and has the priest tell a tale of the good folk being surrounded by and challenged by the forces of diabolical evil just beyond the edge of day.

In Indian mythology, religion, and culture, on the contrary, the dream world, as with the Australian Aborigines, has always been a more frequent presence, representing one-half of everyday life. Louis Owens says that he knows no Indians who do not believe in and experience the power of dreams. They move freely and easily, especially the shamans, from one world to the other, in a connected and easy step that makes it difficult at times for non-Indians to understand and accept. Non-Indians have difficulty moving freely into the Middleworld and Lowerworld and back. Whereas in the world of such writers as Hager, Medawar, Doss, Owens, and others to one degree or another, the separating veil is thin and easily penetrated. The growth of Native American crime fiction is opening the passage from one world to the other and acquainting the rest of us Americans with this new development in mystery fiction.

This development represents the exfoliation of crime fiction in general into new fields: feminism, lesbian and gay, other nationalities and peoples, and history. These new areas represent not only a growing interest on the part of people to write of these cultures and interests but also of readers to buy the books. Old terms such as "crime fiction" and "detective fiction" are giving way to the larger and more inclusive generic "A Mystery." Increasingly this descriptive term on the book, as in a large amount of general fiction, provides only a lure, a motivation, a source of attraction, to drive the reader on, while the real reason, or at least an important reason, for the novel is to provide information on some historical fact or cultural imperfection. Josephine Tey (1896–1952), for example, wrote *The Daughter of Time* (1951) to try to determine if Richard III killed the princes, Edward V and his younger brother Richard, Duke of York, in the Tower of London; as did Alison Weir in her mystery *The Princes in the Tower* (1992), considered one of the authoritative studies on the subject. Anne Perry is more interested in casting light on cultural evils and corruption, as in *The Silent Cry* (1997) in which she is concerned with the abuse of Victorian Englishwomen who were forced to become prostitutes in order to support themselves, their children, and sometimes their husbands who for one reason or another could not or would not supply the basic needs of their families.

The number of authors of mystery fiction is becoming almost overwhelming. Willetta L. Heising, in her two volumes listing such authors, names some eighteen hundred men and nearly that same number of women who through the years have written such fiction, and over five hundred titles published by women in the years 1994–95! They must find new subjects and new treatments about which to write. The opportunities furnished are immense.

These unfolding pages in mystery fiction are thus opening to new possibilities of all kinds. Instead of remaining a subgenre of literature, the subject is attracting more people interested in "literature," and is thus becoming more literary. It is becoming increasingly attractive to literary people, whoever they are, and serving an expanding geography of cultural purposes. It is not narrow enough to be called muckraking or 60 *Minutes* reporting or even eliteraking but is instead what we might call affirmative crime fiction because regardless of its ultimate purpose — to entertain or to press an agenda — it is revealing elements of culture in such a way that to know of the culture is to begin to bring new forces to bear and to change it.

The people studied in this book, though by no means historically the first, are the vanguard of the new approaches and new accomplishments. Individually and collectively they represent new thinking about the citizens of this land who were here to greet the Europeans. Their ways of life, threatened and nearly eclipsed by the more dominant European culture, were nurtured through the many years almost underground or at least unobserved. Now as those cultures are being revivified or at least allowed some breathing space, the authors included in this volume, and their works, aid us in getting to understand those cultures, and through our increased knowledge to develop more respect for them and their dignity.

With the possible exception of Tony Hillerman, whose body of works is extensive now, the authors seem to be in their creative prime and seem to promise more works to add intensity to the light that is shining on the cultures of the people who came before us. If to know is to appreciate and to appreciate is to develop empathy, the authors of Native American crime fiction are helping all of us pay back in one coin or another the bounty of life available on this continent that five hundred years ago seemed to be, finally, the Eden for which we all looked and were willing to fight. The goals are more worthy now than they were in the long long ago.

One precaution should be mentioned, that of developing new stereotypes of Indians and Indian life in this new kind of fiction paralleling the stereotypes so common in movies and Western fiction of the past. As I mentioned earlier, such misdevelopment is possible but not likely, for several reasons: 1) Fiction is not so graphic as movies in developing stereotypes; 2) the new authors of Indian crime fiction recognize that their effectiveness depends on authenticity and uniqueness, not stereotypes, so they must write of reality, not clichés; 3) readers of crime fiction are sophisticated though many live in the unrealistic literary world of ratiocination and Golden Age closed-door adventure; they realize that there is another world that consists more of Chandler's "mean streets," which by now have become meaner. So the emerging authors of Indian crime fiction are more "responsible" than they might have been in the past, and they present the world more realistically. The readers are also more demanding. Both are a long way from accepting and writing the kind of fiction previously so popular. This Native American crime fiction is on a new page in an opening book of literature. The new demands will result in a more satisfactory literature all round.

Interviews with Authors

The following interviews with authors were conducted by mail. I wrote each author and explained that I was writing a book under the title *"Paying Back": Remorse and Atonement in Native American Fiction* and asked that he or she assist me by providing useful information about himself or herself. I later changed the title of the manuscript to *Murder on the Reservation,* as being more comprehensive and appropriate. Because there are sufficient interviews available on Tony Hillerman, I did not ask for a new one from him. One or two others I did not get. The interviews were to a certain extent blind shots toward the sources of the novels, and the questions therefore were often broad and meant to evoke free associational responses. They did. The degree to which the authors responded depended, of course, on the amount of time they had. I am grateful to each and every one for his or her assistance in my project. For each author I give my general questions and follow with the response.

Laura Baker

Q: Please give me some background on yourself and your novels.
LB: Your letter requesting information about my two books, *Stargazer* and *Legend,* was certainly intriguing and thought-provoking. It's not often that a letter launches conversation at my

gallery about the concept of "pay back" to the Native Americans. Believe me, it was a lively conversation, though I'm not sure any of the remarks helped to enlighten me as to my *own* motives. Nonetheless, I will give your questions a go.

But first, it might help to know my inspiration for each of the books. The idea for *Stargazer* began with a setting: Canyon de Chelly. When the Navajo arrived there at least 500 years ago, they were not the first and the evidence of prior inhabitants was all around: beehive ruins clinging to the cliffs and thousands of petroglyphs etched in the rocks. They would have recognized the labyrinth of canyons as a special place. Indeed, they added their own unique marks. Canyon de Chelly is the site for more numerous planetaria and star charts than anywhere else in Navajoland. It is also the place where the Navajo chose to make their last stand against the whites. It had always been their fortress, a safe place from which to conduct raids against Utes, Zunis, Hopis, Mexicans, and rancheros. For over 200 years, the Navajo were at war with everyone around them, which gained them a reputation and a label: Lords of the Land. They are now the largest tribe, residing on the largest reservation, with the most money. Yet the Navajo individually are among the poorest, the most illiterate, with obscene rates of unemployment, alcoholism, and infant mortality. I asked myself, "what would the warriors of the past think of today's Navajo. And vice versa" I also found it curious that many of the Navajo I know have not even visited Canyon de Chelly, one of the most beautiful canyons on the reservation, to be sure, and, even more important, the most significant site both historically and culturally for the Navajo. *Stargazer,* thus, grew into a story about ancient legends and cultural traditions set against modern responsibilities and pressures.

Legend, on the other hand, grew from several recent situations. The first involved our difficulty in convincing some of the Navajo craftsmen we worked with to stamp their creations with their name or hallmark. They did not want to do anything which would make them stand out above other Navajo. Since a Navajo is responsible to any member of his clan who asked for help, and those who were accomplished silversmiths made enough to be *able* to help, I was confused by their reluctance to sign their pieces. Finally, one silversmith confided that he did not want to be suspected of being a witch. The next situation was in 1993 with the outbreak of the Hanta Virus. The first person to die was a young Navajo runner. He was quickly followed by other Navajo, young and old. When the virus attacked white tourists, it became national news and was called a plague. Reporters and photographers from all over the country, even the world, descended on the Four Corners area. The Plague became network news; tourists were warned to stay away or take precautions (the bus drivers issued white gloves to tourists before disembarking at trading posts); media reps swarmed the reservation shoving microphones in the faces of mourning families. Obviously, I found all this appalling. But there was even more vicious gossip at work and it was spread by the Navajo themselves: The Hanta Virus was blamed on witchcraft. Several medicine men were murdered, suspected of practicing the witchcraft. The third situation was a story told to me by a Christian Navajo who swore she saw a skinwalker cross the parking lot of her church. But instead of being afraid, she said that she took it as a sign from the wolf—not threatening but reminding her of her Navajo roots. All this got me to wondering about witchcraft and the Navajo need for balance. *Legend* then became a story about a witch motivated not by evil but by retribution.

Q: Are you interested in trying to "pay back" the Indian for former injustices rained down on them by the dominant white society?

LB: Though both novels include a bit of anger at the injustice suffered by Navajo, I don't consider them as "pay back" stories. I could certainly be wrong, but my gut reaction to the term "pay back" is that the story will incorporate evil white characters and the basic conflict will have more to do with clash of cultural beliefs. But that conflict holds absolutely no interest for me. What gets me jazzed is writing about two protagonists of equal intelligence with sympathetic goals and very deep convictions—it's these deep convictions within the protagonists which I want to rock to the core and crack and make them reconsider by the end of the book. And the convictions must be about how they see *themselves* in the world, not how they see their gender, or their race, or their culture. Writing is a way for me to explore the human heart in conflict with itself: What makes the person who he or she is?

Certainly my relationship with Navajo artists and friends was a "spring board" for my interest in their culture. But as I researched more, it was their core of beliefs which really drew me in and left me powerless to go in any other direction. Their belief in duality and search for balance spoke to something inside me. Indeed, I think the search for balance is a universal quest. You see, when I write about the Navajo, yes I am trying my best to be true to their culture and beliefs, but I am also depicting human beings, just like the rest of us, with hopes, dreams and fears. The journey to find our place in balance with the world is not exclusively Navajo: The conflicts I describe are within all peoples.

That is one of the reasons romance as a genre is so popular: the universality of emotions.

If, by "pay back" you mean "education," then I am definitely guilty. I know that most of my readers will never meet a Navajo except through my stories and so I am *very* careful in my depictions of the People, their land, and beliefs. I "introduce" the Navajo through slices of their culture. For instance, most people don't know the history of Navajo as warriors or that a basic structure of their culture is the clan system. No doubt one of my purposes is to help others understand the Navajo, even form some sort of a bond, while I'm entertaining—because the more we understand others, the more we understand ourselves. Letters from readers thanking me for all they learned about the Navajo make me smile.

Q: Are your novels read and appreciated by the Navajo?

LB: Yes, I do have many Navajo friends and they seem to admire my work. I have two stories in that vein. When I was writing *Stargazer*, I approached one of our silversmiths for an opinion of the plot. Besides being a well-known silversmith, he is also a medicine man and, at that time, was on the staff of the Navajo President. I outlined the story, from the time-travel of my hero, to his ultimate goal of saving the life of the next Starway Shaman. My friend sat there very quietly, even after I finished. Then, without the slightest change of expression, said, "Reminds me of the story my grandfather would tell us." To this day, I don't know what part of the story he meant, or whether he was pulling my leg. He still comes to the store to sell us jewelry and always asks how my books are doing. Another artist, also an older man, picked up *Stargazer* at the gallery and took it with him. About a week later, I was standing outside my gallery when a silversmith approached. Instead of going to my husband, who does all the buying for the gallery, the Navajo walked straight to me. For the first time in the 11 years I have known him, he gave me a hug. He stepped back and said, "I have been reading *Stargazer*. Now my wife has it and my kids want it, so I don't know when I will get it back to finish the book. Can I have another one?"

Q: Who are your favorite authors?

LB: As for my favorite authors, I'm so glad you mentioned Jake Page. He's certainly one, as well as being a good friend. He joined me for my very first signing—a real hoot: a male southwestern mystery writer and a female southwestern romance writer. We had a ball. Another favorite is James Doss. But I have to confess that I do not read any other books with Native American elements. The reason is that I do not want to be influenced by the story, the characters, or the style of the other writer. That has not been a problem with Page and Doss since my style is so different from theirs.

Peter Bowen

Q: What is the overriding purpose of your novels?

PB: Each book is to a purpose. When they work, fine. I don't grade them.

Q: You have chosen to write about a group of people little covered by other authors. Any particular reason?

PB: They were the overarching human fact of northern North America for centuries; now few even know who they were are.

Q: Besides wanting to sell well do you have other immediate goals for your novels?

PB: Heh Heh Heh.

Q: Are you interested in the notion entertained by some authors of Indian literature that whites owe Native Americans some kind of "pay back" for all the injustices piled on their heads through the centuries?

PB: Without having actually *read* Page and Hager, the use of the P.C. term "Native American" sets off stink bombs. I have *never* heard that foolish misnomer on reservations or from *any* of my Indian friends. I suspect Page and Hager probably believe they afford dignity to Indians by portraying them as new age twits uttering fatuities best left to the anguished of Hollywood. (Kevin Costner is known as dripping little Weasel Dick among the Sioux *I* know.)

What any sentient human being wishes is to be treated like a human being and be judged on their merits, accomplishments, and character. Any race wants that from the dominant culture, which of course prefers rather tribal exclusions. This applies in America to Blacks, Hispanics, Indians, poor whites, Samoans, and, lately, loggers and cattle ranchers. Other countries operate similarly with varying vilenesses. Indians have among them good folks, bad folks, murderers, saints, poets, people of courage and cowardice, child molesters, and, given the available pool of white guilt, numerous two-bit hustlers, literary and otherwise, since they possess not a few rank opportunists in their variegated unconformity.

All of the medicine people I knew had wonderfully pointed senses of humor. Example: At a pow-wow a young woman of twenty or so, a former girlfriend of a friend of mine, spotted me, and, a little uncomfortable at being surrounded by Indians, she scuttled over to crouch in my large shadow.

I was talking to an old woman who was a most thorough bearer of Salish traditions. I introduced them and since the day was hot I went for drinks for all of us.

When I returned, this old Salish lady was laughing, and the young woman was blushing violently.

"Mary," I said, "you old bat. What'd you *do* to her?"

Mary pointed to a benchload of old Salish women nearby.

"She ask me what them old women laughing about," said Mary, "so I tell her them old women can tell she has held a man's pee-pee in her mouth. . . ."

Mary chortled. I soothed her latest victim.

Q: You write in a vernacular style that is pretty hard for the average reader to follow, effective but unusual.

PB: My work is my work. I'm a Montanan. When any book reaches galleys, I destroy all notes and manuscripts. And when I move through the country I leave no tracks.

P.S.   I am by nature unhelpful to enterprises such as yours, not that I care one way or another whether or not you do a chapter on my work.

Q: Though I know you despise academics, I should admit that I have been one for over forty years. I could almost guarantee, however, that putting you in my book will not benefit you at all in sales. So don't upgrade your lifestyle on prospects.

PB: 40 years? I'd be in the slammer for multiple homicides and wholly unrepentant. Fine with me if you want to put in a chapter on me—I can't help, largely because I have no idea how I write my books. They take about ten working days and then I forget them. Copyediting is fun. I find a book there quite new to me.

Good luck with your book.

Margaret Coel

Q: How did you become acquainted with the Arapaho people on the Wind River Reservation?

MC: The Arapahos are very private people with reason to distrust outsiders. You can't just show up on the reservation and say, "Hi, I'm here to write about you." You must gain their trust, which takes time. I first went to Wind River in the late 1970s when I was writing *Chief Left Hand, Southern Arapaho,* a biography of one of the great Arapaho leaders. Another historian accompanied me and introduced me to her Arapaho friends. Because she vouched for me, in a sense, and because they trusted her, they were willing to talk to me. Since then I have visited the reservation many times and have made wonderful friends there.

Q: How did the Arapahos like *The Eagle Catcher?*

MC: Well enough to hold a celebration for me on the reservation after the novel came out. They wanted the celebration to take place at Blue Sky Hall, since the hall appears in the novel. We had a feast, music, dancers, and a master of ceremonies. It was great!

Q: Can you give us another memorable experience on the reservation?

MC: I would say all my experiences on the reservation have been memorable. But one stands out. I was visiting with some Arapaho friends outdoors when a golden eagle began circling us. One of the women said, "The eagle is upset because we are telling you about our culture." That was the end of the conversation. But the next day, the women came and found me. They had consulted one of the elders who reminded them that whenever the eagle comes, it is a good sign. "This white woman," he said, "will write the truth about our people." Since then, my Arapaho friends have explained many things that have helped me understand the Arapaho culture better. I am very grateful to the eagle.

Q: How did your background as a history writer influence your mystery novels?

MC: It makes them what they are: contemporary mystery stories grounded in history. I'm fascinated by the way the past continues to shape the present—by the way nothing is ever over. In some ways, we are all trying to live with the past. This is especially evident on Indian reservations where past events still shape the present. I like to weave this theme through my novels.

Q: You were also a journalist. How does your journalistic background influence the mysteries?

MC: It's probably the journalist that makes me write about real issues. *The Ghost Walker,* as well as my first novel, *The Eagle Catcher,* deal with real issues facing Indian people today and how those issues affect their lives.

James D. Doss

Q: The blurb on your books picture you as something of a loner who also likes to do his writing as he can and where he can. Could you tell me a little about your background, why you came to writing and why about the Utes?

JD: Yes, I suppose I am—in some sense—a 'loner.' I prefer a quiet place to write, and that usually means being alone. I work hard all week at my 'day job' at the Los Alamos National Laboratory—and enjoy my contacts there. (I'm an electrical engineer.) But on Friday evening, I slip away to my little hideaway in the Sangre de Cristo Mountains above Taos. The small log cabin is nestled among the spruce and aspens. A stream called the Rio Hondo runs by the cabin. A waterfall sings me to sleep shortly after the sun goes down. I get up early on Saturday morning, have breakfast, and write for about ten hours.

Q: Does your knowledge of Indian lore and culture come to you naturally or must you dig in the library in order to get it right?

JD: I grew up in the Midwest, mostly in western Kentucky. One of my greatest pleasures as a youth was to find flint arrow-points in plowed fields. When I was about 12, I joined archaeological societies in Illinois, Indiana, and Ohio so I could have a subscription to their journals. Despite my lifelong interest in Indians, I never intended to write about the Utes. The first novel *(The Shaman Sings)* was to be about a crime in the fictitious university town of Granite Creek, Colorado. I intended to explore the issue of professors who steal the research of their students. It seemed appropriate to have a Native American in the tale, so I invented the character of Clara Tavishuts who is dispatcher in the Granite

Creek police station. With even a single minor Ute character, it was necessary to learn something about this group of tribes who once controlled much of the central Rockies. Little has been published, but I found a rather academic report (*Ethnology of the Northern Utes,* by Anne Smith) in our local library. It was here that I discovered the *pitukupf.* Once I had learned about this remarkable 'Ute leprechaun,' there was no turning back. I visited the reservation and found a fellow who was willing to tell me about the dwarf. The shaman, Daisy Perika (Clara's aunt) was a necessity because someone had to talk to the 'little man.' Charlie Moon was invented because a Ute policeman had to show up at the end of the tale and rescue Scott Parris. I liked Charlie so much that he became a major character in the second novel *(The Shaman Laughs),* the third *(The Shaman's Bones)* and *The Shaman's Game.* I have no specific plans for either Charlie Moon or any of the other characters. When the writing begins, these folks do pretty much as they wish. I can't imagine what Charlie or Daisy will be involved with after *The Shaman's Game* . . . but it might have something to do with an astonishing archaeological discovery on (or near) the Southern Ute reservation.

Most of my research is performed at the places I write about. This includes, of course, the Southern Ute reservation. I know a sweet lady there who has been very helpful. I have also visited the Ute Mountain reservation at Towaoc in SW Colorado, the Uintah (Ute) reservation in NE Utah, and the Shoshone Wind River reservation in central Wyoming. I must get a good feel for the land and talk with the people who live on it. I visit libraries (Fort Lewis College in Durango has a terrific reference section on the Utes) and buy every reference that I can find (and afford).

I realize this isn't much, but I hope it is helpful to you. I'd attempt more, but I have a mid-September deadline for the current ms (I've been working on it all day) and begin a book-signing tour next week—all of which must be done on weekends and scheduled vacation days.

Jean Hager

(This interview was conducted by Professor Peter Rollins and his wife Susan Rollins, Oklahoma State University.)

Q: How did your career get started?

JG: I've always wanted to write. As a kid I wrote short stories. I was turned on to writing by a librarian in elementary school, name of Helen Rushmore. She, not my parents, became my model. My parents had no writing background. When I was a student at Oklahoma State University I took a course in creative writing and ended up with a degree in English. After that I taught school three years in Cleveland, Oklahoma. I lived on a farm in Cleveland — 40 acres — and had nothing but cattle. But during those years I knew I wanted to be a writer. I enrolled in a writing course — through correspondence — and then joined a writing group in Tulsa.

As a child I had read all the mystery books like Nancy Drew. In 1970 I wrote a children's mystery which sold to schools and libraries locally. Then I wrote two adult novels which didn't sell. One was *Terror in the Sunlight,* under the pen name of Amanda McAlester, which had a heroine as an English teacher. I also wrote another novel called *Evil Side of Eden* under the pen name of Sara North. I also wrote *Shadow of the Tammarack* under that name. These were both romantic suspense mystery novels. I finally found an agent through a conference I attended at the University of Oklahoma for professional writers, in the 1970s.

I was encouraged to read romance novels like the Harlequin novels which Dell publishes. Then I wrote *Captured by Love,* which is set in Texas. The heroine is a veterinarian.

Then I met a representative from another publisher by the name of Judy Stevens, who had sold books to Harlequin. So I began writing for Harlequin but quickly got "burned out" by writing many of these. As a result I decided to write a contemporary mystery novel.

I like Tony Hillerman and have based my books on his style. The first under the Jean Hager name was *Grandfather Medicine,* which is about Cherokee ways yet the hero is an outsider. For that book I got lots of my information on the Indian ways from my old Aunt who was in a nursing home. I would visit my Aunt and talk about her memories of Indian folklore. I had to do research on my own though Cherokee is my heritage. I am one-sixteenth Cherokee.

But I have to do a lot of research. And I like to. Doing research on the Cherokee nation is no different than the history of England or colonial America. Apparently I succeed in creating reality because the Cherokee Nation welcomes me each year for a book signing. They like me because I treat them with respect.

I believe I am the first Indian Cherokee mystery writer. I have been encouraged to write from a female perspective. So I invented the heroine Molly Bearpaw. But only after I was successful with my male hero, Mitchell Bushyhead. I had some difficulty in getting control of Molly. I am only one-sixteenth Cherokee and basically an outsider as far as the traditional culture is concerned. That may be why the first Molly book was harder for me to write— Molly is a full-blood Cherokee, raised by a somewhat traditional grandmother (She's an insider). Mitch, on the other hand, although he's half-Cherokee, was not raised in the culture and is therefore an outsider like me. I can identify with Mitch more easily than with Molly.

But with the Cherokee mysteries I need a change of pace, so I have written the Irish House Series. It is a self-contained environment with people intertwining in their relationships. To write these I need four to five suspects. The whole thing is a total fantasy. Readers have to suspend reality to accept the whole premise. These Cozies are fun, especially exploring the characters

But the Cherokee mysteries are more rewarding. I am especially fond of Tony Hillerman, as I said, and Dana Stabenow, whom I did not discover until I'd written several Cherokee books. I have not read Jake Page or Arthur Upfield.

Q: Why do you write of the Cherokee?

JH: To record the old ways. So much has been lost. I am trying to record the heritage of the people from whom I came. My characters speak English although occasionally I use a phrase in Cherokee for both the effect and because it just sounds right in its original voice.

My Cherokee books are selling well all over the United States, even in England and Australia. So the appeal of the American Cherokees, maybe all Indians, is more extensive than a local audience.

Q: How do you start a book? Do you first have a plot or something to talk about? Or what?

JH: First I start with a character. The plot grows out of the characters. I start with a character description. I have to have a victim, a murder, who else would have motivation, time to get to know my characters. As they begin to interact the story unfolds of itself. I use no outline. I am often amazed at how the story happens and the end is often a surprise to me.

Q: How often do you write? Every day?

JH: No, not every day, but at least four to five times a week. But I am constantly researching to get new ideas. I am reaching out for the mythological. I use as my major sources the Kilpatrick Chero-kee books which are in the reference room at Northeastern State University in Tahlequah. I have found those books my best and readiest source.

Q: Do you get any inspiration from Indian paintings?

JH: No not really.

Q: What are your future plans?

JH: Two or three more books on Molly Bearpaw and on Mitch Bushyhead. I intend to keep them as separate series and they won't meet.

Q: What is the attraction of the mystery genre?

JH: I like the puzzle element. The characters grow on paper and get involved in the puzzle. There has to be a satisfying conclusion. It is mostly an escape for me!

Q: How do you like the role of being a famous published author?

JH: I like being out on the road. It is nice to meet my readers. It gets tiring and I am always so glad to come home to my own rou-tine. It is good that my face isn't famous so I can sit here in a restaurant with you like this and not be bothered. I have the best of worlds. My fans know who I am when I am at a book sign-ing, and I get fan mail, but my daily personal life is my own and uninterrupted.

Q: Are your children writers?

JH: None are into writing. I have a daughter who likes to read but that's as close as they get.

I would like to leave you with what I think is a necessary truth. You have to treat the culture of which you write with great respect even if there are negatives about that culture. Your characters within the culture can make the comments to speak to the posi-tives and negatives, but the author must treat the culture with great respect.

I do not consciously have a political agenda when I'm writing these books. While I want to get the culture right and treat it with respect, it would be pretty egotistical of me to think that I'm pay-ing back some of the debt owed to the Indians. I hope that readers come to understand something of the culture through reading my books. I think that's about all I can hope for.

Louis Owens

Q: I guess I know your lineage and your background since most academics' are painful and long. But why did you take up academia, and how did you get to the University of New Mexico, Albuquerque?

LO: I'd say I took up academics both by accident and path of least resistance. Coming from a family of nine kids, with parents neither of whom went beyond third grade, I did not grow up thinking of higher education. Of nine of us kids, in fact, only my older brother and I graduated from high school, and I'm still the only one in my extended families to attend college. I went to work in a can factory right out of high school and then went to junior college to kill time until my best friend could graduate from high school so we could enlist in the Marines and go to Vietnam together. My older brother did three tours in Nam, and by my second year of j.c., he had convinced me to do anything necessary not to take part in that awful war. I applied to UC Santa Barbara because one of my junior college teachers told me to. When they sent me papers saying I had received a full EOP scholarship and grant, I threw them out, thinking it was a trick to get me into debt like my parents. My teacher called and got new forms and made me fill them out and send them in. I transferred from junior college to the university and eventually graduated. I was not intent on grad school and never wanted to be a professor. I worked for the US Forest Service as a fire fighter and wilderness ranger and on trail crew, attended graduate schools sporadically because my new wife thought it would be a good idea, dropped out of three different programs, and finally ended up with a Ph.D.

I came to UNM because my first teaching job as a new assistant prof was at Cal State Northridge, where I had wonderful colleagues and students but lived in utter hell of smog, etc. I applied for an MS degree program in Forestry Management at Utah State, was accepted, and was set to go when I got a call from UNM. I liked New Mexico and came here instead of quitting teaching and going back to Forestry.

My biggest incentive to become a prof, by the way, was having long weekends to backpack and fish and having summers off to do the same.

Q: In all the Native American crime fiction I have read there is great significance placed on Indian mysticism. Why do you find it so useful, even necessary?

LO: I've always mistrusted the word "mysticism," so I decided to look it up in a dictionary before answering this question. "Any belief in the existence of realities beyond perceptual or intellectual apprehension but central to being and directly accessible by intuition." From the American Heritage Dictionary. I would have to say that the foremost reason for the presence of what you call mysticism in my work lies in my upbringing. I was raised to believe very clearly in the realities described in this definition, in perceptions that are not intellectual or "rational," in communications that might be termed extra-rational, in spirits, in dreams, etc. These were parts of stories told to us kids by our mother and others, and parts of our immediate experiences. I have, in fact, had direct contact with what people might term "ghosts" and so on. That's simply a part of a larger reality that figures in my fictions. Either a reader crosses that threshold or he doesn't, but if he doesn't then the fiction probably does not work.

In addition to writing about reality as I have always perceived it, including dream reality, I also want to extend my readers' consciousness and challenge them by urging them to see beyond ordinary limitations. I cross boundaries as much as possible, with characters who are of more than one cultural and ethnic heritage and with characters who inhabit more than one kind of reality. I think you will find a lot of what you termed mysticism in writing by and about Native Americans in large part because Indian people tend to see the world in this way, tend to believe in realities beyond "perceptual or intellectual apprehension but central to being." I don't personally know any Indian people, for example, who do not take dreams very, very seriously. And I have immediate, personal evidence that Indian people share experiences and communicate through dreams. Again, that's just the way it is. And of course this isn't the exclusive domain of Native Americans.

Finally, it's possible to say a lot about mundane life by incorporating something beyond the mundane. And it's fun.

Q: You seem personally to be hoisted on the rack of a very mixed blood line, or lines. Do you find that a convenience or inconvenience, though you use it with great purpose in your fiction?

LO: Mixed heritage is obviously central to my own being and just as obviously a phenomenon about which I've worried and pondered and wondered and written about forever. Being hoisted on the rack of it is a concept that makes me a bit nervous, however. Nonetheless, through my characters I'm clearly exploring and attempting to resolve these issues, even the undefined ones. It is a kind of mystery waiting to be solved: who and what am I? We all go through this. In *The Sharpest Sight*, Cole's search for his brother's bones is in some ways a metaphor for his search for a coherent identity. In some ways, being a mixedblood, as we're called, makes it difficult to rest. I have an essay or two that examines this dilemma in my latest book, *Mixedblood Messages*.

This also provides me a huge amount of energy and intensity. It certainly is inconvenient—it would be much easier just be some-THING, to say, "I'm African American, I'm Lakota, I'm Jewish," or whatever and leave it at that—but this kind of limbo, what Gerald Vizenor calls torsion in the blood, does provide a necessary focus and, again, intensity. Out of it, we hope, comes some kind of art. It is unmistakably my major subject.

Q: Ordinarily in a situation like this I find that I don't know half the questions I should ask, so will you just please give me answers to the questions I should have known enough to ask but didn't.

LO: You probably should have asked me why I choose mystery or the crime novel genre for my fiction. I would have replied that I never intended to do that. I am not a reader of mysteries or crime novels, never in fact having read one before I began writing. However, in my fiction I wanted to write books that my father and my brothers and my sisters would read, that is, novels with plots as opposed to precious symbolist poetry going on page after page. The challenge for me was to try to write fiction that could be page-turning, plot-structured, and still encompass all the complexities—both technical and intellectual—that I wanted to explore. So I have ended up writing books that have layers. *The Sharpest Sight*, for example, can be and has been read as a crime novel or mystery, and left at that. It received the Roman Noir prize for the best "noir" novel published in France in 1995. However, perceptive readers will discover the centrality of not just a large dose of Choctaw mythology but also Indo-European mythology, the two mixed inseparably I hope. And I also go on to interrogate the whole American meta-myth in the process. Still, it's a novel that can be and is read by people who only read for character and plot. The same, I hope, can be said for my other novels, including *Nightland*, which you mention.

One last point I'd like to stress is that I'm writing also to explode clichés and stereotypes. In my novel Oklahoma is publishing in January, for example, I have an Indian who runs around a reservation shouting Italian at women. He has learned it from other "Indian" actors in Hollywood. I have a young Indian man who sells vision quests and an anthropologist who is more "Indian" than the Indians. In *Bone Game* I have a cross-dressing Navajo anthropologist. And so on. No Indian braves in eagle-feather headdresses, no drumming shamans, no swooning Indian damsels. I really hate that stuff. Even worse is the dysfunction school of Native American literature, the new Vanishing American garbage in which Indians are self-destructive drunks and darkly comic and nothing more. By the way, I find that in publishing with a university press I have a freedom I cannot have with a New York publisher, a freedom that allows me to do whatever I want in my novels. I published *Nightland* with Dutton Signet, singularly the most unpleasant experience I have had as a writer; to those people Indians are defined by Hollywood westerns and romance novels, and Indians are either dead or in the process of making themselves vanish through alcohol and dysfunctional behavior. I had wanted to get away from the University of Oklahoma Press for one book. Now I'm going back to OU Press with great pleasure. New York wants ridiculous, comically self-destructive Indians, mystical shaman-warriors, breathless and precious prose about imploding Indian communities and idiotic love affairs. Either Louise Erdrich or Tony Hillerman (or worse, Sherman Alexie).

Jake Page

Q: According to the blurb on your books you have worked at virtually every kind of job known to man or woman. Let me play stupid and ask the obvious. How have all these jobs contributed to the strength of your novels? Did you turn to novelizing because you had done all things and felt you should write about them?

JP: The mining and ranching jobs were early excursions into the West (I came from Westchester County, NY) and not meant to mean anything much — but taught me a lot about other kinds of people than myself — that is, what might generally be called rednecks, with whom I got along perfectly well. After college at Princeton, I went into book publishing which landed me in a joint Doubleday-American Museum of Natural History publishing co-venture which, in due course, put me in charge of *Natural History Magazine*. This all put me into the middle of the natural sciences, ecology, conservation, and mainly the intellectual delights of biology and anthropology. This was from 1962–69. In 1970 I moved to Washington to help with the beginnings of *Smithsonian* magazine as its science editor, in 1976 starting up a mail order book publishing operation for the Institution at the Secretary's request.

More important, in 1974 I met, fell in love with, and soon married a photographer named, at the time, Susanne Anderson. She had been asked by the Hopi to photograph them and their lives — which no one else had been allowed to do since about 1910. So I went along on many of the trips — about thirty over 8 years — and we published *Hopi* (Abrams, 1982), which was very well received — esp. by the Hopi.

(We're getting to your questions.) While among the Hopi by whom I was profoundly influenced in many ways — but not in the sappy way a lot of people are who meet Indians and want to wear feathers or whatever — the tribal chairman asked me if I would mind writing magazine articles about the theft of stolen Indian religious material — they had just lost four gods. Not altar pieces. Gods.

So I wrote one for *Smithsonian,* my alma mater, at their request and they turned it down because it implicated a sister museum in this nefarious trade. I then wrote one for Tom Hoving's *Connoisseur* magazine (at their request, also), which they finally turned down because it would be offensive to galleries (who advertised in *Connoisseur*).

By then Susanne and I lived here in New Mexico and were working on a book about the Navajo also for Abrams and published a couple of years ago. I was pretty pissed off at the magazines, and eventually sold a piece or two elsewhere, but they would have been a great market. Anyway, I decided to try and write a popular mystery novel about this business of collector's ignorantly or not buying up religious stuff from the Indians — all of which is illegal, but when did that ever stop a collector?

Which is why I started writing *The Stolen Gods*. Frankly I was a bit surprised when Ballantine Books not only wanted it — I'd written only a third — but a second one as well. So after the first one, I did *The Deadly Canyon* which had a lot of natural history in it. (I have written a lot of books and articles on natural history over the years.) So now, I've done five—*A Certain Malice* will appear in spring 98, and the denouement has a lot to do with my mining experiences back in the Pleistocene Age in Colorado.

Q: Mo Bowdre is surely one of the more imaginative creations walking around today in fiction. It is hard to imagine a blind sculptor, but then it is likewise hard to imagine a blind golfer. But there are such things. How was Mo conceived and born? Are you happy with his credibility?

JP: Neither my wife nor I can recall exactly how Mo Bowdre came into being—a blind sculptor. We were doing a piece on Billy the Kid, had a lot of wine at dinner, and the next morning Mo sort of existed. We have a friend who is a very bright academic, born as a back country kid, with an explosive and altogether irritating laugh. A sculptor? I'd done some wood carving over the years and thought, I guess, that a sculptor's view of the world shouldn't be too hard to put forth. Why he is blind I will never know, but he is, and it is an interesting challenge.

For the most part, I'm satisfied in his believability (who would believe an amateur detective these days anyway?), but as a blind man he seems to work. It turns out, I discovered after the first book, that there is a blind sculptor (from a Rio Grande pueblo) out there who is well thought of. I've just heard from him and his wife who said that Mo worked just fine, and noted some other coincidental similarities. This made me very happy.

Q: Connie, too, is superbly etched, a fitting foil to Mo. How was she born?

JP: In the first book we needed Mo to have a connection to Hopi, to get him involved in the stolen gods, and what better way than if he had a Hopi girlfriend. Since she was going to have to be a lot more worldly than a lot of Hopi women are, I made her half-Hopi, with a runaway white father. So if she did something wholly uncharacteristic, the Hopis could say it was because of her deadbeat father. I'm glad you like her. I do too, and one of these days, I'll probably have one book in which she is the principle character and Mo is in the background—if I can actually keep him in the background.

Q: Your style is about as clear and direct as it could be without being raunchy or deliberately sexy. How do you achieve the vernacular without the sexy?

JP: I don't know the answer to this. I don't really analyze how I write or any of that. I just try to put myself in the minds of these characters and let them do the talking. I know how that sounds—the usual bullshit about characters having a life of their own. Mine don't. I am God the Creator, and without me they vanish—but I impersonate them, I guess.

Q: One of the delights of your novels is the Indian lore that enriches it. Are you a library researcher or does your knowledge about Indian lore come natural?

JP: See above.

Q: What other things should I know about you and your work?

JP: Well, let's see. Most of what I write is non-fiction—essays, articles, books—altogether I guess I've written, or co-authored 32 books—Indians, science, natural history, mythology. I'm working now on a book about the American Southwest for the National Geographic Society and a thriller about the Smithsonian for the highest bidder. My wife and I have just finished *A Field Guide to Southwest Indian Arts and Crafts* for Random House.

I have twelve grandchildren, all of whom I am trying to subvert into being westerners—having become one legally a decade ago. The *Denver Post,* a while back, called me "one of the Southwest's most distinguished writers," which I guess is pretty good for a carpetbagger. My wife Susanne is a very intimately involved personage in virtually everything I write, especially the mysteries.

Usually when starting a mystery—and you can probably tell—I have no idea what the hell is going to happen. All I have in mind is a general theme, a particular type of crime, or whatever.

Dana Stabenow

Q: Give us some background about your growing up and the development of your characters.

DS: I was born in Anchorage, Alaska, March 27, 1952, and raised on a 75-foot fish tender in the Gulf of Alaska. When I wasn't seasick I wrote stories about normal children who lived on shore. In 1964, the Great Alaskan Earthquake occurred during my twelfth birthday party, and I realized I was destined for greatness if I survived the day.

I graduated from Seldovia High School in 1969 and put myself through college working as an egg grader, bookkeeper, and expediter for Whitney-Fidalgo Seafoods in Anchorage. I received a B.A. in journalism from the University of Alaska in 1973 only because the dean of students called me into the office the previous fall to inform me that participation in Lathrop Dorm's second floor keggers did not, in fact, count as credit. I spent one last summer knee-deep in humpies and blew my earnings on a four-month backpacking trip to Europe, where I discovered English pubs, German beer, and Irish men.

Fortunately, upon my impoverished return home construction began again on the TransAlaska Pipeline, and answering wholeheartedly to the call of the Cash I worked for Alyeska Pipeline at Galbraith Lake and later for British Petroleum at Prudhoe Bay. I made an obscene amount of money and went to Hawaii a lot.

In 1982 at the age of 30 I began to give serious thought to what I wanted to be when I grew up, quit BP and enrolled in UAA's MFA program, from which I graduated in 1985. My goal was to sell a book before I went broke and just barely made it: a science fiction novel, *Second Star*, was bought by Ace Science Fiction in 1990. In 1991 I contracted with Berkley to write three novels featuring an Aleut detective set in a generic national park in Alaska. The first Kate Shugak mystery, *A Cold Day for Murder* won an Edgar award. The seventh in the series, *Breakup*, will be in a bookstore near you on June 2.

I have just contracted with Dutton to write a new series featuring an Alaska state trooper and his significant other, a bush pilot, which will be set in Bristol Bay, Alaska, the salmon-fishing capital of the world. The first novel concerns a murder—or is it?—committed with the propeller of a Piper Super Cub. Messy business, murder.

In creating these works I have had to rely both on experience and imagination. Every writer's characters contain bits and pieces of themselves and people they know, and Kate, whom you call "a marvelous creation," is no different. But she is her own individual self. She was not based on any specific real person.

Only one character in the Shugak series was based on a real person: Emaa or Ekaterina Shugak, Kate's mother, was modeled after a great old gal named Exenia Barnes, an Eyak from Cordova. For a few years I had the pleasure and privilege of being one of her step-grandchildren, and got to eat her fry bread, drink her cocoa, and listen to her stories along with the rest of her 99 other grandkids. She wasn't the leader Emaa is, but she was a strong woman who took joy in living. Creating the character of Emaa is my way of making sure she never dies.

Q: Are you directly or indirectly interested in changing the way people look at Native Americans? Are you trying to "do good"?

DS: I'm a writer of popular (I hope) fiction; my job is to provide enough entertainment to justify the price of the book. If, along the way, I get lucky and teach someone something they didn't know before, that's just gravy.

I write about Aleuts because I was raised with them, specifically with a half-Aleut half-Filipino family in Seldovia, Alaska. Until I went away to the University of Alaska, Fairbanks, in 1969, I'd never seen so many white people in one place before in my life. I don't necessarily have a cause in writing about Aleuts; they're just the folks I grew up with.

Some trivia for you—Aleuts are not Native Americans, they are Alaska Natives. Same with Inupiaq, Yupik, Athabascans, Tlingits, Haida, and Tsimshian. It's more a legal quibble than anything, but the federal government gets exercised over it (when indigenous Americans are referred to in government documents, it is usually as Native Americans/Alaska Natives, or NA/AN). Inupiaq and Yupik do not take kindly to being called Indians, and Athabascans are averse to being called Eskimo.

Q: You obviously know a great deal about the culture you write about. Do you supplement your experiences with book knowledge?

DS: I was raised in Southcentral Alaska. Southcentral was a high impact area, hit with wave after wave of Western influences, from the great European explorers to the Russian exploiters to the American settlers. The people indigenous to this area had been, by the time I was born into it, so assimilated into the predominant Western/white culture that their own culture had almost ceased to exist.

Almost. They're recovering it now, slowly, due in large part to the lands and money they acquired through ANCSA. Land and money means power, a commodity in which they were largely lacking until 1973. In the past twenty-four years they've made a good start at running the BIA out of business, taking over the administration of NA education, health care and housing programs.

I remember when I was growing up in Seldovia, people would try to hide their Native heritage. Now it is a matter of pride and spiritual sustenance. It is a wonderful thing to see.

It's a wonderful thing to write about, even if only in fiction.

No, I didn't learn about this culture from reading about it in a book.

Q: Kate is a powerful character. How do you see her developing in future books?

DS: Kate is a strong character with a low tolerance for fools and a willingness to take action when it is necessary. She is also a loner by preference, an echo of the independent and nomadic existence of her ancestors. In future, I see her being dragged kicking and screaming into a leadership role in her tribe. There is a movement toward Native sovereignty up here, much analyzed and debated and which naturally terrifies the state government into idiocies such as appropriating $500,000 to fight it in court. There is also the issue of subsistence, or who gets to catch what fish where, that is vital to Alaska Native concerns, in particular in the Bush communities. Both issues generate a tremendous amount of passion and conflict on every side; the stuff of drama. My stuff. Kate will definitely be concerned with both.

Q: What cultural role do you see your characters playing in society?

DS: As I said before, my primary goal is to entertain. I'm not a teacher, or a sociologist, or an anthropologist, or a booster. I'm a writer. I write popular fiction. You could even call me a performer; I want to make 'em laugh, make 'em cry, make 'em shiver. If I make 'em think, too, that's just the icing on the cake.

Aimée and David Thurlo

Q: Will you give me a bit about your background motivating the writing of your novels.

ADT: It's hard to guess what you're looking for, but here goes. Born in Albuquerque, I grew up in Shiprock, and eventually ended up at the University of NM in Albuquerque. I met Aimée there while I was a student. Aimée was born in Havana, and came to the US when she was seven. She went to Catholic boarding schools, then LSU-NO, and ended up coming to Albuquerque. She moved next door to me, and after a whirlwind romance, we married and I finished grad school. I taught science in Albuquerque for 25 years, and just retired.

Aimee began a novel around 1979 and I helped edit and play devil's advocate. It took us around six months to sell the manuscript, and our career in writing took off shortly after that.

We soon learned that my strength was plotting, action, and detail work, and Aimée was best at dialogue and characterization. Nowadays, I write the basic story outline, Aimée does the first draft, then we take turns with drafts, both adding whatever we think is needed, and editing extensively. Working together, we go through four to five drafts before a novel is complete.

We're both committed first of all to each other, then to our careers, and though our work is very demanding, we always manage to decide on what's best for the manuscript. "My words are better than yours" doesn't come up much any more. We've developed ways of solving our writing problems by talking things out. I think one of our advantages is that our strengths are in different areas, and we trust each other.

When we have to work out a scene, or story line, or characterization, sometimes we'll saddle up the horses and go for a ride, or if it's night, take a drive. Everything works out, eventually.

Q: Why have you settled on writing the Ella Clah series at this time? Do you aim to use her as a kind of vehicle to pay back the Navajo for white injustices of the past?

EDT: Aimée has acquired a deep respect and admiration for the Navajo culture and people, something instilled in me at an early age. Our families always insisted on respect for others, and bigotry was never in our background.

We try to write respectfully and honestly about our Navajo characters, hoping that the readers will appreciate and respect the Navajos as a unique culture. As with every group there are scoundrels, and the Dineh are no exception, but we endeavor to represent the majority as the decent, honest, patriotic citizens that we've seen them to be.

We are storytellers, and have no agenda other than to entertain and enlighten the readers with tales involving a unique culture and people in the beautiful Southwest.

The tragedy with most "payback," in our opinion, is that it usually benefits those who weren't maligned by hurting those who weren't responsible for the original suffering. We're not here to teach any lessons or function as advocates or spokespersons.

Neither Aimée nor myself are trying to compensate for some real or imagined guilt, individually or collectively, and we certainly would not assume to represent or speak for the Navajos in any way. No Navajo speaks for another, and we certainly wouldn't presume to do such a thing either.

We present issues such as racism, poverty, alcoholism, youth gangs, and violence, certainly, but try not to preach or present society in any other way than what we perceive it to be. Our characters have to come up with their own solutions.

Our series characters, especially Ella, Rose, Clifford, and Wilson Joe, are ordinary people doing extraordinary things because of their individual abilities and strength of character — and the fact that they are also Navajos shouldn't be misconstrued to represent anything special to the readers.

The dignity we give our characters, and to the Dineh in general, is something every culture is entitled to receive, and we don't need a soapbox to justify that to the reading public.

Every writer has their own reasons for doing what they do and taking the path that they take, but conscious remorse and atonement are certainly not part of our journey. We're trying to entertain the reader, and if they are enlightened a little at the same time, that's good too.

Q: You have a powerful figure in Ella Clah. Do you intend to stay with her?

ADT: We love Ella Clah and her stories, and want to continue the series, which is growing steadily in popularity as more readers discover our books. The next book in the series, *Enemy Way,* will be out in the fall of 1998. We have plans to work on a fifth book and beyond, if the publisher shows sufficient interest in further developing the series. If this doesn't happen, expect another Navajo character and series to take Ella's place with a new publisher.

Q: How do you expect Ella to evolve?

ADT: Ella will continue to grow and develop in *Enemy Way,* and Rose, Clifford, and Wilson Joe will definitely go through new experiences — involving Ella in some way — that change their lives.

J. F. Trainor

Q: Would you give me some personal background and training for your fiction?

JT: I was born November 29, 1949, in Taunton, Mass. and grew up in nearby Attleboro, graduating from the city's high school in 1967. I attended the state college in Bridgewater, Mass. for two years, then changed my major to journalism and transferred to Northeastern University in Boston, graduating from their liberal arts college with a B.A. in journalism in June 1972.

I worked as a reporter-intern at the Taunton, Mass. *Daily Gazette* while at N.U. After graduation, I worked for three years as a general assignment reporter for the Fitchburg, Mass. *Sentinel* (now the *Sentinel & Enterprise*) and lived in Leominster, Mass.

Following a year of trying to establish myself as a freelance writer, I returned home and went to work for Taunton/Attleboro CETA. This was the beginning of a 20-year career in manpower services and employment enhancement training that ended in October 1997. During that time, I worked at Taunton/Attleboro CETA from 1977 to 1978, at the Balance of State CETA Administration, state Department of Manpower Development (DMD) from 1978 to 1983, again at Taunton/Attleboro CETA in 1983, and finally at Warwick Community Action, Inc. from 1984 to 1997. I am now in what is euphemistically called "retail," working for the small Sunnybrook Farms store chain in East Greenwich, R.I.

Although I did my writing nights and weekends, I did manage to travel quite a bit during those years. Overseas to South America three times, to Japan, and to the Philippines. Here in the USA, I've visited North and South Dakota, Kentucky, Florida, Michigan, Wisconsin, Minnesota, Wyoming, Montana, Washington, Oregon, Iowa, and all six New England states. My favorite destination, of course, is the North Shore of Lake Superior in Minnesota, from Duluth to Grand Marais. I visited the region yearly from 1980 to 1983 and again from 1986 to 1997. Were it not for the fact that my aging parents need me here, I would have left New England long ago and moved to Duluth. To me, the Northland is truly God's Country.

Q: Where did such an unusual character as Angie come from?

JT: Where did Angie come from?—Would you believe—a painting!? No lie. It happened back in late July of 1986. That was my first trip to Montana, and a must-see on my list of destinations was Yellowstone Park. So I drove from Bozeman down to West Yellowstone, Montana, and spent a couple of days there. If you've ever been to West Yellowstone (population 915), you know about all the gift shops, particularly those on Firehole Avenue.

Well, although I was writing young adult horror novels (I call them *Creatures and Cutiepies*) at the time, I did want to branch into adult mysteries. I am a great fan of John D. MacDonald's. I've read everything he ever wrote with the exception of the magazine crime stories he did before I entered kindergarten. I'd already decided that I wanted to do an amateur sleuth. I also wanted a sleuth who, like Travis McGee, would be equally at home on the wrong side of the law. At first I toyed with the idea of a male protagonist, but then I thought about doing a female detective in a Great Lakes setting. I called her Brunilda Barros, and she was supposed to be the Douglas County juvenile officer, based in Superior, Wisconsin, the city just across the bay from Duluth. But the idea still hadn't quite jelled.

So I happened to be browsing in a large gift store on Firehole Avenue in West Yellowstone, Montana, and I saw for the first time a large poster based on the oil painting *The Great Man's Daughter* by the Western artist Bill Hampton. I saw that painting and I was stunned. *There she is,* I thought, *there's my heroine.* And the name literally popped into my mind—*Angela.*

Angela what? I racked my brains for a surname. At this time I was planning on making Angie a Lakota. But then I realized that I didn't know enough about Lakota culture to make the character real. But, having been to the Northland and the reservations at Fond du Lac near Cloquet, Minnesota, Lac Courte Oreilles near Hayward, Wisconsin, and L'Anse, Michigan, in the U.P., I knew quite a bit more about, and felt far more comfortable with, Anishinabe culture. So I hunted for an appropriate surname for Angie. I came across *bidaban,* the Anishinabe word for dawn or sunrise, in Father Baraga's dictionary. It sounded just a little too harsh for English-speaking ears. I remembered then that one of the Iron Range towns near Virginia, Minn. is named Biwabik. So I made the name Biwaban, a blend of the two words. To me, it is perfectly pronounceable and euphonious—*bih-wah-ban.* But you'd be surprised at how many editors have stumbled over it.

I had already decided to make both Dakotas, the intermountain West, and the Great Lakes the arena for Angie's adventures. For a variety of reasons. One, I was sick to death of reading mysteries set in—pick one: (a) New York City (b) Los Angeles (c) New Orleans. You'd think they were the only three cities in America. Well, I vowed that I would set Angie's mysteries in communities with a population of 30,000 or less, drawing heavily on local history. I also determined that, like Louis L'Amour, I would visit the areas I intended to write about. So it was that in August 1988, I was spending my annual two-week vacation in northern Utah. The material I gathered here I used a few years later in *Dynamite Pass.*

(By the way, "Clover Creek," the hometown of the Sagers in that novel, is the original name of Logan, Utah. A sort of inside joke between me and the Daughters of the Utah Pioneers, who provided me with a load of background material.)

While I was in Logan, I went to the Tri-Cinema one night to see *Crocodile Dundee II* with Paul Hogan and Linda Koslowski, now Mrs. Hogan. I'll never forget the reaction of the Utah gentleman who sat in the row in front of me when the movie opened. As soon as Paul Hogan appeared in the rowboat, the man in front of me chuckled and said, "There's ol' Croc." And I thought to myself, *that's what I want. I want a heroine so unique and so vibrant a character that she'll be instantly recognizable to an audience.* The Utah trip was sort of a turning point in Angie's early life. Not only did she get an aunt out of it, she got a "second home" in the Intermountain West—Heber City—which delighted me so much that I spent over a week there in 1988.

Returning to Warwick, R.I., I began work in earnest on Angie. Before plotting out the first proposed Angie book, I sat down and wrote a 50-page biography of the lady, starting with her birth at Fond du Lac twenty-eight years ago to her recent release from the South Dakota women's prison. My agent, Denise Marcil, turned down the first book. She said it was too complicated, so I started work on the second, *Target for Murder.* I finished it in March 1991, and Denise walked it around New York for a year before our friends at Kensington offered a contract in 1992.

One reason I chose a woman instead of a man is that I wanted to gently spoof America's Western tradition in the same way Cervantes kidded Spain's stern medieval chivalry. I didn't start out planning to do so. Events in the West influenced me, notably the Sagebrush Rebellion, the shootouts with Robert Jay Mathews, Gordon W. Kahl, and Arthur L. Kirk, and particularly the year-long pursuit of Don and Dan Nichols following the abduction of Olympic contender Kari Swensen, during the 1980s. It was as if the Wild West was coming back to life—the past and the present colliding in a violent cataclysm. Was there ever a more surrealistic image than blond, ponytailed Kari jogging along that Spanish Peaks trail in her bright blue unitard, suddenly captured by two mountain men who could have easily shared some chaw or a jug with Jim Bridger? One of the high points of my Montana trip in 1986 was actually shaking hands with the Nichols boys' captor, by then former Sheriff John France, at the downtown cafe in Ennis.

I have always wondered what would have happened if Don and Dan had elected to shoot it out with John instead of surrendering and taking up residence at the state pen in Deer Lodge, Mont. Had they been killed, would they have become legends? Probably. But they cheated the myth at the last minute. Surrender to the sheriff? Fellas, it's just not done. You're supposed to return to town draped face-down over the mule's saddle, and then the undertaker props up your bullet-riddled corpse for the memorial photo. I'm just glad Doc Holliday is dead and never lived to see this disgrace. (Doc, if you'll recall, died in 1879 in a Denver hospital, wheezing out his last tubercular breath, cursing the nurses and calling for his boots, "Put 'em on, dammit!" He was so wrapped up in the Western myth that he felt that he *must* die with his boots on.)

The USA's Western Myth in a nutshell—the lone rider comes to town. Usually he is a working cowboy. A good hand with a gun but he's no tinhorn—he never advertises the fact. He knows the Indians—knows how to read trail sign and live off the land. He doesn't want trouble, but someone else usually starts it—evil mayor, cattle baron, lumber king, corrupt Indian agent, Mexican bandido, renegade Apache chieftain. They chase our hero all over the landscape, and then he rallies, hunts them down and polishes them off in an apocalyptic battle. Afterward, he either marries the schoolmarm or good rancher's daughter or saddles up and rides on, ever searching for his own personal El Dorado. This, of course, is the plot of every Western movie ever made (Example: *The Searchers*) and more than a few space operas. After all, what is *Star Trek* other than the U.S. Cavalry in outer space?

Well, in writing Angie, I decided to have some Cervantes-style fun with the myth. Angie, of course, is the Lone Ranger, although in modus operandi she's probably a lot closer to the Scarlet Pimpernel. But instead of being a strong, resolute, strapping six-foot Western Marlboro Man, she's a petite five-foot-four heroine. Instead of being a straight-shooter, she's devious and manipulative. Like Scheherezade, the archetypal Moorish Princess, Angie uses words as her weapons. She is defending truth, justice and the American way with an endless series of lies. She wants to love and be loved, yet she rejects the traditional female role her family, most notably Aunt Della, has set out for her—husband, children, a family and home of her own. The basic immaturity of her lifestyle is self-evident. Angie is still playing the Black Canary, just as she did when she was seven years old. Her grandfather, Charlie

Blackbear, knows this and has pointed it out to her on occasion. In *High Country Murder,* he complains, "What am I supposed to do—go tear-assin' around the countryside like Captain America?" Yet still he accompanies his mercurial granddaughter on her quests, adding a small measure of adult sanity to the proceedings. Charlie is also Angie's link to the past and her own millennia— old Anishinabe heritage. In short, a woman can get away with a lot that a man, particularly an American man, cannot. Casting Angie as the late 20th Century's answer to the Lone Ranger strikes me as amusing. Although I have received comments, pro and con, on the idea. Some liked it. One feminist accused me of trying to subvert their movement by casting a "childlike depen- dent woman" in a starring role. And one member of RIRW theor- ized that Angie was a distant descendant of the Lone Ranger's companion, Tonto. I don't know if that remark had Jay Silverheels spinning in his grave, but it probably had Scout whirling like a pinwheel.

Q: Many authors of Native American crime fiction are writing in an effort to pay back, to atone for white misdeeds of the past. Is that one of your goals?

JT: Native American Culture—This may sound strange coming from a child of the Fifties, but I never thought of Indians as *the enemy.* If we were playing cowboy at Horton Field in Attleboro, I never had any objections to being the Indian chief. To me, they were fellow Americans of different customs and languages.

It's funny how the Old West has such a grip on our national psyche. I'll give you an example. Back in 1980, I went to see the movie *Breaker Morant.* I'd read Thomas Pakenham's book on the Boer War a few years earlier and wanted to see this film. I was blown away by it. Today it's still one of my favorite "Army" movies because I don't think there are many films that address the absurd- ity of war the way *Breaker* does. Well, I urged my parents to go see it. They did. And my father, who never even heard of the Boer War, commented, "Those Boers—they were real renegades, weren't they? Just like the Comancheros."

Well, I laughed. Afterwards I thought about it, and I realized how much the Old West myth had affected our perceptions of the world. Here was my dad, born in 1924, child of the Depression, high school graduate, U.S. Navy veteran of World War II, who had never heard of the war in South Africa at the beginning of this century, and who had never left New England except for wartime service in Virginia, Morocco, and Britain. But he has seen every Western movie including silent films starring Tom Mix and William S. Hart. So he goes to see *Breaker Morant* and there onscreen is a bearded white man on horseback, toting a rifle, wearing a bandolier, who tosses a bundle of dynamite at a guard post, and he thinks, *Comanchero!*

Most non-indigenous people in our country think history began on our side of the world when Leif Erickson waded ashore in Newfoundland. I tend to think of our era of European dominance as just one episode in a long history. In college, I took courses on the Aztecs and the Mayans. Someday I hope to visit Teotihuacán and Cholula. Back in the 1970s, I spent my vacations in South America. In Peru, I climbed that steep trail to Machu Picchu, marveled at the ruins of Cerro Sechin and Chavin de Huantar, walked the winding streets of Cuzco, sampled the Inca's pool at Tambomachay, danced on the fortress of Sacsahuaman, stood by moonlight on adobe pyramids in the ruined city of Chan Chan, explored the dark-red adobe massive temple of Pachacamac. In Bolivia, I hiked across the *altiplano* from the village bus stop to the dead city of Tiahuanaco two kilometers away. There I saw the cyclopean Sun Gate and the remains of a stone pyramid and sat in the sunken temple of Kalasasya. Still have those photos, too. In fact, I'm a sucker for a Native American ruin. Last year, I dropped in at Grand Mound, just west of International Falls, Minn., a good ten thousand years old. History in America began with Columbus? I don't think so!

Nothing makes me wince so much as to hear one of the politicians go on about "how our ancestors conquered the wilderness." My response is, "Your wilderness is their backyard." As Angie pointed out in *Whiskey Jack,* the continent had a name long before Amerigo Vespucci stuck his on the hemisphere. To the Lakotas, it's *Tunkashila*. To the Anishinabe, it's *Michimackinakong*. In the area where I was born, the land William Bradford dubbed "the New English Canaan," the Eniskeetompauwaug called it *Tolba Meneham*. But they all mean the same thing—Island of the Great Turtle, North America.

A few years ago, I visited New Ulm, Minn., the site of a two-day siege and battle in the now-forgotten Sioux War of 1862. This conflict saw the only mass execution of P.O.W.s in American history—31 captured Lakota warriors. At the Mdewakanton pow-wow, which I've been to, the way they badmouth Abe Lincoln, who signed the execution order, you'd think you were in the most Confederate corner of Mother Dixie. The municipal museum in New Ulm is very interesting. The first floor is dedicated to the battle and the "pioneer victory." The second floor has dioramas and displays presenting the history of the town. But on the third floor, dark and dingy and as musty as any attic, you'll find all of the Native American artifacts, Lakota backboards, mortars and moccasins, Anishinabe vests and jingle dresses, and beadworked pouches. Shunted away to the attic like Mr. Rochester's unfortunate wife.

I think our culture has done a bit of the same with the Native Americans. No longer relevant, part of the dead past. Not so! Every July the Lakotas gather in Chamberlain, S.D., for the annual Buffalo March, a religious and cultural ceremony dating back thousands of years. It's still going on, only now you can see the marchers' column from the Interstate 90 overpass high above the river.

I think what I've tried to do with Angie is to create a confluence of myths. Tried to blend traditional Native American lore with our still-vivid mythology of the Old West. Just as in Lakota and Anishinabe culture, the war chief serves the same function as the *reeve of the shire* (hence the word sheriff) in Anglo-Saxon Britain—identify malefactors, raise a company of men to arrest them, put them on trail—so Angie becomes "the good princess" working to expose evildoers and to give aid and comfort to the helpless.

Works Cited

Alexander, Bruce. *Murder in Grub Street*. New York: Berkley Prime Crime, 1995.

Alexie, Sherman. *Indian Killer*. New York: Atlantic Monthly Press, 1996.

Allen, Paula Gunn. *The Sacred Hoop: Recovering the Feminine in American Indian Traditions*. Boston: Beacon Press, 1992.

Baker, Laura. *Legend*. New York: St. Martin's Press, 1998.

_____. *Stargazer*. New York: St. Martin's Press, 1998.

Bordewich, Fergus M. *Killing the White Man's Indian: Reinventing Native Americans at the End of the Twentieth Century*. New York: Doubleday, 1996.

Bowen, Peter. *Ash Child*. New York: St. Martin's Press, 2002.

_____. *Coyote Wind*. New York: St. Martin's Press, 1994.

_____. *Long Son*. New York: St. Martin's Press, 1999.

_____. *Notches*. New York: St. Martin's Press, 1997.

_____. *Specimen Song*. New York: St. Martin's Press, 1995.

_____. *Thunder Horse*. New York: St. Martin's Press, 1998.

_____. *Wolf, No Wolf*. New York: St. Martin's Press, 1996.

Brown, Dee. *Bury My Heart at Wounded Knee*. New York: Holt, Rinehart and Winston, 1970.

Browne, Ray B. *"A Night with the Hants" and Other Alabama Folk Experiences*. Bowling Green, OH: Bowling Green State University Popular Press, 1972.

Browne, Ray B., and Lawrence A. Kreiser Jr., *The Detective as Historian: History and Art in Historical Crime Fiction*. Bowling Green: Bowling Green State University Popular Press, 2000.

Caputi, Jane E. *Tracing the Goddess/Facing the Monster*. Madison, WI: Popular Press, 2004.

Cawelti, John. *The Six-Gun Mystique Sequel*. Bowling Green, OH: Bowling Green State University Popular Press. 1999.

Coel, Margaret. *The Dream Stalker.* New York: Berkley Prime Crime, 1997.

————. *The Eagle Catcher.* New York: Berkley Prime Crime, 1996.

————. *The Ghost Walker.* New York: Berkley Prime Crime, 1996.

————. *The Lost Bird.* New York: Berkley Prime Crime, 1999.

————. *The Spirit Woman.* New York: Berkley Prime Crime, 2000.

————. *The Story Teller.* New York: Berkley Prime Fiction, 1988.

Deloria, Philip J. *Playing Indian.* New Haven: Yale University Press, 1998.

Dilworth, Leah. *Imagining Indians in the Southwest.* Washington: Smithsonian Institution Press, 1996.

Doherty, P. C. *Ghostly Murders: The Priest's Tale of Mystery and Murder as He Goes on Pilgrimage from London to Canterbury.* New York: St. Martin's Press, 1998.

Doss, James D. *Grandmother Spider.* New York: William Morrow, 2001.

————. *The Night Visitor.* New York: Avon, 1999.

————. *The Shaman's Bones.* New York: Avon, 1997.

————. *The Shaman's Game.* New York: Avon, 1998.

————. *The Shaman Laughs.* New York: Avon, 1995.

————. *The Shaman Sings.* New York: St. Martin's Press, 1994.

————. *White Shell Woman: A Charlie Moon Mystery.* New York: William Morrow, 2002.

Dove, George N. *The Police Procedural.* Bowling Green, OH: Bowling Green State University Popular Press, 1982.

Ellison, Ralph. *The Invisible Man.* New York: Modern Library, 1952.

Greenberg, Martin. *The Tony Hillerman Companion: A Comprehensive Guide to His Life and Work.* New York: HarperCollins, 1994.

Hager, Jean. *The Fire Carrier.* New York: Mysterious Press, 1996.

————. *The Grandfather Medicine.* New York: Mysterious Press, 1995.

————. *Masked Dancers.* New York: Mysterious Press, 1998.

————. *Night Walker.* New York: Mysterious Press, 1990.

————. *Ravenmocker.* New York: Mysterious Press, 1992.

————. *The Redbird's Cry.* New York: Mysterious Press, 1994.

————. *Seven Black Stones.* New York: Mysterious Press, 1995.

Henry, Sue. *Murder on the Iditarod Trail.* New York: Avon, 1991.

————. *Sleeping Lady.* New York: Avon, 1996.

————. *Termination Dust.* New York: William Morrow, 1995.

Hillerman, Tony. *The Blessing Way.* New York: Harper & Row, 1970.

————. *Coyote Waits.* New York: Harper & Row, 1990.

————. *Dance Hall of the Dead.* New York: Harper & Row, 1973.

————. *The Dark Wind.* New York: Avon, 1983.

————. *Finding Moon.* New York: HarperCollins, 1995.

————. *The Fly on the Wall.* New York: HarperCollins, 1995.

————. *The Ghostway.* New York: Avon, 1984.

————. *Listening Woman,* New York: Harper & Row, 1978.

————. *People of Darkness.* New York: Avon, 1982.

————. *Sacred Clowns.* New York: HarperCollins, 1993.

————. *Skinwalkers.* New York: Harper Paperbacks, 1986.

————. *Talking God.* New York: Harper & Row, 1989.

————. *Talking Mysteries.* Albuquerque: University of New Mexico Press, 1991.

————. *A Thief of Time.* New York: Harper & Row, 1988.

Hoppenstand, Gary. *Popular Fiction: An Anthology.* New York: Longman, 1998.

Hoppenstand, Gary, and Ray Browne. *The Defective Detective in the Pulps.* Bowling Green, OH: Bowling Green State University Popular Press, 1983.

Howe, LeAnne, "The Story of America: A Tribalography," in *Clearing a Path: Theorizing the Past in Native American Studies,* ed. Nancy Shoemaker. New York: Routledge, 2002. 29–47.

Jackson, Helen Hunt. *Century of Dishonor.* New York: Harper & Brothers, 1881.

Jones, Stan. *Shaman Pass.* New York: Soho Press, 2003.

Kilpatrick, Jack F., and Anna G. *Friends of Thunder: Folktales of the Oklahoma Cherokees.* 1964; Norman: University of Oklahoma Press, 1995.

————. *Run toward the Nightland: Magic of the Oklahoma Cherokees.* Dallas: Southern Methodist University Press, 1967.

————. *Walk in Your Soul: Love Incantations of the Oklahoma Cherokees.* Dallas: Southern Methodist University Press, 1965.

Klein, Kathleen Gregory. *The Woman Detective: Gender & Genre.* Urbana: University of Illinois Press, 1995.

LaLonde, Chris. *Grave Concerns, Trickster Turns: The Novels of Louis Owens.* Norman: University of Oklahoma Press, 2002.

LeBlanc, Steven A. "Prehistory of Warfare." *Archaeology* 56.3 (May/June 2003): 18–25.

LeBlanc, Steven A, with Katherine E. Register. *Constant Battles: The Myth of the Peaceful, Noble Savage.* New York: St. Martin's Press, 2003.

Leeming, David, and Jake Page. *The Mythology of Native North America.* Norman: University of Oklahoma Press, 1998.

Lewis, Stephen. *The Blind in Darkness.* New York: Berkley Crime Fiction, 2000.

————. *The Dumb Shall Sing.* New York: Berkley Crime Fiction, 1999.

————. *The Sea Hath Spoken.* New York: Berkley Crime Fiction, 2001.

Macdonald, Gina, and Andrew Macdonald. *Shaman or Sherlock? The Native American Detective.* Westport, CT: Greenwood, 2002.

Malotki, Ekehart. *Hopi Animal Tales.* Lincoln: University of Nebraska Press, 1998.

Marson, Ian. *Falconer and the Face of God.* New York: St. Martin's Press, 1996.

Maza, Sarah. "Stories in History: Cultural Narratives in Recent Works in European History." *Journal of American History* 101.3–5 (1996): 1494.

Medawar, Mardi Oakley. *Death at Rainy Mountain.* New York: Berkley Prime Crime, 1996.

———. *The Ft. Larned Incident.* New York: St. Martin's Press, 2000.

———. *Murder at Medicine Lodge.* New York: St. Martin's Press, 1999.

———. *Witch of the Palo Duro.* New York: St. Martin's Press, 1997.

Owens, Louis. *Bone Game.* Norman: University of Oklahoma Press, 1994.

———. *Dark River.* Norman: University of Oklahoma Press, 1999.

———. *Mixedblood Messages.* Norman: University of Oklahoma Press, 1998.

———. *Nightland.* New York: Signet, 1996.

🖝 ———. *Other Destinies: Understanding the American Indian Novel.* Norman: University of Oklahoma Press, 1992.

———. *The Sharpest Sight.* Norman: University of Oklahoma Press, 1991.

———. *Wolfsong.* Norman: University of Oklahoma Press, 1995.

Page, Jake. *A Certain Malice.* New York: Ballantine, 1998.

———. *The Deadly Canyon.* New York: Ballantine, 1994.

———. *The Knotted Strings.* New York: Ballantine, 1995.

———. *The Lethal Partner.* New York: Ballantine, 1997.

———. *The Stolen Gods.* New York: Ballantine, 1993.

Parker, Robert Dale. *The Invention of Native American Literature.* Ithaca, NY: Cornell University Press, 2003.

Pearce, Roy Harvey. *Savagism and Civilization: A Study of the Indian and the American Mind.* Berkeley: University of California Press, 1988.

Perkins, Wilder. *Hoare and the Portsmouth Atrocities.* New York: St. Martin's, 1998.

Perry, Thomas. *Dance for the Dead.* New York: Ivy Books, 1996.

———. *The Face-Changers.* New York: Ivy Books, 1998.

———. *Shadow Woman.* New York: Ivy Books, 1997.

———. *Sleeping Dogs.* New York: Ivy Books, 1992.

———. *Vanishing Act.* New York: Ivy Books, 1995.

Potts, Malcolm, and Roger Short. *Ever Since Adam and Eve: The Evolution of Human Sexuality.* New York: Cambridge University Press, 1999.

➤ Pronzini, Bill, and Martin Greenberg. *The Ethnic Detectives: Masterpieces of Mystery Fiction.* New York: Dodd, Mead, 1985.

➤ Reilly, John M. *Tony Hillerman: A Critical Companion.* Westport: Greenwood, 1996.

Richter, Daniel K. *Facing East from Indian Country: A Native History of Early America.* Cambridge, MA: Harvard University Press, 2001.

Roe, Caroline. *Remedy for Treason.* New York: Berkley Prime Crime, 1998.

Rollins, Peter C., and John E. O'Connor. *Hollywood's Indian.* Lexington: University Press of Kentucky, 1998.

Ruppert, James. *Mediation in Contemporary Native American Fiction.* Norman: University of Oklahoma Press, 1995.

Rust, Megan Mallory. *Coffin Corner.* New York: Berkley Prime Crime, 2000.

Stabenow, Dana. *Better to Rest.* New York: New American Library, 2002.

————. *Blood Will Tell.* New York: Berkley Prime Crime, 1996.

————. *Breakup.* New York: Putnam, 1997.

————. *A Cold Day for Murder.* New York: Berkley Prime Crime, 1992.

————. *A Cold-Blooded Business.* New York: Berkley Prime Crime, 1994.

————. *Dead in the Water.* New York: Berkley Prime Crime, 1993.

————. *A Fatal Thaw.* New York: Berkley Prime Crime, 1993.

————. *A Fine and Bitter Snow.* New York: St. Martin's Minotaur, 2002

————. *Fire and Ice.* New York: Berkley Prime Crime, 1998.

————. *Hunter's Moon.* New York: Berkley Prime Crime, 1999.

————. *Killing Grounds.* New York: Berkley Prime Crime, 1999.

————. *Midnight Come Again.* New York: St. Martin's Press, 2000.

————. *Nothing Gold Can Stay.* New York: Signet, 2000.

————. *Play with Fire.* New York: Berkley Prime Crime, 1995.

————. *So Sure of Death.* New York: Signet, 1999.

Steinbeck, John. *The Grapes of Wrath.* New York: Viking, 1939.

Straley, John. *The Angels Will Not Care.* New York: Bantam, 1998.

————. *The Curious Eat Themselves.* New York: Bantam, 1993.

————. *Death and the Language of Happiness.* New York: Bantam, 1997.

————. *The Music of What Happens.* New York: Bantam, 1996.

————. *The Woman Who Married A Bear.* New York: Signet, 1992.

Teague, David. *The Southwest in American Literature and Art.* Tucson: University of Arizona Press, 1997.

Thurlo, Aimée and David Thurlo. *Bad Medicine.* New York: Forge, 1997.

————. *Blackening Song.* New York: Forge, 1995.

————. *Changing Woman.* New York: Forge, 2002.

————. *Death Walker.* New York: Forge, 1996.

————. *Red Mesa.* New York: Forge, 2001.

————. *Shooting Chant.* New York: Forge, 2000.

————. *Second Shadow.* New York: Forge, 1993.

————. *Tracking Bear.* New York: Forge, 2003.

Trainor, J. F. *Corona Blue.* New York: Zebra Books, 1994.

————. *Dynamite Pass.* New York: Zebra Books, 1993.

————. *High Country Murder.* New York: Kensington, 1995.

————. *Target for Murder.* New York: Zebra Books, 1993

————. *Whiskey Jack.* New York: Zebra Books, 1993.

Upfield, Arthur W. *Murder Must Wait.* 1953; New York: Collier Books, 1987.

————. *The New Shoe.* London: Heinemann, 1952, 1968.

————. *Venom House.* 1952; North Ryde, London: Heinemann, 1970; Australia: Angus and Robertson, 1985.

Vizenor, Gerald. *Fugitive Poses.* Lincoln: University of Nebraska Press, 1998.

Wallace, Irving. *The Man.* New York: Simon and Schuster, 1964.

Washburn, Wilcomb. Foreword. *Hollywood's Indian: The Portrayal of the Native American in Film.* Ed. Peter Rollins, and John O'Connor. Lexington: University Press of Kentucky, 1998.

Westbrook, Robert. *Ancient Enemy*. New York: Signet, 2001.

————. *Ghost Dancer*. New York: Signet, 1998.

————. *Red Moon*. New York: Signet, 2000.

————. *Warrior Circle*. New York: Signet, 1999.

Will, George F. "Tom Wolfe's Rooftop Yawp." *Newsweek*, 23 November 1998, 96.

Winks, Robin. *Colloquium on Crime: Eleven Renowned Mystery Writers Discuss Their Work*. New York: Scribner's, 1986.

Index

Note: Character names are listed in uninverted order, and authors and other actual peoples' names are inverted.

A RAY AND PAT BROWNE BOOK

Murder on the Reservation: American Indian Crime Fiction
Ray B. Browne

Goddesses and Monsters: Women, Myth, Power, and Popular Culture
Jane Caputi

Mystery, Violence, and Popular Culture
John G. Cawelti

Baseball and Country Music
Don Cusic

The Essential Guide to Werewolf Literature
Brian J. Frost

Images of the Corpse: From the Renaissance to Cyberspace
Edited by Elizabeth Klaver

Walking Shadows: Orson Welles, William Randolph Hearst, and Citizen Kane
John Evangelist Walsh

Spectral America: Phantoms and the National Imagination
Edited by Jeffrey Andrew Weinstock